your
preschooler
BIBLE

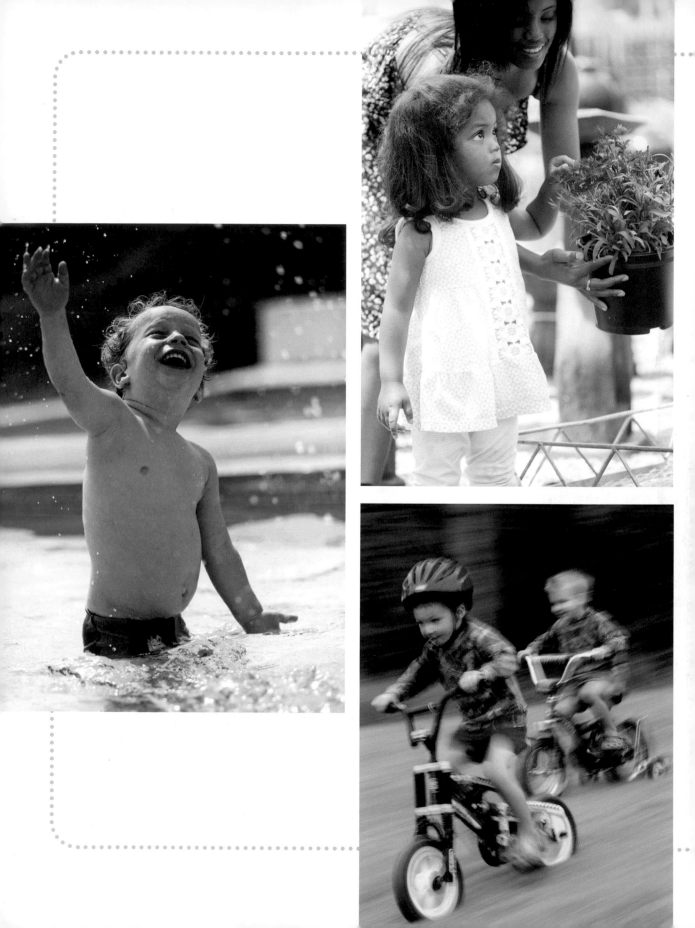

your
preschooler
BIBLE

CARROLL & BROWN LIMITED

Contents

First published in 2014 in the United Kingdom by
Carroll & Brown Publishers Limited
Winchester House
259-269 Old Marylebone Road
London NW1 5RA

Copyright © 2014 Carroll & Brown Limited

A CIP catalogue record for this book is available
from the British Library.

ISBN 978-1-907952-36-4

10 9 8 7 6 5 4 3 2 1

Printed in Europe

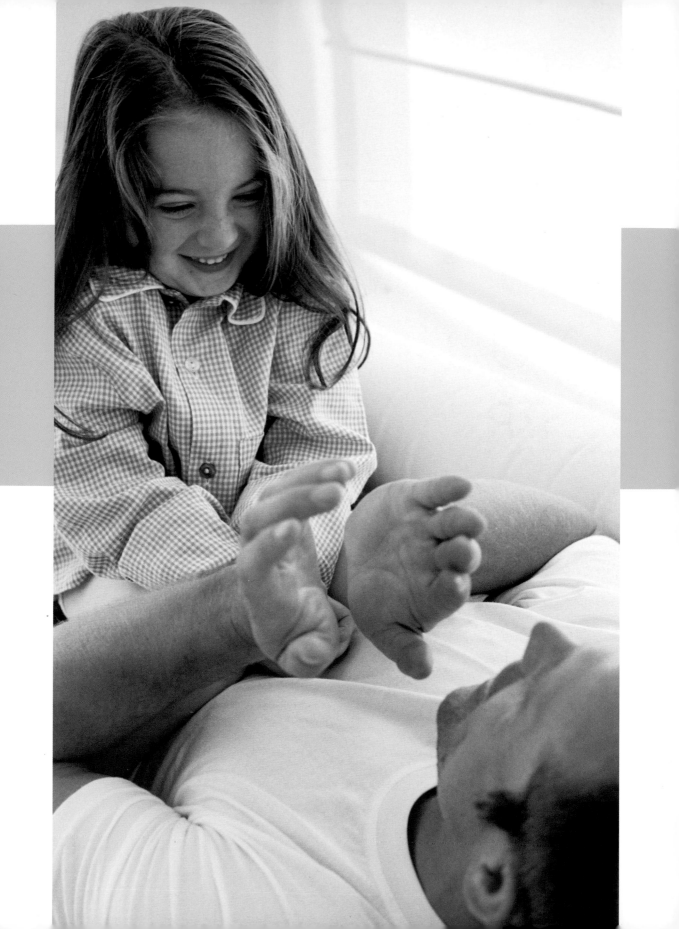

CHAPTER 1
YOU AND YOUR PRESCHOOLER

Once your child reaches the age of three, she has left babyhood behind and is on the brink of becoming an independently minded individual with a recognisable personality. Your task over the next few years will be to equip your child with the skills necessary to go to school and become a welcome part of a larger community. But it's not going to be all hard work! In fact, the preschool years can be the most fulfilling time for you both. Unlike when she was a baby, your child is now old enough to appreciate your care and attention but not so old that your influence will be eclipsed by her peers. To find out what's in store, read on. At this age, development is subject to advances and seeming retreats, and the 'snapshot' of your child at various stages will cover the expected highs and lows.

Sharing your life with your preschool child

You probably can't remember a time when you didn't have a child in your life. That phase seems just a dim and distant memory from long ago, a surreal time when you had nothing to think about except yourself and your partner, a time when you could do exactly what you wanted exactly when you wanted. Learning to share your life with your child has certainly been challenging up till now, though you have probably adapted to it better than you expected. In the first year or so, you had to adjust to focusing your time on your baby instead of solely on yourself and your partner, you had to adapt to a change in routine in which your baby's needs came before your needs, and you had to learn to carry out babycare tasks when there were moments all you wanted to do was to stay in bed and

hide under the duvet. A young baby becomes so much a part of your life — it's not that you share your life with her, it's that your two lives become intertwined to such an extent that some days you feel she and you are completely at one together.

Then came along the toddler years, with that wonderful explosion of development, in which your child started to speak, walk, to have ideas of her own and to show her sense of humour. Suddenly, the calmness at home was disrupted as your toddler made it clear that sharing your life with her had entered a new and more challenging phase altogether, one marked by tantrums, determination and a strong desire to be independent. But once again you both gradually adapted to each other, learning when to push and when to compromise, when to follow the rules and when to be flexible.

That type of sharing is a normal part of parenting, and is a natural process that usually takes place without any actual deliberate thought or planning. The very fact that you chose to become a parent in the first place meant you were ready to share your life with someone else. Yet just when you thought you had it all worked out, just when you and your toddler had meshed into a way of sharing your lives together that suited you both, she has now become a preschooler, with strong ideas of her own, an insatiable curiosity to discover how the world works, a much greater use and understanding of spoken language and a very distinctive personality and temperament. Sharing your life with your preschooler will be new, exciting and altogether different.

There are several reasons, covered in more detail below, why your child's feelings and behaviour change significantly during preschool years, and all are linked to progress in her psychological and physical development. Because of them, sharing your life with your preschooler usually will be a combination of

TIME MANAGEMENT

Over the preschool years, your child will require less hands-on attention from you. She will still need you to attend to or supervise her personal care, to spend individual time with her — either talking or reading, playing or teaching her things — and to watch over her while she plays outdoors. However, there will be more things she can do on her own with less supervision (though still within sight or earshot) such as playing by herself or with others, using the computer or watching tv or a dvd. This means that in a 24-hour day, your

- ◆ 3 year old will require about 6½ hours,
- ◆ 4 year old will need about 6 hours,
- ◆ 5 year old will require about 4 hours of your time.

emotional highs and lows. Sometimes everything will seem to go so smoothly and yet other times you will feel that you and she are completely out of synch. You may even feel aggrieved that your child takes more than she gives back, and that you hadn't imagined your life would be like this during these precious preschool years.

Your partner is sharing, too

Decisions were much simpler when your child was younger, for instance, choosing whether she wore the striped or single-colour sleep suit, or which brand of formula milk she would drink during weaning. Even if important, they were unlikely to be a source of controversy between you and your partner.

When your child became a toddler, decisions grew more complex. For instance, you and your partner had to reach an agreement about how to encourage your child's behaviour in positive ways and how you would ensure she followed rules. Somehow, though, these decisions were reached reasonably quickly. During the preschool years, however, you have to make decisions that will have a significant impact on your child's

future development, such as the type of day care you use for her when you return to work, or the type of nursery you want her to attend. Then there are her friendships, some of which you'll be pleased with and others, which you would prefer her not to have. And towards the end of the preschool phase, you need to select a school for her — perhaps one of the most important decisions of this life-phase.

No wonder then that the preschool years can be a time of tension and disagreement between partners. Sharing your life with your child also involves sharing major decisions with your partner, not making choices and then informing your partner after the event as a fait accompli.

Whenever engaging in discussions about aspects of your child's future, think through all the pros and cons very carefully. Weigh up all the advantages and disadvantages of each option before coming to a conclusion. Be prepared to shift your initial opinion if necessary — after all, your partner's view may be right, even if your original idea was different. A couple is more likely to support a strategy for their child when they have reached a joint agreement, and that makes it more likely to work effectively.

Adapting to your changing child

Sharing of any sort involves giving something of yours to someone without any guarantee that you'll get anything back in return; that's why sharing is so difficult for young children. And sharing your life with a constantly changing and growing preschooler will be especially demanding for you because she will seem to ask constantly for so much from you — and will often seem prepared to give so little back. However, you are the parent and she is the child. You can't reasonably expect your child to be sensitive and responsive to your needs in the same way that you are to hers.

Over the next couple of years, she will become less self-centred and focused on what she wants, and more empathic and focused on what you want as well. When she reaches school age, she will be much easier to be with. In the meantime, however, she's finding her way in her own little world, testing out the limits of her strengths, talents and abilities, and is determined to assert her independence.

Sharing your life with a child during the preschool years, therefore, involves recognising that she is trying to develop a view of herself and who she is and that she achieves this through trial and error. She learns by example and also by her mistakes. This means you will find yourself in role of rule-setter and rule-enforcer, perhaps when you'd rather be sharing songs, games and fun activities. It also means that you will find yourself in the role of peacemaker and soother when your child has a temper tantrum, perhaps when you'd rather be relaxing by yourself or enjoying a day out together. That is what sharing your life with a child means.

Keep things in perspective, however. True, your preschooler will be more demanding, challenging, confrontational, and volatile than she was when younger but she's also more communicative, physically affectionate, interesting, curious and fun to be with. Don't lose sight of the positives just because you also have difficult moments. Concentrate on the times when things go well. Learn from the more challenging episodes and try to avoid repeating negative incidents in the future. Sharing your life with your preschooler can be very fulfilling as you both adapt to each other's changes needs, interests and feelings.

STEP-PARENTING A PRESCHOOLER

Whether your partner's preschooler lives with you or stays on a regular basis or even if the child is an infrequent visitor or remains with her other parent, it will impact on your relationship with your partner. Be prepared for complications! No matter how you relate to your step-child, the vital thing is to keep open the lines of communication with your partner and to ensure that he/she takes the lead role. Most importantly, you need to agree about the rules you set your child and when and how to discipline her if they are transgressed, the level of child care you provide and how you relate to others, particularly her other parent and grandparents.

As a rule, it's easier to be a step-parent to a preschooler than an older child but that doesn't mean it's easy. Young children (younger than nine years) are more accepting of step-parents and can more readily adapt to having two homes though it's best if daily routines are kept the same in both. But, of course, they also require more care and attention.

Key to creating a relationship with your step-child is not to be overly ambitious in demanding her love (or even like) but to take your time and cues from your child. Some children need a while to accept change — particularly if circumstances have been traumatic — so it's important to set realistic expectations. Even if your preschooler will live with you all the time, it's best not to think of yourself as her 'new' mum or dad. You can be a significant other but your step-child's biological parent will always have a particular place in her heart. Similarly, don't expect that your 'new' family will be better or even similar to what she had previously, only that it will be different. One thing that can build bridges, is to share a particular activity that both of you like — maybe creating a scrapbook of found items from your nature walks together or even watching favourite dvds.

Often, step-families have problems not because of the children but because the adults in the family become jealous or resentful of the biological parent's attachment or feel rejected by the child and her other parent or even guilty about breaking up the former family in the first place. So, if you suffer from any of these emotions, it's important to discuss them with your partner and if he or she can't resolve them, to seek help. Charities like Relate and Parentline Plus offer help lines and you may discover a local step-family group you could join.

Preschool twins

As you have already discovered, twins are twice the usual work — but twice the usual fun as well. Happily, most parents of twins find that their workload decreases over the preschool years, as their children begin to eat by themselves and get out of nappies and luckily, there's always a willing playmate on hand. On the downside, it can be more of a challenge to keep two children of the same age safe from harm (see chapter six).

There are particular parenting challenges for parents when it comes to twins, simply because of their closeness in age, their special relationship — which is often more intense than normally found between siblings, and their underlying need to develop as distinct individuals despite being part of a tight-knit twosome. You have to find a way to balance their similarities with their differences in order to ensure that each of them is allowed to become a unique individual. Bear in mind, too, that if you have boy/girl twins, girls generally develop more quickly, reaching milestones at an earlier age, which can be discouraging for their brothers. Moreover, boy/girl twins' behaviour may be less sterotypical than singleton boys and girls; your son may be less boisterous and aggressive than his peers or your daughter more of a tomboy.

The practicalities of looking after and stimulating two preschoolers is demanding for even the most competent parent. So be willing to ask for help, whether from your partner, relatives or friends, and if you are lucky enough to receive spontaneous offers, take them. That doesn't mean you can't manage on your own, it's simply a very practical solution to help you juggle the continuous child-care demands. Don't wait until you feel totally overwhelmed by everything — that's leaving it too late.

Same, but different

Bear in mind that even if you have identical twins who look alike in every way, they will each have their individual characteristics. For instance, one twin might enjoy imaginative play while the other might prefer problem-solving play with shape-sorters and other basic puzzles. Or perhaps one prefers

rough-and-tumble while the other is more comfortable with quieter activities. Try to provide appropriate play opportunities that meet these different interests, so that their individuality is allowed to develop.

You may find that while your twins are good at playing together as preschoolers, even having a shared, private language, they are not so good at playing with other children. You may need to give them a helping hand with this. As well as affording them experience of sharing, turn-taking and playing games with rules at home, make a special point of letting them play with their peers. This gets them used to being with others their own age. Since their initial reaction might be to stick together, encourage them to interact. It can be a good idea to take them to play groups or twins clubs.

Of course, time is tight when you have two preschoolers the same age to look after. Whatever time you have during the day, however, make an effort to spend some moments alone with each twin, rather than spending time only with them together. All it takes is a few minutes each day playing with one of your twins, while the other is either cared for by someone else or is engaged in his or her own activity. And when you do spend time stimulating them, focus on language-based activities. Twins often develop speech and language skills at a slower rate than non-twins, probably because they often construct their own shorthand system for communicating with each other. That's why a broad range of language activities is so indispensable for your twins. Talk to them throughout the day as they progress through their routine activities. Read them stories, sing them songs and recite poems and nursery rhymes when you can.

Having a fair discipline system isn't always easy. For example, when something goes wrong, you might not be sure which of the two misbehaved — and the true culprit is unlikely to own up. Instead of punishing them both, try to identify the one who really was at fault.

Likewise, one twin could be harder to handle than the other, and therefore may require firmer limits. Recognising and responding to your twins' individual behaviour patterns by having different ways of managing them is perfectly reasonable. If you simply treat each twin the exact same way, they might actually end up feeling hard done by.

It maybe they both enjoy music or dance 'classes' but, more likely, one twin could be interested in dressing up and playacting while the other is more sporty. If they are forced to follow the same interests, at least one of them will feel thoroughly miserable. True, encouraging your twins' individual interests in this way is not entirely convenient for you and may not be cost-effective, but that applies to all parents who have two children close in age, not just to parents of twins.

Point of separation

One of the key decisions you have to make about encouraging the individuality of your twin preschoolers arises when they start nursery or school. Assuming they both attend to the same nursery or school, should they go into the same class or should they join separate classes? Or maybe you'd like them to attend the same nursery but different schools later on. There is no easy answer.

8 ways to encourage your twins' individuality

1 **Dress them differently** or if they want to dress similarly, make sure they have different haircuts. This will make it easy for people to tell which child is which.

2 **Make sure they have their own possessions** as far as possible, and don't just share things from a general pool.

3 **Afford them time alone with you or friends.** Make sure each twin spends indiviidual time with you and that each has the opportunity to play with other playmates.

4 **Tailor your shopping excursions**: just because one needs new shoes doesn't mean they both do.

5 **Teach your children to say their names** and to correct anyone who calls them by the wrong one.

6 **Speak to your children individually.** Address each by name. When speaking to others, talk about them individually rather than as a duo.

7 **Take individual photographs** as well as joint ones and put them on display at home.

8 **Make each twin a cake on his/her birthday** and ensure family and friends give each child a separate present and card. You could also appoint other days in the year, which each child has as his/her own special day.

The advantages of your twins being in the same class — whether in nursery or primary school — is that they could support each other, could help each other when minor problems arise throughout the school day, and would each have a ready-made friend in the school playground. But a potential disadvantage is that they might be treated like two peas in a pod, not just by the nursery or teaching staff but by their classmates as well. (In fact, if you've downplayed their twinness at home, you may need to explain about twinship as their new schoolmates or teachers may refer to them as 'the twins' rather than by their names.) In other words, they might be expected to fit into people's stereotyped expectations of twins, which would then constrain their individual differences from emerging.

In contrast, going into separate classes would have the advantage that each twin would be more likely to be accepted as an individual, without constant daily comparisons with her twin. This allows for more individual growth and expression. Yet temporary separation from each other during the school day could leave them feeling lonely, isolated and perhaps even afraid. Weigh up the pros and cons very carefully before making your choice.

Discuss this with your twins in order to find out their feelings on the matter. Chat to nursery or school staff as well. Although your children are more likely to develop their individual interests if placed in separate classes, sensitive teaching can still encourage their differences even if they are in the same class. The choice is yours.

Some parents are so determined to allow each twin to develop individually, that they enrol them in different schools after finding ones that suit their children's specific individual blend of talents, abilities and personality. However, that is a rather extreme strategy; generally, twins don't need to be separated entirely, they just need to be allowed to have their own opportunities.

How your child changes during the preschool years

As your child's individual blend of temperament, skills, interests, abilities, emotions and thoughts continue to emerge and develop, he will change in many exciting and fascinating ways. He will become much more of an independent free-thinker with very clear ideas about what he likes and dislikes, what he wants to achieve, and with whom he prefers to spend time. In many ways, living with your preschooler will become much more dynamic than during earlier years because in comparison to babyhood and infancy, he can do more, communicate more effectively, think more maturely, and has a better sense of humour. But, of course, these personal 'highs' can also be matched with personal 'lows' such as shyness, temper outbursts and even sagging self-confidence. It's the combination of all these characteristics that makes your preschooler a wonderfully unique and special person.

Growing independence

Your child has two conflicting yet complementary urges that develop strongly in this phase. On the one hand, your child has a natural, inborn desire to be able to do more for himself without any help from you and this intensifies. It happens because not only does he continue to want to be independent but he now believes he has the ability to cope on his own. His improved physical skills contribute to this belief. On the other hand, your preschooler still needs you to be beside him whenever he wants. You are the one who guides him, helps him, loves him and makes him feel valued and important. In other words, he still needs you as his parent as much as ever.

The challenge for your child is to balance those competing psychological forces by improving his independence skills (physical abilities and emotional self-reliance) while at the same time keeping close emotional ties with you. Sometimes this results in confusion for him (and can be trying for you),

especially in situations when his ambition outstrips his ability, for example, when he moves bravely and confidently upwards on the climbing frame on his own, only to burst into tears and call out for you seconds later when he realises he is stuck halfway. Or, when he insists on putting on his vest without help yet dramatically bursts into tears when he discovers it's on back to front. Ironically, you will think it was easier and quicker for you when you did everything for him.

Greater ability to communicate

Listening to your child now, it's hard to imagine that he was once a baby with no words, phrases, sentences, questions or arguments. His language and communication skills lift off at a rapid pace during the preschool years. It's not just that you see a huge increase in the number and range of words your child uses to express his thoughts and feelings, it's also the way he uses these new language features, which make him so much more interesting. Words and questions are used to challenge and explore the world around him. If he wants to know more, he just asks, whether or not you feel in the mood for a detailed discussion; the endless chatter of a talkative four year old can be draining and giving him looked-for explanations will take up much more of your time than previously.

Your preschooler can also give a more accurate account of his experiences when he isn't with you. Conversations between you and your child start to have adult-like qualities and you can begin to reason with him when you have a disagreement. Favourite words at this age are usually "No", "I don't want to" and "Why can't I do that?", so brace yourself for living with a child who is able and willing to voice his opinions. These sophisticated communication skills also reflect his better understanding of the world around him and of his relationships with the people in his world.

Wider sociability

Friendships start to matter to your child now. He wants to have lots of pals and to be popular, though he might not have the necessary social skills to achieve this target. He's at the age when children learn how to cooperate in play with each other, to share their toys and to play games with rules, especially as they near school age, but there can be a steep and difficult learning curve. Some children are more outgoing and make friends more easily than others.

One of the features of peer group relationships at this age is that they are often quite fragile — a best friend one week might be a forgotten memory by the next. And because preschoolers aren't always effective at resolving conflict peacefully, minor bickering is common even amongst friends. So the social life of a preschool child can be full of ups and downs.

Another social dimension that often emerges is shyness, as when your normally outgoing child suddenly freezes, say, as he is about to enter his best mate's party. In an instant, he bursts into tears and claims he doesn't want to go inside with the others even though he knows most of the children there. This type of unexpected shyness is common but fortunately, the frequency of such episodes steadily diminishes over the next couple of years.

Your life, too, changes as more than before, you spend time organising and implementing your child's social diary, ferrying him from one social encounter to the next, and dealing with any friendship squabbles.

Increased confidence

Your child's self-confidence is very important because if he feels good about himself, he will have the courage to try everything at least once. There are new social, learning and relationship experiences every day, and your child needs the confidence to tackle them effectively.

A child with low self-confidence is easily put off when facing a new task because the challenge can seem insurmountable to him. You know what it's like when you are trying to learn a new skill, such as striking a golf ball so that it travels a long distance. At first you think you'll never do it because every time you swing the club you miss the ball. Then comes that sweet moment of success, when you feel the club and ball connecting in the way they should. It's a great feeling — and your child feels the same when he achieves something. His self-confidence is highly variable and can be extremely fragile. One day he might show you how he can dress himself yet the next day he'll insist he can't put his clothes on without your help. Or perhaps he jumps wildly and happily on the bouncy castle till he suddenly demands to leave because he is afraid of injury. He may try to avoid difficult tasks for fear of not mastering them. But the more success he achieves in any area of his life, the stronger his confidence will become.

Emotional control

Regulating feelings and developing sensitivity to others ('emotional intelligence') will be an on-going internal struggle. Your child has been used to expressing whatever he wants whenever he wanted. When he was although some children have difficulty with this. A preschooler's outburst of temper can easily intensify to explosion point. Tantrums occur when a child's temper flares to such an extent that he loses all control of his rage. While most children manage their anger effectively by the time they start school, in the meantime an enraged preschooler can be quite a handful.

There is no doubt that a child who manages to regulate all his emotions (positive and negative) effectively and who shows empathy to the emotions of others generally has a more enjoyable life experience. A child who has little emotional regulation experiences exhausting emotional extremes. You'll see moments when your child will struggle to keep control because although he would rather do and say exactly what he wants, he yet successfully manages to keep his intense feelings in check.

Learning gains

Many children spontaneously learn early reading and number skills; for instance, they can recognise their written name and can complete very simple additions. Others need more help to achieve this. Every child is different in his rate of learning. Whatever your child's natural talents, however, tackling the early stages of literacy and numeracy becomes an important factor in his life.

As your child grows and thrives throughout the preschool years, the influence of these changes will become ever clearer. They way your child deals with those influences will affect the type of person he develops into. If he can build a solid emotional base during this phase of his life, he will be secure, confident and psychologically ready for starting school.

a baby, he cried when he wanted feeding without a thought for anyone else. When he was a toddler, he had a tantrum when he couldn't get his own way. In other words, he vented his emotions at the time they arose, without making any effort to control them or without thinking of the impact they had on others around him. That changes now. Your preschooler will see, for example, that his friends back away from him when he loses his temper, or that you become upset when he won't do what is asked of him. As a result, he will try harder to gain control over his feelings —

What you need to do

There are many specific ways you can help your preschooler to maximise all aspects of her potential and these are dealt with in subsequent sections of this book. However, here are some general parenting strategies, which will be needed to support your growing child throughout the preschool years.

Provide structure, stability and consistency

Children thrive best when they grow up in a stable and predictable environment. It's not that they are resistant to change — in fact most preschoolers find small changes in their lives exciting — just that they need to feel emotionally secure in their surroundings. For example, your child takes for granted that her bedroom will look the same tonight as it did last night, and that she will go to the same nursery tomorrow as she did today. Stability boosts her confidence, enhances her sense of wellbeing and makes her feel safe and secure.

The same should apply to your parenting. Your growing child knows the type of parent you are and expects you to behave in certain ways. When it comes to discipline at home, she understands the family rules and expects them to be applied consistently. Once she knows your expectations of her behaviour, she will do her best to conform, at least most of the time anyway. If family rules or your expectations of her change unpredictably, she will become confused and disorientated. That's why consistent parenting is crucial for your preschooler's psychological development. A child raised in uncertainty and constant change is likely to feel emotionally unsettled.

However, that doesn't mean everything has to stay the exact same all the time. There will be times when you bend the rules, for example, when you allow her to stay up late one night as a special treat, or when you don't allow her to play outside because of bad weather. She will adapt to small irregular changes like that, as long as she experiences overall

structure and stability within a background of consistent parenting.

There may also be major (possibly unplanned) changes in your family life, for instance, if you move house, switch child carers, separate or divorce, or a grandparent dies. Don't fall into the trap of thinking that because she's young, change doesn't matter to your child — it does. Each preschooler reacts to change in her own way. You may be able to tell just by looking at your child that something is troubling her, and if a major change has just occurred in her life — for instance, her dad has just left the family home — then you can reasonably make the connection. But distress at change can show in more subtle ways. For instance, ten minutes before going to spend the morning with her new child carer, your child complains that she has a sore tummy. Or your outgoing preschooler suddenly becomes sad and withdrawn. The better you know your child, the more sensitive you'll be to her reactions.

You can help your child adapt to major (and unwelcome) changes in the structure and stability of her life by acting with sympathy and understanding. If you are moving home, for example, the chances are that you are also having difficulty with the change (after all, moving is a stressful time for you, too) and you may find your preschooler's negative reaction frustrating. Try not to get angry with her, despite the pressure it puts you under. Give her lots of reassurance. True, you can't guarantee that life will be marvellous after a marriage split or that your child will be able to see both of you each day. But reassure her anyway. Tell her that she'll be fine, that everything will work out well and that in time she'll be just as happy with the new arrangement.

Good communication

Communicating well with your child doesn't happen by chance — you need to work at it, especially with all those other attractions that compete for her time. That's why you need to keep communication high and your child are used to each other and feel relaxed in each other's company — the more you do it, the easier it gets. Give your child your full attention, ignore all distractions and avoid all interruptions. Instead, let her speak to you without you butting in, so that she feels you are genuinely interested in her comments.

Do your best to ensure that enthusiasm for communication is two-way. Encourage your child to approach you whenever she wants to express something — she should understand that she can talk with you at any time, not just at mealtimes or those special moments when you are together. And when she does reveal a recent experience that upset her, or she tells you her latest exciting news, give her a big cuddle and tell her how pleased you are that she discussed this with you. Establishing good communication habits at this age sets the foundation for a continued close connection between you and your child for the rest of her childhood.

Positive parenting

Raising your preschooler has many wonderful moments, but it's also hard work. The constant running after him, dealing with his moods, taking him from here to there several times each day, and making his meals can be very demanding. If you are not careful, the pleasure of parenthood can slip away letting a more pessimistic viewpoint take over. When that happens — in fact before that happens — turn the situation around and instead make yourself a 'positive parent' — one who has an optimistic outlook in life. Positive parenting is not simply about pretending that everything in the parenting garden is rosy (because it isn't). Instead, it's about developing strategies for managing your child and your role as a parent in an effective way, so that you feel good about yourself. And if you feel good about yourself this benefits everyone in your family. Positive parenting is about taking the initiative, planning ahead and keeping control of your life.

on your parenting agenda. There will always be a thousand other things that you could do instead of spending time with your child — and there are probably a thousand other things she could do as well instead of spending time with you — so if you don't make communication a priority it simply won't happen. Try to build 'communication opportunities' into your weekly (and daily) routine. Perhaps the most effective strategy is to organise a traditional family meal at which you and your preschooler (along with all other family members) sit down and eat together round the one table. Communication works best in face-to-face situations, not when you are in separate rooms, at separate times, engaged in separate activities. Do your best to have a family meal at least a couple of times a week.

In addition, set aside ten or twenty minutes every day for the specific purpose of spending that time with your child. It really doesn't matter what you do during these minutes, whether you play or watch television together, chat about school or friends, or go for a walk — it's the shared time with each other that counts. Communication flows better when you

10 techniques that encourage positive parenting

1 **Reflect.** The problem with being a parent is that you are so busy doing things you rarely have time to think about them. So take a few minutes to consider your routine. Maybe you don't have to do absolutely everything. Your house will survive if you don't take all the papers to the recycling this week. Be prepared to drop some of the less important daily tasks.

2 **Take short breaks.** Try to organise your day so that you are able to put your feet up for 10 minutes. This could be when your child goes to nursery, or when he watches his favourite tv programme. Tell yourself that you need a short break, that you deserve it and that it must be a priority for you each day.

3 **Monitor 'nagging'.** Nobody likes to think that he or she is negative towards his or her child, but it is easy to fall into this trap. Think about the number of times you have reprimanded your child today — maybe you could have ignored some of these instances or perhaps made a more positive remark to him.

4 **Focus on good behaviour.** When you see moments of good behaviour — for instance, when your child plays quietly with his toys in his room — make a big fuss of him. Let him know how pleased you are with his actions. This helps both of you to realise that there are good moments too, that there aren't arguments all the time.

5 **Ask for/accept help.** The chances are that your partner, relatives and friends are more than willing to look after your preschooler once in a while so that you can have time to yourself — even if you have to ask. Take advantage of these offers. A short break on your own for only, say, an hour will enable you to recharge your batteries so you'll feel more positive.

6 **Structure your day.** Try to have a reasonable idea of what each day will hold — a schedule of activities for you and your child. Although you probably won't be able to follow the schedule to the letter, having a plan keeps you in control of your life. You are in charge of what you do, it's not just down to chance.

7 **Praise yourself.** Tell yourself each day that you are doing a good job. Reflect on at least one incident that day which you handled really well. Be proud of yourself as a parent. Other people may not think to praise you or give you encouragement, so give yourself a pat on the back every day.

8 **Enjoy your child's achievements.** Your child may be annoying at times when he moans and complains, yet he's also a fabulous child who does new things every day. You can't fail to notice the new skills that he acquires as he progresses through the preschool years. Be proud of his progress, maybe even noting down each new stage in a diary.

9 **Have realistic expectations.** Positive parenting also means that you need to recognise your own limitations as a parent. Everybody wants to be the best parent in the world but that title can only go to one person. Set yourself attainable goals instead of creating a set of overly-high expectations of yourself that are totally unrealistic.

10 **Give lots of cuddles.** No matter how strained your relationship with your child might become at times, make sure you give him lots of hugs and cuddles. Loving, physical contact of that sort helps melt away the negatives and puts you both in a positive, caring frame of mind. A good cuddle cheers you both up.

The importance of routine

A regular routine provides your preschooler with stability. He likes the world to operate according to routines and has an underlying need for a predictable structure in his life. In the same way that unexpected events might make you feel uneasy and momentarily insecure, an unstructured pattern to the day unsettles your child. Most children this age like to know, for example, that they go to nursery three days a week, that they go to the swimming pool another day, and so on. This sort of structure enables your child to plan ahead and to organise his life in a limited way. However, he may not fully realise that routines are there to help him rather than enslave him, or that a change in routine can be positive. When he is older, he'll be much more able to organise himself if he has had experience of doing this during the preschool years.

Another benefit of routine is that it gives your child some control over his life. He enjoys feeling in charge. He's only young, but at this age he still wants to be firmly in the driving seat. Your child prefers to be the one to decide when he should eat his dinner, what television programme he should watch and what time he should go with you to shop

in the supermarket. His need for control is very strong, and becoming familiar with daily routines satisfies this need. Bear in mind that most young children are not very adaptable. Flexibility usually improves with age; as your child's confidence grows over time, he will learn that minor changes can make life much more interesting, but for now he just likes the security of fixed routines.

The importance and significance of routines in your preschooler's life becomes even clearer when the established pattern is broken. For instance, he might become furious with you because he can't play in the park one Tuesday and yet he always plays in the park on that day. The fact that the family car has broken down, or that it is raining heavily, will make no difference to him. Routine leads him to expect the same to happen each time, and he will become distressed and angry when there is a break to that routine, whether that involves changes of food, mealtimes or activities. Suggesting something different may produce a confrontation.

Your child is more likely to enjoy the security and comfort of routines when he understands their purpose. So explain them to him. For instance, it's better to tell him "I'm not going to read you another story now because you are tired and I am tired, and we both need our rest" than to say "You're not getting another story now because I say so." Likewise, you can help him adapt to routines by reminding him of the next step. When you are out shopping in the afternoon, for instance, tell your child, "I bet you can't wait to get home, so that you can play in a lovely warm bath"; this will encourage him to anticipate what's coming next, and to look on it positively.

But make sure you avoid lengthy periods without any change in routine; the longer a routine is fixed, the more your preschooler wants it continue without alteration. That's why he might argue furiously with you because he has taken a bath in the morning for as long as he can remember and now you have decided bath-time should be moved to the evening. Well-established routines are hard to break and discourage flexibility. When you anticipate a break in routine, therefore, warn your child in advance. You won't always know ahead of time that you need to change his routine (for instance, if his friend suddenly becomes unwell and can't play with him that day), but if you are aware of an alteration, let him know as soon as you can. A sporadic break in your normal routine is good, and is usually as exciting for your preschooler as it is for you. Turn it into a special treat.

Likewise, be prepared to change routines if you feel they are too tiresome. For instance, if you find that putting your child to bed at seven in the evening is difficult because that's the exact time when your partner comes home, then change bed time (or other task) for earlier or later. The less demanding the routine is for you both, the more likely you are to enjoy the activities together. Think about the routines you have at the moment. Perhaps you'll discover that they can be altered to make life less stressful and more fun.

Formal schedules

By the time your child is aged four or five, you can consider creating more formal schedules, which will transfer some of the responsibility of setting routines

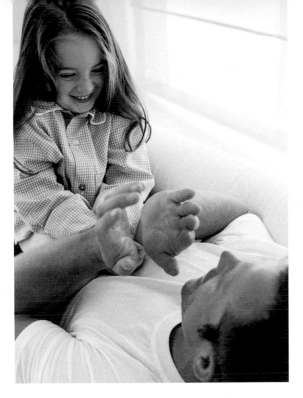

from you to your child; this also will help him organise his time more effectively. The schedule can be activity-focussed; for instance, your child may have a specific task to complete each day, such as tidying his room, and he could draw up a plan in which he decides to do this as soon as he returns home after nursery. It can also be time-focused; in this instance, your child could have a specific time each day in which he's allowed to watch tv or a dvd. If he is not well organised, start with an activity-based plan since a time-based schedule is probably too overwhelming for him at the moment. Pick one activity and begin to draw up a schedule for that.

A schedule will only be effective if your child feels committed to it — if he doesn't, he will feel it is imposed and will make no attempt to stick to the arrangements. An effective way to engage your child with a schedule is by involving him in decisions about the way it is compiled.

Whatever the focus of the schedule, talk to your preschooler about this. Discuss with him the difficulties he experiences at present (for instance, he is always rushed, he feels irritable when doing things, there are many other distractions) and point out the advantages a schedule would bring.

Likely flashpoints

During the preschool years, there are likely to be occasions when you and your child clash. Here are some common areas of conflict, with suggestions about how you could deal with them positively and effectively.

"I don't want to eat that."

Many children go through a phase of fussy eating, when they insist that they will only eat certain foods. This can happen for several reasons, including your preschooler's desire to assert his independence, a genuine change in his tastes, his realisation that refusing to eat is a great way to get your attention or even his dislike of having to sit at a table while eating.

Deal with it by staying calm. Bear in mind that you cannot force your child to eat no matter whether you cajole, threaten or beg him. He will only eat when he wants to. So when he insists he doesn't like anything on the plate in front of him, avoid an argument. Instead, chat to him about something else, and when you have finished your meal, remove his plate. He won't starve. You'll find that the less attention you pay to your fussy eater at mealtimes, the less fuss he makes. And try to make the eating experience pleasant by providing child-sized cutlery and good seating for him, and by sitting with you child so that you and he eat together.

"I don't want to do that."

Your preschooler will have more ideas of his own and is willing to challenge your decisions because he thinks he knows better than you. When he can't get his own way, his temper will start to rise. Your child completely believes that

he shouldn't be told by anyone what to do, especially when he is enjoying himself doing something else.

Deal with it by standing your ground. Without losing your temper with your infuriatingly challenging preschooler, simply repeat that you want him to do what you asked. You can give him a brief explanation of why you want him to do this (for example, he should stop playing now because it is time to tidy up) but avoid a long discussion. If you allow him to ignore your request because he has a tantrum or is tearful, you'll soon discover that the frequency of his tears and outbursts increases. If he makes no attempt to do what you asked, lead him gently towards the task you asked him to complete. Praise him when he responds positively.

"I don't want to go to bed."

Life is so exciting for your preschooler that it is hardly surprising he wants to savour every precious waking minute. He enjoys bedtime and being tucked up under the duvet, but he'd still rather be awake for the time being. Refusal to go to bed usually happens when he is busy with an exciting activity or watching an interesting dvd.

You should be prepared to make an exception to his normal bedtime occasionally, but most times you'll tell him he has to go to bed now because he needs the sleep. If he resists and starts crying, take him to bed anyway. You can help minimise this flashpoint by having a predictable bedtime routine every evening (for instance, bath, pyjamas, drink), giving him plenty of reminders that bedtime is fast approaching, making sure he only plays quietly or watches a short dvd shortly before, and by making bedtime interesting (for instance, by reading him a story before he goes to sleep).

"I don't want to go to nursery."

As far as you are concerned, the nursery (or child carer) is perfect for your child. He always enjoys himself there and talks excitedly about it when you collect him. Yet he can be easily put off, perhaps by a small incident in which he was mildly reprimanded or if he has a minor fall out with one of the other children there.

You should tell him that he is going anyway, but add that you are surprised he doesn't want to go because he likes it there so much. Listen to what he says in response. Sometimes a child this age isn't able to verbalise his feelings clearly so he might not be able to say why he is reluctant to go. See if you can discover what's troubling him through chatting to him. Certainly you should speak to the nursery staff (or his carer) and explain his reluctance to attend. Ask them if something has happened to unsettle him recently. Even if there is nothing obvious, it's good for you and them to keep an extra close watch on your child for the next few days.

"I want that toy."

Children have an insatiable desire for new and interesting toys. No matter how many toys your child already has, or how many he gets as presents, there will always be something else he desires. He sees new toys on television, at his friends' homes or when he goes shopping with you. He is as much a consumer as you are.

Pester power can be very strong, particularly if you are in a crowded supermarket with your preschooler and you fear that your refusal will result in an embarrassing tantrum or raging argument. However, be prepared to say "No, not on this occasion." Like it or not, your child has to learn that you have limited resources and that he can't get everything he wants. Point out to him all the wonderful toys he has already, many of which he probably hasn't actually touched in months. In addition, suggest to him that he could ask for that

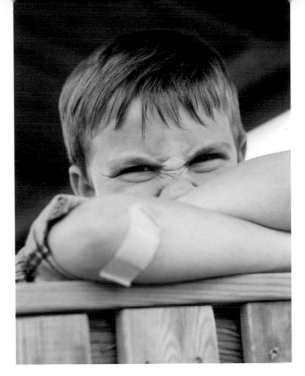

toy for his birthday or another present-giving occasion; by that time he may lose interest anyway.

"I can't do that."

You will know what your preschooler is capable of, so you are certain to be surprised when, say, he won't try a new jigsaw because he insists it will be too difficult. There will be times when your child will have a crisis of confidence because he fears that a challenge facing him is beyond his ability. He will rather refuse to attempt it at all, than to try it and fail.

Reassure your child that whatever activity he backs away from (the jigsaw, for example), he will be able to do it. Remind your child that he has solved similar puzzles in the past and point out that you won't be annoyed or upset with him if it turns out to be too difficult for him. To get him started, you could also offer to share the challenge jointly, giving him occasional help when necessary to enable him to move on to the next stage. Explain that you can't do everything you try, and that you just want him to do his best. You'll be happy as long as he makes an effort, rather than giving up before he starts.

3 YEARS OLD

✔ *happy*
✔ *loving*
✔ *giving*
✔ *eager to please*

Your turbulent two year old matures into a more relaxed three year old — a child who is a better master of his abilities, more eager to share and to learn from others and calmer emotionally. He's learning a lot and his challenge is to make sense of new things — are they real or imagined, which may explain why he may be prone to fears (of the dark, for example). His newfound awareness of things can lead to rapid changes of mood or be expressed as physical and emotional sensations — he may suffer from a tummy ache if told off or become excited and run about when given a gift.

Language becomes increasingly important and your child will love to talk with you — and often to himself. If you want to know what he is thinking and feeling, it's a good idea to listen to him or perhaps ask him to tell you a story. Much of his conversation is self-initiated — calling attention to himself or asking questions or for information —but he may occasionally respond to something you ask him. He will know his name and be able to repeat it, and it is a good thing for him also to learn to repeat his address. His

command of language should be sufficient so that he is able to express his thoughts, wants and needs but, if not, he'll be prone to whine. He will be able to use time concepts such as 'yesterday' and also times of day, and can learn some numbers. He will also know the difference between large and small, singular and plural, and can identify colours and match shapes. He'll begin to name items in books but he also will use language in 'silly' ways such as repeating funny, made-up words or deliberately mispronouncing them.

Physically, he is more sure of himself when walking and running and riding a tricycle or scooter. This sureness with motion means he very often moves with abandon so it's important to make sure he doesn't become over-tired and exhausted. He will love playing outdoors. His hand-eye coordination is much improved and he is better able to build clay models and work with blocks, draw and paint within boundaries and perform the fine movements necessary for self-help skills; he should be more adept with his fork, pour from a pitcher using two hands, be able to button and unbutton when dressing and undressing and wash and dry his hands. He probably can use the toilet and wipe his bottom. Though he will be clean and dry most of the time, there will be plenty of accidents. His increased skills, and his liking to do things unaided, means he can be a help to you by tidying away his toys and clothes and helping to lay the table; he even may be able to pour out his cereal. Make chores fun and when he does well, praise him afterwards; if helping becomes routine at this age, there will be less resistance to doing so when he is older.

He enjoys playing with others — both real children and imaginary friends. With friends, he is beginning to play with them instead as previously alongside, and is starting to share some, less treasured, possessions. He may understand that he has to take turns on the swings or slide and acknowledge that others also have feelings. His happiest times, however, will still be with his parent — just being close to them as well as helping them with tasks, accompanying them to the shops and playing with them.

Play at this time also becomes more imaginative whether it involves dolls or role-playing games. Books and music should also feature largely in your child's daily life. Your child may want to hear the same story read over and over again (with no changes) and may occasionally 'read' to himself. Music can be the accompaniment to more active play as well as self created rather than just something to listen to or sing along with.

He will generally adhere to family 'rules' but as far as routines are concerned, keeping your child in bed can become something of a challenge as can mealtimes if your child starts to develop fussiness over food — although most three year olds eat anything and everything.

3½ YEARS OLD

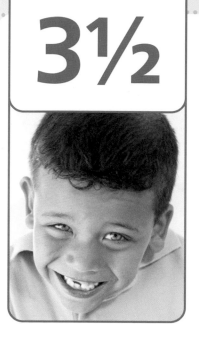

✓ *rebellious*
✓ *determined*
✓ *inconsistent*
✓ *anxious*

While six months previously, your child was calm and conforming, a sea change is occurring and insecurity will replace stability. She becomes hard to please and hard on the person who tries to please her. She is also struggling emotionally because she wants to be mistress of her surroundings but doubts her ability to do so, and this leads to frequent battles over almost anything but particularly her daily routines. From getting up to going to bed, and everything in between, your child may fight you every step of the way.

Parenting a three and a half year old can be difficult, so it's extra important for your child to feel loved and appreciated even when you find it most difficult to handle her. Your child is mainly interested in provoking you, as her chief carer, rather than adults in general, so it can be a good idea to have her attend nursery or be with a sitter some of the time, particularly if you're going shopping or on other errands. When she is in a good mood, make the most of it — talking and playing together. She will commonly be beset by fears, anxieties and timidities, and rather than belittling her worries, you should take care of her emotional fragility by giving her 'weapons' to combat them or by suggesting alternative activities when she refuses to budge. Distraction rather than confrontation should be your aim.

The reason for all this turbulence and trouble is normal disequilibrium, brought on by a marked spurt in development that can prove too strong for your preschooler to control. Such a lack of control can prove unsettling and be exacerbated by a desire to dominate, so that your child becomes prey to a great deal of stress and strain. Although she can speak more fluently and effectively, she often may stutter; when she walks, she may stumble or fall; and when she manipulates items, she can tremble and be uncoordinated. She will be quicker and more vigorous in her actions but this can mean her all-too-easily bursting into tears when things don't go her way or swiping another child's toy from under his nose. Whining and tension-relieving actions such as nail biting, thumb sucking, nose picking, etc. become more prevalent.

But the developmental changes at the bottom of her insecurity mean that in spite of her frequent ineptness, she will be more active and willing to challenge herself. She'll be more skilled and effective in physical activities such as jumping and balancing, riding a scooter and reproducing drawings or models based on a pattern (rather than copying what you do). She can string beads or pasta and arrange them by colour and shape.

Language becomes more advanced and she frequently asks questions, can follow more complex directions more accurately (discriminating between under and over, beside and between, for example), and uses language in her play. She also can use her voice to express emotions, hence she will whine when anxious or whisper when fearful, and has many ways of saying "No".

Your child will be happy to play in small groups and will become much more interested in her playfellows. While there will be more cooperative play — more sharing, more give and take, less arguing — there will also be more excluding. In fact, your child's 'group' can define itself by those whom it won't allow in! Your child and her friends will find shared humour in accidents, incongruous behaviour or by being aggressive.

4 YEARS OLD

✓ *exuberant*
✓ *adventure-loving*
✓ *emotional*
✓ *imaginative*

The average four year old can best be described as 'wild and wonderful.' She is excited by the new — people, places, games, playthings and activities — but along with versatility, demonstrates extreme emotions. A child of four has great drive and a fluid imagination.

Your four year old will be constantly in motion — hopping, jumping, running or trying out new stunts — both indoors and out. Her fine motor abilities have strengthened and she enjoys playing games that require complex motor skills such as activities in which she has to manipulate many small pieces, such as constructing models out of Lego®. She can draw, colour and paint with more detail, using her whole arm to do so, and should be able to dress and undress with very little help.

All fours love to talk loudly or in a whisper and do so constantly. Your child will probably be better at talking than listening; for example, she will ask many questions, but will not be interested in long answers. Her exuberance and liking for all things new will manifest itself in language by her use of

big words and her liking for silly sounds and nonsense rhymes, while her emotionality reveals itself in name-calling, swearing, boasting, tattle-telling and talking back. She demonstrates imagination by telling tales but, in fact, has trouble distinguishing fact from fantasy.

Her memory skills have increased, so not only can she talk about something that happened in the past — a movie she saw and enjoyed — she will also enjoy counting by rote (probably up to 20), repeats nursery rhymes with few mistakes and if taught, will know her address along with her full name. She is beginning to understand the concept of numbers and certain grammatical patterns.

Her vivid imagination is also displayed in dramatic play — she loves pretending she's in a dangerous situation — and she relishes scary fairy tales. She remains an avid reader, particularly of humorous books but now appreciates those with complex illustrations. She enjoys playtime with other children, and is most interested in simple games and activities that combine singing and movement. She plays cooperatively although she often changes the rules. While joining in with others' laughter, she also will cry loudly and may hit, kick or spit when things don't go her way.

In addition to her liking for silly sounds and rhymes, she also demonstrates a sense of humour in her activities along with greater sensitivity to the feelings of others. She tries to figure out what is the 'right' and 'wrong' way to act.

Since four year olds enjoy new adventures, make the most of this characteristic by both creating and sharing adventures with her. Plan excursions and activities that will interest her (a science or natural history museum with hands-on activities will be preferred over an art exhibit) and encourage her to point out things of interest en route. Show her you enjoy her exaggerated stories or silly rhymes by offering ones of your own.

It's important not to worry overmuch about your child's overall exuberance — even if she occasionally goes out of bounds. This is totally natural for this age. Instead, make every effort to enjoy your amusing, lively and enthusiastic preschooler, even if you don't approve of everything she says and does (and don't blame behaviour that you don't like — exhibitionism, bad language, sex play, etc.— on her playmates!).

Nor should you try too hard to motivate her if she becomes uninterested or inactive, or feel you can increase her intellectual abilities as these are things that come naturally with maturity or are inborn. By all means provide books and stimulating activities but don't force her to make use of them. Even if she is still sucking her thumb or wetting her bed, this may not be the time to try and put them to an end; she may need a few months' more maturation for them to stop naturally.

4½ YEARS OLD

✓ *unpredictable*
✓ *confused*
✓ *demanding*
✓ *reality-based*

In maturing from four to five, children appear a bit confused and highly unpredictable as they move into a stage of fitting things together. In particular, you will find that your child is now more demanding and is less easily shifted than he was six months previously. Instead of being distracted with humour when he insists on having something he's not permitted, he may become obnoxious, make faces and stick out his tongue. But in many other ways, he is quieter (though still physically active he has calm periods), becoming better able to withstand frustration although he will still be highly emotional. Very often, having just had a good laugh at something, he will become suddenly tearful.

Your child will love learning new information — and this is the top age for questions. He'll ask you endless 'whys' and 'hows', not only to gain knowledge, but just to keep the conversation going — and occasionally to be obstructive. He will demonstrate a strong interest in whether things, such as stories in books or that you tell him, are real or not and this is because he is

beginning to differentiate fantasy from reality. He may even become scared by wild stories he loved at four.

while others may be very willing to follow another child or have intense likes for a particular friend. Although your child will continue with imaginative play, he will prefer reality in his activities, often suggesting the use of real objects — "Let's put some windows on the house" — when's he's constructing things.

He's also likely to cooperate more with family members, if he's not feeling overly challenged or rushed, and is less likely to push limits. He may even set the table, if asked. At 4½, a child is becoming aware of authority — you may see some fear as well as intentness in his expression when you reprimand him — so bargaining can prove an effective ploy in changing behaviour. You give a little and your child may be willing and able to give a little in return. Moreover, you can appeal to his sense of adventure by suggesting a change in routine; if he absolutely refuses to eat his lunch, you can occasionally allow him to have his dessert first (as long as its something healthy). This is an age when praise and compliments work wonders, so feel free to compliment your child extravagantly when he does something well.

Although it's a good idea at any age to avoid situations that you know will be troublesome, it's particularly relevant now. One example is telephone talking; children of this age hate it when their parents spend 'hours' on the phone and generally respond by behaving badly, and invariably they end up being yelled at and possibly punished. It's therefore better if long, chatty phone calls are restricted to times when your child is busily engaged doing something else or is out of the room. Your child loves to talk, and he mainly likes talking to you and having your full attention. Talking to him will ensure that you know what's on your child's mind, and it's this that can help you get through the day.

Self-motivation is more evident and he'll need less adult supervision with tasks; in fact, he'll demand his independence. As well as gathering new information, he will perfect old skills, tending to stay on task with activities that he likes better than before, though his unpredictability is evident in the lack of interest he shows in expanding his skills. He will, however, like to call attention — often dramatically — to his own performance.

Your 4½ year old considers friends very important and is starting to play collaboratively, although his level of cooperation is unpredictable. At this age, some children demonstrate leadership capabilities

5 YEARS OLD

✓ *equable*

✓ *calm*

✓ *anxious to please*

✓ *serious*

A preschooler of this age understands the world better and more accurately judges what he can and cannot do, but is determined that everything he does, he does just right. While your child will not be particularly adventurous, his liking for learning will be immense and he will enjoy practising skills and abilities. He wants to please and for things to go smoothly. This makes him a much easier playmate — though best with a child his own age — and more independent in terms of personal care skills so for parents, a five year old is a joy to be around and for many, it will be one of the most rewarding periods in their entire relationship with their child.

A five year old enjoys being at home, around his mother, having his own room and living in a familiar neighbourhood. (If at nursery, he'll be very fond of any playgroup leader or teacher, be generally obedient when he's with him or her and often will tell you what he or she says.) He tends to concentrate on the present (not past or future), liking life the way it is, feeling good about himself and his parents and any siblings and grandparents.

For a five year old, parents are the ultimate authorities. That being said, your child will also be adaptable to change, so good with unfamiliar people, places, food and activities. He tends to love life and everything that is a part of it. It's not surprising then that five year olds are strong believers: God, Father Christmas and even the Easter Bunny figure large in their world. If asked where one of the above lives, your child will come up with a concrete destination and when he writes his Christmas gift list, your child expects to receive what he asks for. A birthday party, too, is very important at this age

Intellectually, your preschooler will demonstrate great competence in language learning. He shows interest in new words and has an extensive vocabulary. He now asks questions — how, when, what and why — to seek information and unlike his four-year-old self, will be content with longer answers. He'll enjoy spelling out signs and words in books. He's starting to figure out things for himself and thus begins to make generalisations (even if based on inadequate evidence).

Increasingly, he exhibits creative and constructive abilities and enjoys hands-on learning. All these factors are important in deciding on his school readiness. Creativity in a five year old is something that parents can nurture, not only by providing artistic materials, music-making instruments and puppets, but through games such as "20 Questions" and activities that require a child to figure out common problems — for example, new uses for everyday items such as paperclips, a way to group disparate items or how to share out an uneven amount of money or candy.

Physical play will be an important part of your child's life. Having greater control of his movements and well-developed gross motor skills such as skipping, jumping and climbing, he's able to confidently enjoy playground equipment without a lot of parental guidance. His improved manipulative skills in cutting, tracing, pasting and stringing are evident in many of the creative activities he most enjoys. However, he is more interested in problem solving at this stage than engaging in imaginative play, although playing

house is an activity enjoyed by both boys and girls. Books and reading are one of your child's great pleasures, particularly stories that can add to his learning or contain puzzles he can work out.

Five year olds can appear much more accomplished (compared to their younger selves). They can carry out a great many commands, do simple errands, and are more aware of time and when certain activities, such as eating, tv viewing or going to bed occur. Many can count and some even can read and/or write their name. If taught, your child should know his name, age, address and birthday. These, moreover, are some of the things that are vital in considering school readiness.

Although gentle, compliant and eager to please, your five year old won't find it easy to admit the occasional wrongdoing. Due to his desire to be good and to do the right thing, you may be surprised if he occasionally lies or to can't resist taking another's belongings.

5½ | YEARS OLD

✓ *hesitant*

✓ *dawdling*

✓ *combative*

✓ *disobedient*

Going on six can appear to be in a constant state of tension with behaviour characterised by opposite extremes such as happy/sad, quiet/loud or agreeable/defiant. Your child will be more restless and less composed than previously, finding sitting still increasingly difficult. She will have problems making decisions and transitions, will play well one moment but argues the next and will feel torn between choices (she'll often try to choose both play or activity options). She may be shy one minute and bold the next or turn from very affectionate to antagonistic without warning. She will complain readily and disobey often. If she lacks the courage to outwardly defy you, she will dawdle, which amounts to the same thing in that whatever you want her to do will very often remain undone. It's important, however, to understand that your child is processing a lot of information and new expectations, and what may look like defiance may actually be her simply being focused on an activity, and lacking the self-regulation to pull herself away and move to something else. In other words, she may simply be too engrossed in an activity to hear you. On the other hand, particularly if she's started school, her growing involvement with a peer group, and the support she feels in being part of one, can cause her to be challenging.

Your child is still young, and while she may resort to tantrums and meltdowns, she's working on her self-control and self-discipline. Make sure that you

She also will test limits to see how far she can go. In addition to talking back, she may assert food preferences suddenly deciding that she will no longer eat 'red' vegetables or only raw tomatoes cut into slices not cooked ones or will have peanut butter sandwiches at every meal. Strong likes or dislikes can also extend to other categories such as particular garments or activities.

Your child will use more diverse and complex language but if verbalising freely, her stories or songs may contain hints of hidden violence or dark thoughts — aggression or accidents. Over the past six months, her reading ability is likely to have improved markedly and she should know all the letters of the alphabet and read simple signs and books. She should be able to print her name and count to 20 with few mistakes.

She is now able to express her thoughts and feelings and to understand what you may be feeling and take that into account, even expressing comfort and sympathy when she encounters someone who is hurt. But she also knows that she can hide her thoughts and feelings from you so starts to have secrets. Due to an emerging sense of right and wrong, she will be prone to tattle on others.

Your child's sense of independence is developing and she should be able to amuse herself for extended periods. She can look through a book by herself, play a game with her dolls, or watch tv alone. Increasingly she may disappear to her room. She has mastered a great many self-help actions like being able to dress and feed herself but may only extend herself if encouraged; otherwise she may passively wait for you to do up her buttons or brush her hair. If she's in a good mood, she may be willing to perform some simple household tasks like putting her laundry away or setting the table.

understand the cause of her being defiant, disrespectful or acting out in anger. There may be an understandable reason or mitigating factors, such as a change in her routines or in the household. If she is starting 'real' school, for example, she may be suffering from separation anxiety, or worried about interacting with new and unfamiliar peers and teachers. She may have trouble adapting to a classroom environment where she has to pay attention, follow directions and sit still for long periods.

There will be physical manifestations of her lack of equilibrium. She may suffer from aches and pains, won't be able to sit still for long periods, may lack fluidity in movements and reverse numbers and letters. She may start to show an increase in tensional outlets such as nail biting, pencil chewing or hair pulling, which also may be due to starting school and finding it difficult.

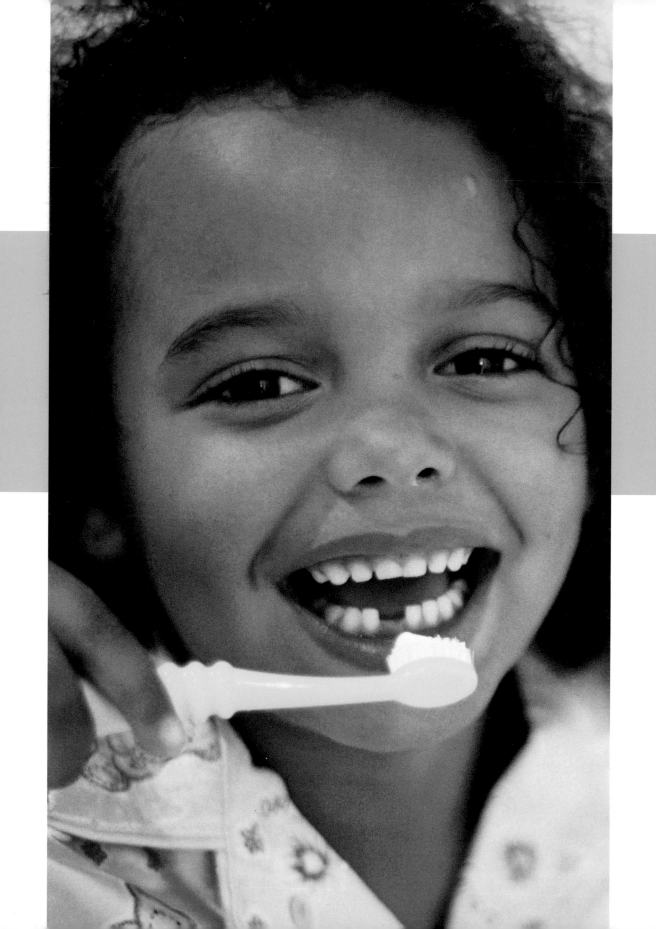

CHAPTER 2
DAILY CARE

Though your preschooler will begin to manage many of the tasks himrself, you still have to devote time to making sure he eats well, is appropriately dressed, pays attention to hygiene matters including brushing his teeth and hair, keeps active and goes to bed happily. You'll also want to ensure that he has lots of time to play — by himself and with others — as well as opportunities to learn about the outside world.

Nutritional needs

Good nutrition combined with healthy eating habits developed during the preschool years will lay the building blocks for future good health. A balanced diet ensures that your child's nutritional needs for energy and growth are met. A good diet also helps to protect your child against illness and infection, and aids his mental development and ability to learn.

Your preschooler needs to eat easily digestible and nutrient-rich foods from the four food groups shown below. In addition to his three regular meals, foods from the different groups can be given as his two-to-three daily snacks. Refined sugars should be avoided. If your child regularly eats something from each of the main food groups, he is likely to get all the nutrients (protein, carbohydrate, fat, vitamins and minerals) he requires for good health.

Calories

Preschool is a time of growth and change for your child; he is developing mentally and physically and needs sufficient calories to grow while not eating so many that he becomes over weight. How many calories he needs depends on his age, activity level and gender. Three year olds of both genders need between 1,000 and 1,400 calories per day, with sedentary children requiring 1,000 to 1,200 calories and active children needing 1,000 to 1,400 calories. From the age of four, sedentary girls and boys need

---

THE FOUR MAIN FOOD GROUPS

PROTEIN FOODS
Aim for three daily servings of meat, poultry, fish or egg or plant sources such as nuts, pulses or beans.

DAIRY PRODUCTS
Aim for at least 350 ml (½ pint) full-fat milk daily or two servings of cheese, fromage frais or yoghurt.

VEGETABLES AND FRUIT
Aim for at least two servings of vegetables and three of fruit daily — fresh, tinned or frozen. (Fruit will provide your child with more energy than vegetables.) Fruit juice should count as only one serving even if given more than once.

GRAIN PRODUCTS AND STARCHY FOODS
Aim for at least one serving (and preferably two) each mealtime of bread, corn, rice, cereal or starchy vegetables. Make several of the servings whole grain products but avoid very rough ones.

1,200 to 1,400 calories daily. Active girls need from 1,400 to 1,800 calories per day while active boys require 1,600 to 2,000 calories daily.

Portion size

A young child's serving is usually a quarter to a third of an adult's. With fruit and vegetables, an easy way to judge a portion is to think of it in relation to your child's hand. A portion at any age is what will fit inside. But if you are looking for a general guideline, ¼ to ½ cup will do for most foods. For protein foods, one ounce of meat, fish or poultry; two tablespoons peanut butter or ½ egg are each a serving.

Snacks

Preschoolers need to snack in addition to their regular meals in order to get the nutrients and calories they need (see also page 47). Snack time may be a good time to introduce new foods. Many times children will refuse food at mealtime, but accept them at snack time.

How much fibre?

Some fibre is necessary in your child's diet to prevent constipation, but too much may fill him up so that he does not want other foods. A high-fibre diet may also lead to diarrhoea and can interfere with the absorption of minerals such as iron.

If your child eats a variety of grains and fruits and vegetables daily, or a combination of white and wholemeal varieties of bread and breakfast cereals, he is likely to be getting enough fibre.

Should he eat fats?

Fat is a concentrated source of energy and vitamins for young children and also provides essential fatty acids. It is best that your child obtain most of his fat from foods such as whole milk, cheese, oily fish, eggs, nuts and seeds, which also contain other essential nutrients. Foods such as crisps and biscuits may be high in fat but are usually poor in other nutrients, so these should be limited. Meat should be lean. Children under the age of five should not drink skimmed or low-fat milk. If you are sure that

your child is getting enough energy (calories) from a good mixed diet, he can drink semi-skimmed. If in doubt, ask your doctor or health visitor for advice.

Vitamin supplements

Your child should be given drops or tablets containing vitamins A, C and D up to the age of five. Only give the dose recommended by the manufacturer as too much of these vitamins can be as dangerous as too little.

Iron and zinc requirements

An iron deficiency can slow down your child's growth and development. Try to give him some foods containing iron every day. Good sources of iron include red meat, oily fish (such as canned sardines and pilchards), shellfish, fortified breakfast cereals, bread, eggs, dried fruits (such as raisins, apricots, and dates), beans and pulses (such as canned baked beans, pinto beans, chick peas and lentils), oranges, apricots, green peas and dark leafy greens (such as cabbage and broccoli). Liver, including paté, although a rich source of iron should only be given to children once a week as it is very rich in vitamin A, too much of which can be harmful. To increase iron absorption give some food or fruit juice containing vitamin C at every meal.

Zinc is necessary for a healthy immune system and for growth. Good sources include meat and poultry, wholegrain cereals, zinc-fortified cereals, hard cheese, eggs, pulses and beans.

Water and other fluids

Most children don't drink enough fluids, but decent hydration is just as important as a good balanced diet. A 2 per cent loss in body fluids, for example, can cause a 20 per cent reduction in both physical and mental performance. Choose from filtered or bottled water, diluted fresh fruit juice or milk (full-fat up to age five) and avoid carbonated sugary drinks. The amount of fluid a child needs depends on age and weight but, as a rough guide, the average three to six year old should drink around five (250-ml) glasses a day. A child who does not drink enough may experience headaches, lethargy, poor concentration and constipation. Dehydration also

SPOILED FOR CHOICE

The greater the variety of fruit and vegetables your child eats, the wider range of nutrients he will get. Choose fruit and vegetables from the various colour groups and try to offer them in different guises: raw, steamed or stir-fried, or in stews, sauces or soups.

RED
Tomatoes, strawberries, sweet peppers, raspberries, redcurrants, apples, grapes, watermelon, cherries, radishes, rhubarb

ORANGE
Carrots, sweet peppers, pumpkin, swede, squash, sweet potato, oranges, clementines, melon, nectarines, apricots

YELLOW
Bananas, courgettes, sweet peppers, marrow, beansprouts, sweetcorn, pineapple, plums

GREEN
Broccoli, Brussels sprouts, cabbage, green beans, avocado, apples, pears, salad leaves, spinach, peas, kiwi fruit

PURPLE
Berries, aubergine, figs, plums, beetroot, red cabbage

affects the body's ability to transport essential nutrients throughout the body and brain.

What to avoid

Although it can be hard to be a food 'policeman', it's important that you monitor your child's diet and make sure that you cut out or down on the following.

Refined sugar

Processed foods such as sweets, cakes, biscuits and sweetened breakfast cereals are high in refined sugar, which has little or no nutritional value and can result in tooth decay and weight gain. Eating sugary food leads to a temporary surge in blood-glucose levels, resulting in a rush of energy (think of kids at a birthday party) that is promptly followed by a slump or sugar-low (tears and tantrums as guests go home). This fluctuation produces an inconsistent supply of energy to the brain, leading to poor concentration and attention span, irritability and fatigue. Sugary foods such as doughnuts, biscuits and chocolate, often also include a fair amount of fat, which increases the risk of disease (see below).

Consuming large amounts of sugar may inhibit the assimilation of certain nutrients, suppress the immune system and lead to glucose intolerance, which means the body has problems regulating blood-sugar levels.

Junk food

Highly processed and usually full of salt, sugar, sweeteners, additives (artificial colours, preservatives and flavourings) and fat, these manufactured foods lack nutritional value. They also tend to be high in saturated and hydrogenated fats, or 'trans' fats, which slow down digestion, circulation and mental processes and clog the arteries, increasing the risk of disease.

Caffeine and carbonated drinks

As well as being found in coffee and tea, caffeine is present in chocolate — a bar can contain up to 50 mg — and in some carbonated drinks, like cola. Caffeine is a stimulant and diuretic and can cause mood swings since it affects the body's ability to

control blood-sugar levels. It also depletes the body of some B vitamins and the minerals, zinc, potassium, calcium and iron.

Sweet, fizzy drinks contain added sugar, colours, sweeteners, caffeine and preservatives. They also are high in the mineral phosphorus, which inhibits calcium absorption.

Additives and preservatives

A number of substances are routinely added to manufactured food:

- Antioxidants (E300–321) prevent food turning rancid;
- Colourings (E100–180) add or intensify colour;
- Emulsifiers, stabilisers, thickeners and gelling agents (E322–495) affect the texture of food and bind ingredients together;
- Flavour enhancers (E620–635) enhance the taste or smell of a food;
- Preservatives (E200–283) prevent and slow down deterioration in food. Any processed food with a long shelf life is likely to include preservatives.

According to research, additives may adversely affect one in seven children. Young children are especially vulnerable since their systems are immature and they are more exposed to them. While not all additives are potentially harmful, some of them (such as the orange food colouring tartrazine [E102]have been

BE ALERT!

FOODS TO AVOID

- Pizza, burgers, sausages, pies and sausage rolls, which are high in fat and contain poor quality ingredients.
- Cheese slices and 'strings' that are processed.
- Sliced meats with a high-water, high-fat and high-preservative content.
- Breaded chicken or fish nuggets with a low meat or fish content.
- Breakfast cereals with a high sugar content.
- Crisps and reconstituted potato products, which are highly flavoured.
- Carbonated, sugary drinks such as cola and fruit-flavoured drinks or fruit drinks.
- Diet versions of drinks that contain artificial sweeteners.
- Sweets that are highly coloured and contain artificial colours and gelatine.
- Ice cream and ice lollies that are highly coloured and made with poor quality, often artificial ingredients.
- Yogurts that are artificially flavoured and high in sweeteners.
- Cereal bars, cakes and biscuits high in sugar and/or fat.

linked to hyperactivity in sensitive children as well as being the potential cause of allergies, poor memory, depression and mood swings.

Most additives and preservatives are listed on food labels and you should try to avoid foods containing flavour enhancers, colourings and preservatives (see box, above). If you are concerned that your child reacts adversely to food additives (he has temper tantrums or otherwise behaves disruptively), keep a food diary and monitor his behaviour over a period of time before contacting a doctor or dietitian.

Managing mealtimes

It's not just what children eat that matters but when. Young children are particularly vulnerable to dips in blood-sugar levels that can lead to mood swings, irritability and poor attention. Regular healthy meals, supplemented by nutritious snacks and sufficient fluids, are crucial throughout the day to maintain steady blood-sugar levels, ensuring mental clarity, sustained energy levels and concentration.

Although children have very high daily requirements for energy (calories) and other nutrients, their stomach is small; they cannot eat large amounts of food at one sitting. Preschoolers, therefore, need three main meals a day with nourishing snacks in-between.

Appetites and tastes

Young children also have different appetites; some eat like birds, picking at everything that's put in front of them; some eat moderate amounts of foods without too much fuss and others wolf down everything on their plate, providing it is of their choosing.

Like adults, children also have their own likes and dislikes when it comes to food, so it is quite possible that there are some foods your child will refuse just because he doesn't like them.

Research shows that children acquire a taste for foods over time, and it takes an average of 10 'tastes' for a child to accept new foods. The theory is that if you can persuade your child to eat just a single mouthful of spinach on 10 occasions, he will learn to like it.

You can also try combining foods you know your child likes with ones previously untried or rejected; you may find that new combinations are enough to encourage your child to try new things. If, however, your child refuses to eat something, and you are unable to persuade him otherwise, take the food away but don't offer an alternative. Although this may be difficult, it's important that your child gets used to eating what he is given and not to expect endless alternatives if he doesn't like the first option.

It's also worth remembering that flavours and textures can affect your child — even changing brands can put him off a certain food. But don't fall into the trap of believing your child prefers bland or so-called 'children's food'; many children like strong flavours and will happily try curries, stir-fries, chilli and the like.

To make your child more enthusiastic about mealtimes, it can be effective to give him a sense of control over what he eats. Try to include him in your meal planning, for example, starting with the trip around the supermarket and maybe involving him in the preparation of a meal.

Expect your child's appetite to fluctuate or almost disappear at times. He will go through phases that are affected by things such as growth spurts, moods, even changes in the weather. He may get 'stuck' on a certain food, refusing to eat anything else, and then without apparent reason reject it. It is easy to worry about this type of faddiness, but it doesn't necessarily mean your child is not getting the proper nutrition. As long as your child eats a well-balanced diet over a period of time, is healthy and growing well, the fact that he may only pick at certain foods on a given day, should not be a cause for concern.

Persuading your child to eat

Don't overwhelm your child with large portions or too many choices — he may find them frightening. Instead, offer small amounts of a few different foods in a child-sized bowl or plate. Serving a variety of foods will help keep your child interested. Food needs to look appealing too, so spend a little time on presentation and making food look appetising.

You also need to pay attention to your child's liquid intake, as too much may kill his appetite.

Structure mealtimes so that your child knows what is expected of him — that you want him to eat when you eat, for example, or stay at the table until he's finished but don't force him to eat everything on his plate if he really doesn't want to.

It can be very frustrating if your child does not eat a meal that you have lovingly prepared, and trying to force your child to eat will be a no-win situation for you both. Children are remarkably clever at picking up on the anxieties of their parents and your child may well tune into your own frustrations about his not eating. Conflict and tension will only to make the situation more difficult and may lead to your child using mealtimes as a way of seeking attention. Gently coax or encourage your child to try just a mouthful; sometimes this is enough for him to be persuaded to eat the rest of the meal. And even if he eats just the one mouthful, make sure you give him lots of praise.

6 ways to encourage good eating habits

1 **Resist the temptation to offer alternatives** and never use food as a reward or a bribe, or refuse to give it as a punishment, as this can encourage an unhealthy attitude toward food.

2 **Don't get hung up on good eating manners.** Your child will almost certainly continue to make a mess when he eats. While ideally you would always like him to eat with a fork or spoon, don't be upset if he uses his fingers or hands, holds his utensils the wrong way or spills things.

3 **Try to eat together as a family,** if only at weekends. This will reinforce the notion that meals are social occasions and a time to discuss things. It's also a time to teach good eating habits, so make sure you eat up your greens!

4 **Involve your child in food preparation.** One of the best ways to get your child interested in the food he eats is encourage him to help prepare his meals. He could arrange salad ingredients, portion out the sausages or pour some cereal into a bowl.

5 **Apply some peer pressure.** Children often learn by example and if your child sees his friends eating up, it may well encourage him to do the same. Ask one or more friends of your child whom you know to be good eaters to come to tea.

6 **Use rewards like sticker charts.** These are simple and successful ways of encouraging children to try new foods, especially unfamiliar fruit and vegetables.

Problems at mealtimes

Feeding your young child may be fraught with problems and mealtimes can easily become a battleground. Parents have an in-built instinct to nourish their child, which can lead to feelings of failure if your attempts are rejected. Of course, your child is only concerned with how he feels that day.

Food refusal

Although there's been a huge increase in overweight children (see page 50), most parents cite food refusal as their biggest problem. Yet although parents will try everything to get a recalcitrant child to eat — persuasion, bribes, distraction, nagging and threats — they are only encouraging the refusal. Coaxing a child to eat only compounds the problem and makes a preschooler ever more determined to continue to refuse food. He does so because in refusing food all attention is focused on him and he may even persuade his parents to give him just what he wants, even if its unhealthy or inappropriate. Moreover, if a child is forced to eat foods he doesn't like, this can lead to him avoiding them for the rest of his life. And, if you talk openly about foods you

or your partner dislike or go too deeply into detail about how foods you serve your child are obtained or prepared, this may cause him to be put off them, particularly if he has a good imagination.

If your child is a 'poor eater', bear in mind that nothing is really wrong with his appetite nor will he ever starve if you don't make him eat. Instead, you need to desist immediately from all attempts to make him eat (even sidelong glances) and simply ignore his behaviour at the table. Treat mealtimes with a casual attitude, neither being grateful if he eats something or angry if he doesn't. However, if he doesn't eat, make sure you don't give him any food between meals. He will learn quite quickly, even if he refuses several meals in a row, that he will only get food at mealtimes.

Tantrums

All sorts of things can trigger tantrums during mealtimes. If your child is hungry he will become ratty, just as adults do. Trying to make him eat food that he doesn't want, or not letting him have a food that he does want, will provoke a similar reaction. If you tell your child off for playing with his food, or

DAILY MEALS

Over the course of their preschool years, most children learn to eat what's prepared for the rest of the family — as long as it's not overly seasoned. While there's no harm in continuing with more 'child-friendly' options, these tend to be bland and may make it difficult for your child to progress to more sophisticated choices.

BREAKFAST

It is now widely recognised that breakfast is the most important meal of the day; it should provide a quarter of your child's daily nutrients. A good breakfast replenishes vital brain nutrients and blood-sugar (glucose) levels that are depleted during sleep and also kick-starts the metabolism, which slows overnight. Skipping the first meal of the day can lead to children developing an unhealthy pattern of snacking on high-fat, high-sugar foods. Because the body needs fuel on waking, when it doesn't get the

sustenance it needs, it switches to survival mode and only releases energy for emergencies. This means that the body and brain are without the glucose they so badly need. So if your child displays a lack of concentration and poor memory, this indicates that he is struggling due to low 'fuel' levels.

A breakfast of carbohydrates (cereals and toast, for example), which are fortified with vitamins and minerals, including the B vitamins and iron, helps with energy production. Carbs also provide glucose, which is the main body fuel, while the milk poured over cereals is a good source of calcium, B-group vitamins, zinc and magnesium.

A protein-based breakfast (eggs, milk, yogurt, beans and fish), on the other hand, provides important nutrients and will satisfy your child's appetite more quickly and for longer than a breakfast solely of carbohydrates. The best policy, since the ideal ratio of protein to carbohydrate is unknown, is to make sure you include examples of both at breakfast time.

LUNCH

This meal, too, should consist of both carbohydrate and protein foods. Protein will keep your child mentally stimulated and alert and helps prevent the

---

BREAKFAST SELECTIONS

- Porridge with sliced banana
- Boiled or poached egg on wholemeal toast
- Low-sugar breakfast cereal with fruit and milk
- Fresh fruit smoothie
- Yogurt with fruit
- Beans on wholemeal toast
- Grilled tomato and bacon or sausages with wholemeal toast
- Pancakes made with wholemeal flour, topped with fruit
- Wholemeal muffin or bread with low-sugar jam, yeast extract or peanut butter

---

LUNCH SELECTIONS

- Lean meat or ground poultry patty
- Cheese omelette
- Mini quiche
- Mixed rice and vegetables
- Home-made sausage rolls
- Falafel in pita
- Poached or grilled fish or fish fingers
- Pasta and tomato sauce
- Tuna fish or sliced chicken sandwich

DINNER SELECTIONS

- Cottage or fish pie
- Macaroni and cheese
- Pork and vegetable stir fry
- Salmon fingers and sweet potato fries
- Chicken and vegetable kebabs on rice
- Baked potato topped with beans
- Vegetable fajitas
- Home-made pizza topped with cheese and vegetables

SNACK CHOICES

- Dry cereal with milk
- Meat or peanut butter sandwich
- Vegetable or fruit breads such as pumpkin or banana
- Fresh, dried, or canned fruit
- Fruit or vegetable juices
- Plain yogurt or yogurt with fruit
- Cheese and crackers
- Oatmeal biscuits and milk

mid-afternoon energy dip that many children experience. However, carbohydrates are the body's most important source of fuel and should play a major part in every meal throughout the day. So a wholesome lunch, whether it be home-cooked, packed or prepared at nursery, is vital.

PACKED LUNCH

If your child attends nursery, then providing him with a packed lunch is a good way of monitoring his diet. It's very easy to get stuck in the 'sandwich, crisps, apple and chocolate bar' rut so try offering different types of fruit and breads for sandwiches (see box overleaf for more ideas) or rice, potato or pasta salads. A flask is perfect for holding soup for a warming winter lunch.

DINNER

For many children, this is the main meal of the day and it can be an opportunity to encourage your child to top up his intake of fruit and vegetables to reach the recommended daily intake of five portions.

There are other reasons, too, to include a higher proportion of carbohydrate to protein. Complex carbohydrates, such as pasta, rice, couscous and potatoes, trigger the release of the brain chemical serotonin, which is said to induce feelings of calm

and encourage sleep. If your child is particularly active or 'hyper' at the end of the day, it could be a good idea to increase the amount of complex carbohydrates he eats at this time. However, don't forget the importance of protein, too. It's vital that your child eats a variety of protein foods to get a balance of the essential amino acids that have to be provided by diet.

SNACKS

Preschoolers need to eat little and often, since their stores of glucose are used up more quickly than those of adults. In fact, it's good for children to have a couple of snacks — albeit healthy ones — during the day to keep blood-sugar levels steady. Snacks, however, should provide more than just calories and high-fat, high-sugar snacks and drinks will produce a sugar-high followed by a sugar-slump, often leading to mood swings and irritability.

It also may be beneficial to provide a carbohydrate-based snack such as toast or a muffin an hour or two before bedtime to encourage the production of the calming brain chemical serotonin and to keep hunger at bay during the night. Dips in blood-sugar levels may be a reason for your child waking in the night.

9 tips for a 'successful' lunch box

1 **Include the right amount of nutrients** such as a protein food, carbohydrates to provide energy and vital vitamins and minerals (such as calcium).

2 **Vary the contents as much as possible** but don't include food you know your child dislikes.

3 **Choose an attractive (age-appropriate) container**. Make sure it is rigid but doesn't contain freezer pads or partitions that can limit space.

4 **Freeze yogurt tubes and diluted juice** to act as 'coolers'. They are healthier choices than so-called low-fat (but high-sugar) fruit dessert cartons or carbonated drinks.

5 **Store cut-up fruit and vegetables in small plastic containers;** the containers will keep the items crisper for longer.

6 **Use wholemeal bread instead of white** because it is higher in fibre and is more filling. Alternatively, ring the changes by offering

tortillas, mini rolls, bagels, ciabatta or muffins occasionally.

7 **To prevent a filling from drying out,** use lettuce or mayonnaise rather than butter.

8 **Wrap bread (without the crusts) around a filling,** or cut sandwich into quarters to make it easier to eat.

9 **Choose small or sectionable fruit, like grapes or satsumas over a banana;** the latter is hard to store and discolours easily. Vary your choices frequently; try half an avocado, a kiwi fruit, cubes of melon or dried fruit for a change.

try to make him stay at the table when he wants to go, a tantrum can result.

In addition, certain rituals, which often only your child understands, can cause a tantrum and food refusal. He might be upset that a piece of meat is touching his potatoes, that his sandwiches are cut into squares and not triangles, or that the meal is not on his favourite plate. Or maybe he doesn't like 'red' food. This type of ritual may seem ridiculous to you, but it can be very important to your child.

As it's so easy to get it wrong with your child at mealtimes, it's probably best to go along with as many of his whims as you can. If he doesn't like orange juice with bits in, for example, offer him smooth orange juice instead — it's just as good and

certainly not worth having a battle over. It's also important to continue offering a 'rejected' food (usually a vegetable) on consecutive days, as your child should remember it and it'll become more and more familiar. Because preschoolers have fairly short memories, if you don't reintroduce an item soon, you are likely to be back at square one when you do.

Of course, you need to stand firm over the important things, such as deliberately upending his dish onto the floor, or spitting food out.

You also need to act when safety becomes an issue; if your child runs around while eating, for example, he might make himself choke. When faced with a tantrum over food refusal, try to remember that your child won't starve himself. Even if he only eats crisps and cookies for a period, these do have some nutritional value.

Modelling good eating behaviour

Your child will eat better if he sees you — or siblings or peers — eating the same food. Unfortunately, the opposite situation is also true. If you are a picky eater and tend to avoid trying a food before offering it to your child, you will encourage his dislike.

It's also true that snacking parents produce snacking children. If you frequently eat crisps, chocolate or biscuits, your child will want to eat them too. Likewise, if you choose healthier snacks, your child will opt for healthier ones as well. Simply by eating healthily yourself, you may not need to employ any other strategies in getting your child to eat well. However, if you are dissatisfied with an aspect of your body image, for example your weight, your dissatisfaction can be transferred to your child. This is particularly true for mothers and their daughters. If you have a tendency to eat for reasons unrelated to hunger, it's more likely that your child will eat food because he feels cross or upset.

Food allergies and intolerances

Allergies and intolerances tend to run in families so if you or your partner suffer from an allergy or intolerance, then the chances are fairly likely that your child will develop one, too. Children are also more susceptible to food intolerance because of their immature digestive and immune systems.

A food allergy occurs when the immune system overreacts to a normally harmless substance in a food by producing antibodies. This can cause a wide range of symptoms from a runny nose, upset tummy and diarrhoea to more serious problems such as asthma, eczema and breathing difficulties and potentially to a life-threatening reaction such as when a child allergic to nuts finds his throat swelling or suffers anaphylactic shock (see page 246).

Somewhat confusingly, a child can test negatively for an allergy but may still react to certain foods. This is known as a food intolerance, which is often caused by a digestive problem.

Food intolerances generally develop over time and are characterised by adverse reactions such as fuzzy headedness, poor concentration, headaches,

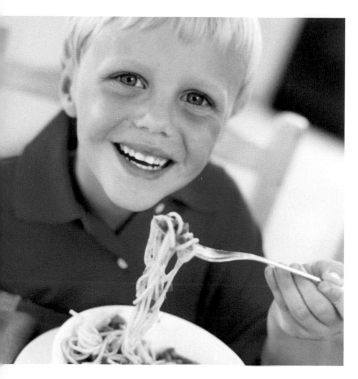

rashes and behavioural problems. Reassuringly, while the number of cases of food intolerance appears to be increasing, the number of people with severe food allergies is still rare. That being said, nut allergy has increased threefold over the last 20 years. The most common food allergens outside of nuts include dairy products, eggs, tomatoes, citrus fruit, wheat, soya and shellfish. Always consult your doctor or dietician about allergy testing and before eliminating any food from your child's diet.

Obesity

Today, obesity is an enormous problem, even with young children. Some health professionals feel it has reached epidemic proportions as almost a quarter of four to five year olds are obese. Although overweight children suffer few weight-related health and medical problems when young, they are at high risk of developing chronic diseases such as heart disease and diabetes later in life. They are also more prone to develop stress, sadness, and low self-esteem as adults. While there may be a genetic basis in certain cases, today's large number of obese children is more likely to be due to a lack of activity (see page 55), eating too many sugary and fatty foods, unhealthy eating patterns, overprotectedness on the part of parents, and possibly, certain chemicals and hormones in food and care products. Children whose parents are obese are more likely to be overweight as they usually share the same dietary tastes and lifestyles.

What you can do

If you are worried about your child's weight, your most important task will be to monitor his food and meals. Don't put your child on a weight-loss diet without getting advice, as this can affect his growth. Talk to your GP if you have any concerns about your child's weight. In the meanwhile:

- Make certain that he eats foods low in fat and sugar and avoids junk food whenever possible (see page 41). Serve grilled, roasted or pan-fried foods over deep-fried ones.
- Include some starchy foods in meals such as potatoes, bread, rice and pasta, choosing

signs your child may be overweight

1 **Babyfat still present.** 'Bracelets' of fat around your child's wrists and ankles and 'love handles' round his midriff means he has a weight problem.

2 **Tired much of the time.** Listlessness and lethargy accompany inactivity. Continous lethargy should be investigated as there may be an underlying medical cause or your child may be depressed.

3 **Breathlessness.** If your child is not asthmatic, getting out of breath when walking or running or an inability to keep up with other children generally is a sign of overweight.

4 **Victim of teasing.** Has your child been called 'Chubby', 'Chunky', 'Big Boy' or given other size-related nickname by relatives or peers?

MEASURING OBESITY

A child's body mass index (BMI) is calculated using the same method as for adults — weight in kilograms divided by height in metres squared — but specific age-adjusted charts that take into account changes in growth, are needed to determine whether a child is overweight or obese.

WEIGHT STATUS CATEGORY/PERCENTILE RANGE	
Underweight	Less than the 5th percentile
Healthy weight	5th percentile to less than the 85th percentile
Overweight	85th to less than the 95th percentile
Obese	Equal to or greater than the 95th percentile

wholegrain varieties of the latter three.

- Serve some fibre-rich foods, such as oats, beans, grains, fruit and vegetables, wholegrain bread, and brown rice and pasta.
- Ensure your child eats at least five portions of a variety of fruit and vegetables each day.
- Encourage him to drink water rather than juice or milky drinks.
- Keep an eye on the portion size of meals and snacks, and how frequently he eats. Using a slightly smaller plate can make it easier to adjust portion size downwards.
- Make sure that you set a good example both in what you eat and the way you eat. If you constantly snack or eat junk food, eat outside of normal meal times or eat in front of the television, your child will do so too.

That being said, it's vital that you not set your child apart because of his weight nor tell him he needs to be on a diet. Instead, you should focus on gradually changing your entire family's eating habits and physical activity levels (see page 57). By involving all your family, everyone learns healthful habits and your overweight child will not feel singled out. Children raised in families that are accepting of body shapes at any weight are more likely to have a positive body image and greater self-esteen that is unrelated to weight. On the other hand, derogatory comments and a negative view of obesity in childhood lead to a poorer self-image in later life. Never discuss your child's weight or overeating with others in front of him.

Dressing and clothes

Putting on and taking off clothes is one of those skills that are mastered in stages though, generally, the latter is achieved much earlier than the former.

While your two year old was able to remove her hat, gloves and socks easily but not dress herself, for example, by the time she's three, however, she should be able to put on her pants, trousers or skirt with elasticised waist, socks and self-stick fastening or slip-on shoes. Shirts and blouses with buttons and lace-up or buckled shoes, however, still will probably be beyond her.

By four, your child will be able to put on most of her clothes on her own although help may still be needed with tricky zips, buttons, buckles and laces. Any garments, particularly nightwear that goes over the head, are best avoided.

At five, your child will have almost all of the necessary skills to dress herself but can lack the interest to do it well or completely. Few, if any, children take care of their clothes at this age.

As with the other elements of daily care — feeding, hygiene, sleeping — dressing is an area in which preschoolers frequently oppose their parent's wishes, often as a way of asserting their independence.

Battling over clothes

Problems can arise with your child's choice of clothes and you're likely to find that what your child wants to wear clashes with your own taste and ideas. You may want your child to look smart and to dress appropriately for the weather, but she wants to wear a favourite scruffy jumper that's two sizes too small and old jeans with a tear in their seat. Or she may be desperate to be decked in head-to-toe pink. You're then faced with a choice between triggering a tantrum and having a child who looks like a ragbag or a feminist's nightmare.

Protracted dressing

Another problem area can be the length of time it takes your preschooler to get dressed. If your child is slow or easily distracted, the time it takes for her to get ready can be a source of irritation for you both, especially first thing in the morning when you are in a hurry to get out of the house. The more you cajole your child to hurry up, the slower she will become. If you try to intervene, she may have a tantrum because she doesn't want your help; if you get angry with her or lose your temper she'll just get even more upset.

If this is a problem for you, try and find a compromise and, as with much preschooler parenting, pick your battles. Does it really matter if your daughter chooses a skirt that clashes with her top or your son wants to wear odd socks occasionally? At this age, if your child has a little bit of involvement with her wardrobe each day, it will help temper any tantrums and encourage individuality to develop. It will also limit the chances of your child refusing to wear something.

If there are clothes you really don't want your child to wear, either pack them away, 'lose' them temporarily or pick out a few different garment options so that she has a choice about what to put on. However, do remember that she is a child and you are in charge; if you think an outfit is truly inappropriate e.g. for the weather or occasion, you still get to make the decisions — at least for a few more years!

6 tips for easier dressing

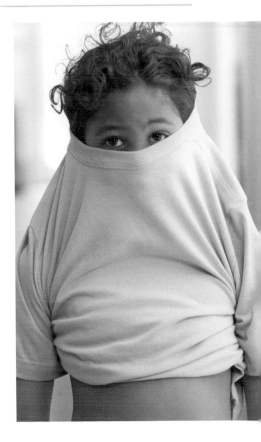

1 **Pack away unsuitable clothes.** If the weather where you live is very seasonal, put away all the previous season's clothes when the weather starts to change.

2 **Limit the choice.** Offer your child a choice of clothes, but make it limited.

3 **Lay out clothes correctly orientated.** It can help if garments are laid out on the floor or bed with the fronts facing and the top above trousers.

4 **Allow more time for your child to get dressed.** Get up ten minutes earlier, if necessary.

5 **Encourage your child to dress herself** but don't laugh at or criticise her efforts.

6 **Be ready to help.** Bear in mind that some garments as well as socks and shoes can be difficult for a child to put on, so be on hand if she gets stuck.

If you sense a battle over getting dressed coming on, you could try sitting down with your child and explaining why she needs to hurry up or why she can't wear shorts and a t-shirt when it's snowing outside. If this doesn't work, and your child refuses to hurry up or has a full-blown tantrum, there is nothing else for it but to pick her and her clothes up and take her to the front door. Finish getting her dressed there so that she understands that going out is the next step.

If your child wants to wear unsuitable clothing or refuses to put on certain items, such as a coat or gloves when it's cold, let her learn from experience how wearing the wrong clothes or going out without these items will affect her (although make sure you have the necessary items on hand).

Clothing needn't cost a fortune

Even if your preschooler would be happy wearing that ragged jumper mentioned above, you no doubt want her to look at least presentable. Whether you go as far as fashion-plate mode is personal preference but bear in mind that lively young children rarely respect costly designer outfits. One rule of thumb, at least for day-to-day wear, is to stick with items you won't feel the need to fuss over if your child is being a typical preschooler — running through muddy puddles, spilling juice down her top or crawling around with her toys on the floor, slowly but surely wearing holes in her trouser knees!

That's not to say your child can't look smart/cool, just that there's no point spending an arm and a leg, especially when there are stylish junior ranges in high street stores, supermarkets and in specialist catalogues. You could also check out eBay for discounted new or lightly used items, or encourage friends with older children to send their best hand-me-downs your way. Jumble sales and charity shops are also good places to check out.

It's unusual for a child under six to be particularly brand conscious herself or to face peer pressure to have the latest trainers or the like, but if this does happen, listen to your child and try to understand why she desperately wants that particular item. Bear in mind, however, that it is your decision and saying

OVERLY GROWN-UP CLOTHING

There has been much press coverage in recent times of sexualised clothing for young children — from child-size heels to t-shirts with "future WAG" slogans and padded bras for primary school-age girls. While you might consider such items 'amusing' or not far removed from the tottering round in mothers' pumps and (usually badly applied) lipstick that toddlers regularly engage in, it's worth bearing in mind that toddler 'dressing up' generally is occasional, uses items that are clearly the mother's not the child's and is done in the privacy of the home. Psychologists believe that dressing young children in overly sexualised clothing can lead to issues with self-esteem and body image. So, if over the next few years, you face occasions when you're out shopping together and your child grabs something you'd rather she didn't wear, remember it's your call. It's might be better to deal with a short-lived outburst of temper now than the long-term consequences of an eating disorder.

"no" does not make you a bad parent (even if there's a tantrum for a few minutes after you do so!).

Sometimes, it's not children themselves hankering after costly designer clothing, but parents. If you are drawn to brands you can't easily afford, consider why this might be. Is it for you or your child? If it's the latter, she really isn't going to know or care whether her outfit is from Dolce & Gabbana or H&M. If you believe that other people will judge you for not dressing your child in the flashest gear, is their opinion really worth worrying about?

Keeping your child active

A healthy lifestyle depends on physical activity. Being active will help your child to use her excess energy, burn calories, sleep better and enjoy an improved mood. It will also:

- Enable her to maintain a healthy weight, now and in the future;
- Improve her concentration and ability to learn, at playgroup or kindergarten;
- Reduce the risk of health problems such as diabetes, joint problems, stroke, heart disease and some cancers later in life;
- Allow her to lead a happy and healthy life;
- Improve her ability to handle stress;
- Elevate her mood and improve her general wellbeing.

For your child to be a healthy weight, having her eat a healthy diet — one with the appropriate amount of calories (see page 38) — is one part of the equation; making sure she has sufficient physical activity is the other. There are two main approaches you need to adopt. The first is to minimise sedentary activities while the other is to encourage active play.

Minimising sedentary activities

It is vitally important to prevent your child sitting for long periods watching television or dvds, using a computer or playing static video games. Not only does watching television discourage your child from active play, but it exposes her to junk food advertisements, which can impact on her eating a healthy diet. Total screen time for television watching and computer and console use should be limited (see page 146).

That being said, active video games like the Wii, can be useful in preventing child obesity. According

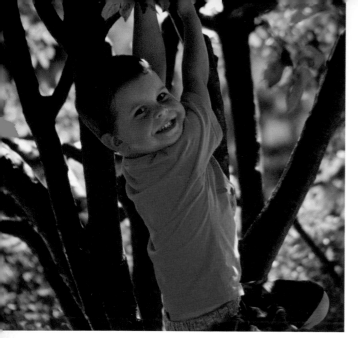

to a recent research, children burned three times as many calories playing 'active' video games versus playing traditional hand-held ones.

Encouraging energetic play

The other side of the healthy weight coin is to get your child engaged in active play. Children need to play and you should offer the time, environment and equipment to allow your preschooler to do so every single day. Bear in mind that for a small child all play is learning, so there's added benefit.

Your preschooler should be encouraged to play actively for at least one hour every day, even if that is just running around with her friends. If you can be on hand to help, great. If you can't, then let her get on with it.

Some ways to play

You should consider taking your child to a gym class, local swimming pool or to a sports centre, but there are simpler and less expensive activities (see also movement games, page 58).

Make walking a positive option. If possible, don't jump in the car whenever you want to go anywhere but try and fit in a weekly (if not daily) walk to the playground, shops or just out and about.

Another good alternative is to cycle to activities. By age four, your child will be able to ride a trike with ease, turning around sharp bends, and she may even be able to handle a bike with or without training wheels. Scooters, too, provide lots of opportunity for your child to get active, but make sure she wears a protective helmet when doing both (see also page 210). You too, should wear a helmet when bike riding (or using a scooter) so that you serve as a model of safe behaviour.

Take a ball to the park for a kick about or to practise catching, throwing and bouncing. When at the playground, encourage your toddler to use all the equipment so that she builds up her climbing and balancing skills.

Put on some music and encourage your child to move to it. Dancing develops balance and co-ordination and is a great way to do something active together.

Your child may be able to manage skates, but again, protective gear is needed. Make sure that she wears all the necessary protection — in particular a helmet as well as knee and elbow pads. Flat paths in parks are the ideal place to learn to skate.

Home gym

There are a number of fairly inexpensive pieces of kit that can help to keep your child active at home.

Balls of all types have a great deal of play potential particularly as they can be used in new and different ways as your child's handling and kicking skills develop. A small exercise ball also offers lots of fun-filled opportunities for your child. She can bounce and roll over on it. However, make certain you supervise your child at all times.

A mini trampoline, too, is ideal for working off excess energy and can be used indoors and out. This also has to be used under supervision.

Your child may be able to spin a hula hoop round her middle or if not, several hoops can be laid flat on the ground and your child encouraged to jump or hop in and out of them.

Jump ropes involve play that will develop your child's arm and leg skills, improve her coordination and encourage healthy bone growth. Because skipping is a high impact activity, make sure your child wears trainers when she uses the rope.

Even reading can be an opportunity for active play as story-telling and role-playing go together. Your child will enjoy acting out a simple tale and perhaps get fitter in the process.

Children are fascinated by animals so you could talk about a walk in the park or a day at the zoo, and as you introduce each animal, ask your child to imitate what she thinks the animal is doing. For example, for a frog, she should crouch down and try jumping across the floor or, when you mention a snake, have your child lie on her stomach and stretch her arms out in front. She can raise her head and 'hiss' and then try to slither across the floor. And for a monkey, she can somersault, look between her knees or even put her foot into her mouth. Accuracy is less important than the actions.

5 ways you can encourage activity

1   **Set an example.** You are your child's most important role model — so if you are a couch potato, don't expect your kid to be active! Get yourself moving for the habit to rub off on your child. Walk or cycle to work so that right from the start, your child sees these modes of transport as 'normal'. If, however, your child sees you come in from work and then settle in front of the TV for the night, she will see no reason not to do the same.

2   **Take an interest.** Encourage your child if she wants to engage in a sport or exercise activity. If she is interested in swimming, take her a couple of times to the local pool to see if a course of lessons might be a good idea or to some local sporting events to fire her interests and enthusiasms. If she engages in anything, make sure you're an enthusiastic supporter or join in (don't just drop her off and leave).

3   **Plan family activities** that provide everyone with exercise, like walking, biking, or swimming. Make an effort to reduce the amount of time you and your family spend in sedentary activities, such as watching TV or playing video games.

4   **Be sensitive to your child's needs.** If your child is overweight, she may feel uncomfortable about participating in certain activities. It is important to help her find

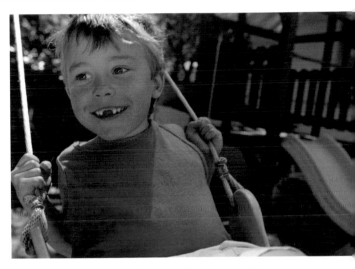

physical activities that she will enjoy and that aren't embarrassing or too difficult.

5   **Make sure her environment is safe.** Being active often involves some degree of risk, and this is true whether your child is at home or outdoors. Childproof your home; your child will need somewhere to work off excess energy when it's rainy outside; teach your child about safe practices when out and about (not picking up or eating plants, not getting too close to animals, not talking to strangers, etc.) ensure she always wears sufficient protective gear (when bike riding, using a scooter or skating) and instill in her safe behaviour in the playground (not walking behind swings, waiting to go down the slide until the last child gets off and then getting off quickly herself, holding onto ladders and climbing frames with both hands).

MOVEMENT GAMES

There are a number of games that can be played with one or more children and depending on the numbers and ages of the participants may not need to have a 'winner'; young children enjoy following instructions and running around. If the children are older, you have the option of penalising anyone doing the wrong action. Musical games offer an extra dimension.

HOPSCOTCH

By the age of four, your child will probably enjoy playing a simple version of this outdoor game. Don't worry about the numbers too much; focus on her

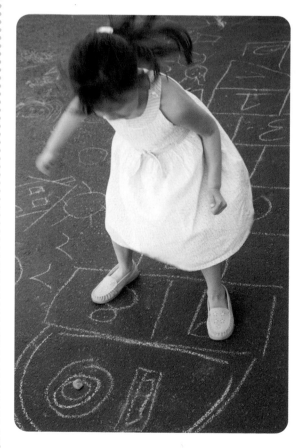

jumping around and having fun. Draw out the squares and let her practise jumping and hopping from one to another. You can play, too! As your child learns her numbers and her agility improves, she will enjoy playing the traditional game alone or with her friends.

TWISTER®

Your child also might like to try Twister or a home-made variation. Cut out large circles of differently coloured paper and place them in rows on the floor. Then call out "right hand, left hand, right foot, left foot" followed by the colour for each. A simpler game would involve limiting the game to having your child jump on the colours you call out.

TRAFFIC LIGHTS

Also known as "Stop and Go", you need to stand in front of your child (and any friends) and give instructions: "Green light" — run around; "Yellow light" — slow down; "Red light" — stop; "Traffic jam" — walk slowly.

FOLLOW THE LEADER

Have your child (and any friends) stand behind you in a line and then make various movements — walk, jump, hop, skip, wheel about, walk backwards, etc.— that she (or they) must copy. Make sure you swing your arms vigorously as well.

SIMON SAYS

Stand in front of your child and make up things for her to do prefaced by "Simon says". For example, "Simon says, hop on one foot". If you just say, "Hop on one foot" and your child does so, you must point out that she's lost a point or must pay a forfeit for getting it wrong. Try to be as inventive as possible.

MUSICAL CHAIRS AND FREEZE DANCE

Both games depend on letting your child run around or dance until the music stops. In the simplest version of "Musical Chairs", you ask your child to walk around the chair(s) until you stop the music when she must sit down. The more children, the more chairs though usually there's one less than the number of children playing. With "Freeze Dance", children have the option to dance around until the music stops and then either sit down or freeze. Strictly speaking the last to sit down or the one who moves is out, but you may decide to let everyone keep playing.

3 Party time

3
4
5
6

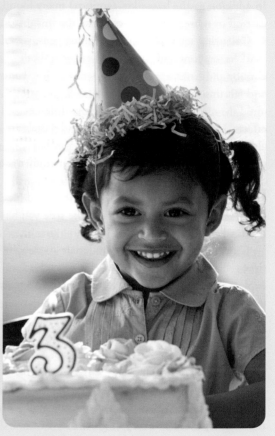

3 years old

Your child is likely to enjoy a party, much as she would a play date, but isn't really aware that it is something special and exciting. Keep the party and guest list short — 1½ hours and 4 guests (some recommend same number of guests as age of birthday boy or girl) — and go with the flow, which should be very slow and unregimented.

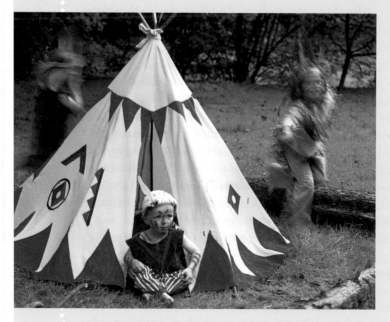

4 years old

Uncritically excited about the food, party bags, gifts and activities or entertainment — all of which he now expects as he knows a party is 'special', your preschooler will still tire easily and/or become overexcited. Plan on 1½ hours and no more than 6 guests. Play should be informal but don't be surprised if it all ends in tears.

5 years old

Be prepared; fives are filled with excess energy so a party with plenty to do is key — though be prepared for children to behave in a solitary way rather than share. Now's the time to introduce simple games and/or activities in which the guests (best if same sex) can let off steam. Plan on 2 hours and about 6 guests (fives find it hard to wait for attention or turn taking). Themes and decorations will add to the excitement.

6 years old

Friends are very important and while you may be able to get away with 6 guests, you may also have to invite his entire class! Work around your child's interest (boys will want more action than girls) for activities or games, cake theme, etc., and 2½ hours will be plenty.

events but it's easy to set up a small group with other mums and children. It's a good idea to keep sessions short and to choose stories with lots of action, repetition and noise, and for which you can use facial expressions while reading. Teller and listeners alike will have lots of fun with a story that has a silly 'magic word' that the children will enjoy shouting out. It also gives the children something to look out for. They will listen intently for the magic word, so that they can repeat it back to you. This, in turn, makes them pay attention to what you are saying, and it makes the experience fun.

Alternatively, you could make some sort of sign or perform an action that the group has to look out for. In any event, choose stories that lend themselves to actions. The more actions and movements you can put in to illustrate what is happening, the more the group will respond and become involved. Pick simple actions like clapping hands or jumping up and down. You could even use soft toys or puppets to help illustrate what is happening in the tale, if appropriate.

As a reader, you should try and make the story more interesting to your child (or children). Exaggerate your facial expressions and movements, and get into the spirit of the tale.

Reading for a purpose

Reading can do more than be entertaining. It's a great way to get your child ready for bed and can help him accept and adjust to problems that he will encounter at home or when she's at school.

A book at bedtime

Reading as part of your child's normal bedtime routine can encourage a restful night's sleep. The perfect bedtime story has to have a strong element of satisfaction and just enough action and adventure to keep your child interested without over-stimulating him. You want to soothe your little one into sleep and leave him feeling that all is well with the world.

Choose short stories, fables or abridged classic tales that last for about fifteen minutes. Read the story beforehand so you know whether the words and images conjure up happy things. If you're not sure that there is something in the tale that might alarm your child, keep the book for daytime sessions.

Use your voice to soothe and ease your child into sleep. Linger over words that present soft, happy images, and wind down your tale by slowing the pace and lowering the pitch of your voice. You may find that your child drifts into sleep half way through the story. If so, just let the words dwindle gently and earmark the book for next time.

Learning about life:

Storytelling is great entertainment but it can also be used to educate your child about the way the world 'works' as well as to help him cope with the new or

PERSONALISED FAIRY TALE

All children enjoy being the centre of a story and an easy way to make it happen is to take a well-known classic story and insert your child's name into it as the hero or heroine. The main character should be a child of similar age and with good qualities. If the story permits, you can use the names of your child's friends as well as mummy and daddy and the grandparents. Even though the story is based on a familiar tale that you may have read before, you can change the name to make it unique. If you feel confident enough, you can introduce elements to the story to make it your own. So, for example, Sleeping Beauty (your daughter) might be lost in a dream world in which she has her own adventure. The prince could be daddy or mummy, coming to save her and giving her a big kiss. Or if you chose Aladdin, your son would need to think very carefully about his three wishes, and you could discuss the ramifications together. Bear in mind that King Midas wished that everything he touched would turn to gold.....

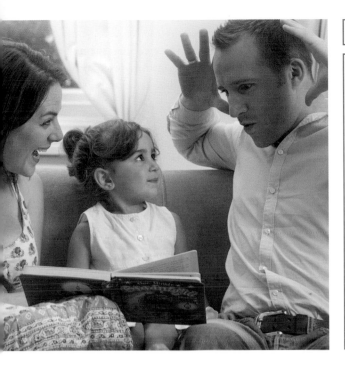

- **3 year olds**
  Stories about everyday life, not only domestically but at the seashore or a farm; various modes of transportation and the different seasons; animals, both domestic and wild, and alphabet books.
- **4 year olds**
  Humorous or 'silly' books, whimsical or imaginative stories and classic fairy tales.
- **5 year olds**
  Humorous, 'silly' or ridiculous books; books about animals that act like people and books that can 'explain' concepts like colours, sizes and opposites.

difficult. Sharing appropriate stories can help your child experience situations in a positive way. For example, reading can be a wonderful opportunity to learn about other cultures. Sharing stories from or about people around the world can give your child an understanding of other societies and how the people in them relate to each other. There's a great tradition of storytelling in other cultures and this should be explored and celebrated. It's never too early to do this.

What's known as 'healing' tales — books that teach a specific lesson, or offer help and advice on such things as learning to play nicely, keeping toys neat and tidy, learning to make friends and not being greedy — enable your child to learn important life lessons in a comfortable and fun environment.

There are many books available that deal with 'difficult' situations; these can help your child prepare for a variety of events or situations that he may experience — the arrival of a new sibling, moving home, going to hospital, illness or death of a close relative, separating or divorcing parents, starting school. Using stories in this way means that your child will be able to think through the process in a safe environment, thus making things familiar

for him and taking away the fear of the unknown. Starting school (or nursery), for example, will be a big event in your child's world. It is associated with a whole host of exciting and frightening changes. Repeatedly telling stories that include this scenario and putting him in the tales will help him identify with the changes. You will be able to allay his fears as he learns about what to expect.

Toys

Giving your child different types of toys and objects with which to play helps him to develop self expression, hand-eye coordination, and stimulates his creativity and imagination; toys will also help him to learn to distinguish different shapes, colours, sizes, textures, sounds and weights.

There are so many toys and games on the market that it can be hard to decide what to buy. The best toys are those that are right for your child's age and abilities, but that also can be used in more than one way; these are the most likely to retain his interest. Construction toys including bricks that can be joined together and incorporate a variety of other linkable pieces such as motors, switches and lights will continue to be used by your child for many years. If a toy is too advanced for your child's age or developmental stage, he will quickly become frustrated and abandon it, and if it's too simple, he will soon become bored with it.

Outdoor activity toys such as scooters, skates and bicycles are fun and give your child an opportunity to get fit and let off steam.

If you have a garden, install a sandpit and water tray, together with 'super soaker' guns. These are useful for children, as not only are they fun but can teach your child about such things as floating and sinking and hydraulics. If you do not have a garden area, offer your child a bowl full of play sand or water on a plastic sheet.

Dressing up clothes including hats, scarves, costume jewellery and bags can be begged from friends and relatives or bought from charity shops to supplement a dressing-up chest of commercially bought outfits. Young toddlers enjoy role play and dressing up; older children will enjoy dressing up tied into a history topic such as pirates, Romans, explorers, etc.

Every home should have a collection of puppets and even a small puppet theatre (or a cardboard box made into a theatre). These toys help to develop language skills, imagination and storytelling, and can be used to help your child to explore issues that he is having trouble articulating, such as problems with friendship, loss, etc. Using a puppet to 'speak' removes a child a degree from the things he says, and can make him feel safer about voicing his problems.

Electronic and digital games

It's important that toddlers are able to grab hold of the gadgets they see all around them, and to start to discover the digital world in which they'll be growing up. There are many great apps out there that our children can learn from and have fun with — partly because they're such a demanding audience — so the quality has to be high to maintain their interest.

But it's yet another challenge for parents to deal with: how often and for how long should you allow your toddler to play with this stuff?

Generally, 'screen time' shouldn't be allowed to replace real-life human interaction and active physical play. This means, that except for rare occasions, not leaving your child alone with a gadget while you do something else; technology should not be a replacement for you. Apps and electronic games should just be other ways to interact with your child, as if you were helping with building blocks or reading him or her a book. Even if an app or electronic toy can be used by your child on his own,

---

4 ways to get on top of toys

1 **Only let your child play with a limited number of toys at a time.** If he has too many to choose from he may run from one to another and keep changing his mind which one to play with.

2 **If your child is given several toys for an occasion** such as Christmas or his birthday, save a few for later and present one as a new toy on a rainy day, or when he is bored or feeling ill or under the weather.

3 **Check the toys regularly.** Are they still safe? If broken, discard a toy immediately. Has your child out-grown them? If your child has become bored with a toy, but it's still within his age range, put it away for a week or two and then bring it out again. He will probably welcome it as a new toy.

4 **Have on hand a supply of differently sized batteries** but don't let your child change batteries, and ensure that battery compartments on toys are inaccessible.

it's best to sit next to him, helping him when he isn't sure what to do or encouraging him when he gets things right. You also should make conversation during the game or activity, discussing what's happening and what your child thinks about it.

Excursions

Your child experiences things everywhere he goes. He's like a sponge, soaking up the sights, sounds, smells, feelings and tastes he encounters. You may think you just are going for a simple day out, but to your child, all outings are rich in incidental learning.

Even a visit to the supermarket can be an opportunity for you to talk together about what you are buying and about the places the food came from. The colours of food will be interesting to your child. Ask him if strawberry red is the same as cherry red. Which is more orange coloured — an orange or a tangerine? How many 'green' vegetables can your child name. Can you find any food you have not tried before? Talk about the item and try to guess what it will taste like, then go home and see who was right! You can look for 'fair trade' or organic labels on food. Does your child know what they mean? How is such food different?

Science and the natural world are everywhere you look. Use a walk in a forested area to identify trees, leaves, plants and bugs using simple guidebooks. Make a collection of items such as leaves, nuts, feathers and stones for your child to 'show and tell' to others. The materials also can be made into collages or dream catchers. A walk round a pond can turn into a science trip. Bring a small net and a white dish and look closely at the plants and creatures you find before returning the creatures to the water. Or, take a sketch pad and crayons so your child can make pictures of what he sees in or near the water. The beach, like many other outdoor environments, is rich in opportunities for hands-on, experiential learning. For example, you are using maths — estimating volume, measuring and looking at shapes — when you construct a sandcastle together. Even history can be introduced as you discuss fortification and dig a moat. Look at plants and creatures on the shore, and then go rock pooling. You also can

encourage language play by making up lists of sea-related things. Create a game: 'In my treasure chest I found …' and make up poetic and outrageous things such as 'a mermaid's song' or 'a pirate's smelly sock' as well as South Sea pearls and jewel-encrusted daggers — it's not just a memory game; it's about stretching the imagination — and this is something that only expands with regular use.

Make up silly poems and songs encouraged by practising alliteration (words that start with the same sound like 'salty sea' or 'rough rocks'). Give your child examples such as 'sticky starfish' and 'wild waves'. You don't have to say you are using alliteration — just tell your child you are looking for descriptions that start with the same sounds. Encourage your child to find an alliterative description for seaweed, sand, fish … whatever you can see or imagine.

A visit to any public garden with a glasshouse offers the opportunity to demonstrate different habitats from around the world, such as a tropical rainforest or desert. Heritage sites can often bring history to life for a child. Encourage your child to think about how life was different in the past, compared to today. What sort of jobs did people

Your child at play

3 | **4** | **5**

3 years old

Your child still prefers playing with large objects such as wooden blocks or Duplo®, which she can combine into basic structures, or threading large beads or cotton reels. Her delight in large-scale play continues with artistic activities: she will prefer fingerpaints to paint and brushes, for example, and her paintings won't have much shape or structure and whole pages may be covered with a single colour. Messy play with sand, clay and water can keep her occupied for long periods and she will be better at producing life-like objects with clay while her water play will extend to blowing soap bubbles and sailing boats.

Your child's imaginative abilities will be more apparent with doll and soft toy play. Instead of just putting dolly or teddy to bed, she may now feed and cook for dolly and organise tea parties.

Outdoors, she should enjoy playing on a slide, swings and climbing frame.

contstruction toys. Amateur dramatics can involve a wide range of scenarios including the fantastic as well as the domestic. Books continue to be great favourites particularly those with more detailed pictures.

5 years old

Whether or not your child is at play group or kindergarten or is still at home, she will enjoy the usual group artistic activities of cutting, tracing, drawing, pasting, string beads and collaging. Now too is the time for enjoying tent houses (indoors and out) and role play with dolls and puppets. Outdoor play can include skating, trampolining, rope jumping and bicycling, and more organised games with peers. Scientific exploration may be undertaken using magnets, binoculars, magnifying glasses and torches. Drawings may now include letters and numbers and within her capabilities are games that require imagination and the ability to think — 'I Spy' or '20 Questions' — as well as chequers.

4 years old

Your child will be particularly fond of outdoor play on trikes, bikes and scooters and will enjoy climbing frames and jungle gyms, which he uses with increased agility. Give him blunt-ended scissors to cut out pictures in magazines to encourage his manual dexterity and he will enjoy making collages. He will engage in make-believe and may have imaginary companions and objects while pretend play — doctors and nurses, for example — with or without dolls and dressing up are great favourites. He may enjoy simple card or board games and large, relatively uncomplicated picture puzzles. Using large building blocks, he'll be able to construct impressive stuctures such as houses and forts and may play in them or use other toys such as trucks and wagons alongside. However, he may also start to build with Lego® and other have, what did they wear? Farms can provide opportunities for your child to see at close hand animals and plants. Many establishments offer activities like feeding the animals, riding on farm equipment or fruit picking.

Apart from the excellent exercise swimming provides, a day at the pool can be an opportunity to talk about floating and sinking, demonstrating with swimming floats and rings.

Use a museum trip to find out more about a subject that really grips your child — be that bugs, dinosaurs or space travel. When you visit an art gallery, take a sketchbook.

Wherever you are, get into the habit of talking about what you see. Ask your child open-ended questions about what he sees: 'What if …', 'Why do you think …', and be prepared for the many questions your child asks you! Never be afraid to say you don't know the answer; if you encourage him to help you 'explore' by sitting next to you while you use books and the internet to find out answers, you will be teaching him a vital lesson: how to research.

Group activities

Today, in addition to playgroups that offer your child independent child care and the opportunity to engage with his peers, there is an enormous number of activities on offer depending on your available time and money. Most communities have preschooler courses for arts and crafts; drama, music and dance; athletics from swimming to gymnastics, yoga and football and language learning. Some preschoolers have such busy social lives that their parents begin to feel like diary secretaries!

Attending a preschool or activity class will expose your child to his peers and may have the social and developmental benefits claimed, but research has found that the more time children under five spend away from their parents, the more behaviour problems — rudeness, defiance or aggression — they exhibit. In addition, children who spent more time in childcare are rated as less socially competent by their mothers and primary teachers. Researchers have also uncovered elevated stress levels in certain preschoolers when away from the home.

Historically, children remained at home with their parents and extended family until much older than they do now. They were not segregated with other children. Unlike children their own age, parents and other family members are able to teach preschoolers self-control, empathy, compassion, patience, social etiquette, and an upbeat, constructive attitude for dealing with peer problems. That's why it's vital that you carefully choose and monitor groups your child joins and that you provide his primary caregiving. Using the internet and other resources, it's very possible to provide your child with lots of varied activities while he remains at home.

4 things you can do to ensure positive group experiences

1   **Keep the number and length of time of each activity short.**

2   **Choose classes that are small and intimate.** No more than 15 students and 4 teachers is ideal as long as the venue has room to play.

3   **Look for teachers who expect friendly, polite behaviour.** Avoid classes or groups where children are allowed to get away with angry, anti-social or disobedient behaviour. Ask how the teachers cope with undesirable behaviour.

4   **Communicate regularly with the teacher.** If you are not present at each class, find out how your child is doing especially if he is being rejected by his peers or is involved in rejecting another child (for which you need to take corrective action). Make sure your child isn't hanging out with a 'bad crowd'. If your child plays in peer groups, which are characterised by negative emotions or anti-social behaviour, his social development will suffer.

Sleep and bedtime

Sleep will help your child grow strong and healthy. Most preschoolers need between 11 and 13 hours of sleep over a 24-hour period and younger children usually have one daytime nap. Naps should not take place too late in the day or go on too long — either situation will result in the lack of a good night's sleep. As your child gets older, napping will tail off, although some children still benefit from taking one. You should establish a set routine time for napping or expect your child to spend some quiet or relaxing time in his own bedroom. Even if your child can't sleep, some 'down time' — about an hour — will help him to relax.

Research has shown that regular bedtimes make for well-behaved children but problems such as resisting going to sleep and waking frequently at night are common as are night-time fears and nightmares, sleepwalking and bed-wetting.

Bedtime routine

A preschooler needs a fair amount of time to get ready for bed. Expect to spend at least 30 minutes on calm and enjoyable activities before kissing your child good night and turning out the light. Action-packed tv programmes and dvds should be left for much earlier in the day. To help your child to wind down, he may enjoy taking a bath and reading bedtime stories. Always stick to a regular routine made up of a set time and sequence of events — dressing for bed, brushing teeth, picking a book, etc. — so that your child knows what to expect.

Make sure the room is cool and comfortable and is lit by a nightlight or area light on the very lowest dimmer setting. Playing soft, soothing music is fine. Remember to reserve the bed for sleeping only; it should not be used as a platform for playing. The room should not contain a television.

CHAPTER 3
DEVELOPMENTAL CHANGES

Your preschooler's physical, mental, emotional and social development is at a key stage — and you have a vital role in helping your child reach her potential. Learning to master a wide number of tasks, make sense of her world and communicate her wishes, manage her fears and anger and appropriately display her affections, and become a popular member of her peer group is an enormous task but one that needs to be accomplished before your child is ready for school.

Physical abilities

The preschooler years should be marked by lots of activity; in the previous chapter, you would have learned how important it is to get your child moving and some appropriate activities that she can do on her own or with you. Your child's increasingly sophisticated abilities are a result of both aspects of her physicality — locomotive and fine motor skills — working in concert with each other.

Locomotive skills

By age three, your preschooler is so agile, she's able to make the most of playground visits. Her agility will continue to develop, so that by age four, she should be able to climb trees and longer ladders with skill.

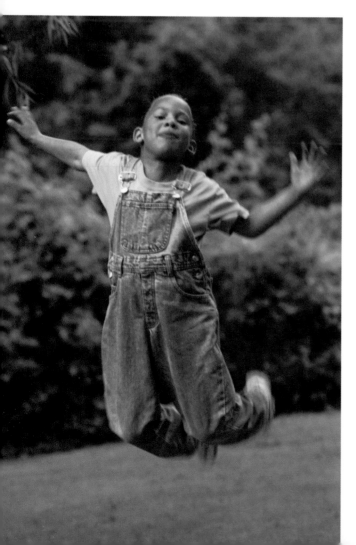

She should have mastered jumping and possibly standing on one leg for a short time. Her balancing skills develop, which are necessary for her to learn to hop, which usually happens at around age four. When she does so, she'll probably favour one foot.

Most three year olds can kick a ball effectively and will start to enjoy trying to kick it backwards and forwards and by four years, your child should start to enjoy ball games that include catching, throwing, bouncing and kicking; she'll be better able to judge direction when throwing. She should be able to catch smaller balls with her hands, and may be able to use a small bat or racquet.

By age five, your child should be able to play and enjoy more complex ball games and have honed her motor skills and in particular, her balancing abilities. She should be able to stand on one leg for up to 10 seconds at a time, hop 10 times in a row, skip on alternate feet and walk along a line one foot in front of the other. Your preschooler will be able to dance rhythmically to music so may enjoy a ballet class.

If your child started riding her tricycle at age three, she should be proficient by age four, even turning round sharp bends. She then should be ready for a bike, though initially with training wheels. Many four year olds also can use skates.

From the later part of the preschool years, your child is well on the way to mastering all the basic skills involved in movement but she will go on refining them and integrating them into more complex movement sequences. For example, while a five year old can both run and kick a ball — although not do both well at the same time — by the time she's six years of age, your child should be ready for organised team sports such as football or rounders. Remember to help your child find a sport she enjoys and be a role model by participating in activity as well. And always make sure she wears the necessary protective equipment.

Fine motor skills

As well as locomotive abilities, finger and hand skills continue to be perfected throughout the preschool years. Dexterity, a fine motor skill, greatly improves between ages two and four so that four year olds are able to pick up and put down objects carefully, even very tiny ones. (Being able to coordinate and manipulate increasingly smaller objects are important skills, which are particularly useful when it comes to self dressing and eating. (See the box, below on ways to help your child hone her abilities.)

Most three year olds can throw a ball reasonably well over-arm and can catch a large, bounced ball when their arms are held out straight. Your child also should be able to create ever more complex constructions — increasingly taller towers and more elaborate bridges – so by the age of four, for example, she can build a bridge of three bricks with either hand and build steps with more than six blocks. Imaginative play using large linking blocks will continue to be enjoyed as your child 'graduates' to smaller blocks (such as LEGO™) and her scenarios become more sophisticated.

From the age of four, your child will enjoy other types of construction toys, including those with smaller and more realistic pieces, such as cars and planes she can assemble herself and use for imaginative play. Make sure, however, that these are age-appropriate for your child and that she plays with smaller pieces under supervision.

ways to encourage dexterity

1   **Offer your child increasingly complex jigsaw puzzles;** being able to pick up and fit together smaller pieces will evolve over time.

2   **Let her thread objects.** Start by encouraging your child to place spools or tubes onto a piece of string or yarn, then offer large beads and a shoelace and by four, big buttons with a thread headed with a blunt plastic needle.

3   **Introduce sewing cards.** From the age of four or so, sewing cards are a simple and fun way to learn. You can buy them or make your own by drawing a shape on a piece of card and cutting holes in the outline, perhaps with a hole punch. Offer your child a blunt plastic needle and yarn to sew around the outline.

4   **Let her 'cook'.** From age three, your child can help assemble and mix up salad ingredients, roll out dough and use simple cookie cutters with it. She will be able to help you decorate cakes and biscuits with an icing pen.

5   **Provide craft materials.** Being able to use a child's scissors. glue, papers and pasta or found objects like leaves and shells to create collages; play dough to make models, and crayons and paints for making pictures not only feeds your child's imagination but helps her perfect many fine motor skills.

6   **Practise different fixings.** Helping your child to master zips, buttons and buckles will feed her desire for dressing independently.

Taking care of herself

3
4
5

3 years old

Routines will be problematical but your child should be able to wash her hands and parts of herself in the bath. She will be better at undressing than dressing but can put on socks and shoes (but not fasten them), pull up elasticated pants or skirts and possibly pur on simple dresses and jumpers; she will need help with most fastenings and 'complicated' clothes. She can hang her jacket and towel on a low hooks, put dirty clothes in a basket, fetch her clothes and toys, eat reasonably skillfully with spoon and hold her cup by one handle. Many threes like to eat with a fork. Overall, table manners are minimal. She may use the potty independently and like most of her peers will be dry during the day, she may, like many, not be at night. Even during the day, she may have occasional 'accidents' (particularly true for boys).

4 years old

Your child will go to the potty and possibly the toilet by himself (and may demand privacy) and remain dry day and night. He can wash and dry his hands, bathe himself reasonably well save for the hard-to-reach places, and dry himself after bathing. He attempts to brush his teeth and comb his hair. He can blow his nose on his own and get dressed in clothes with large buttons and zips and can put on shoes on the right feet with self-stick fastenings or slip-ons; some children can do up buckles. He eats well with a spoon and fork and uses a knife to spread jam on bread but cannot cut with one. If he has his own bedroom, may be happy to go to bed and even tell you when he is tired.

5 years old

Your child can perform a number of hygiene tasks competently like washing her face, brushing her teeth, wiping herself after using the toilet and washing her hands. She is cooperative and enthusiastic when washing herself in the bath although she may not wash all parts thoroughly. She can choose appropriate clothes for the weather and undress herself easily; she also can dress herself competently although her clothes may need to be laid out the right way round. While she can hang up a jacket or dress using a hanger, mainly she doesn't take care of her clothes. If taught, she may remember to cover her mouth or nose with her elbow when she coughs or sneezes. She can pour from a carton and use a knife for cutting soft foods but probably is not able to cut meat well.

Commands

From around three years, due to increases in her thinking skills and memory, your child should be able to understand and perform commands involving at least two pieces of information. She should, for instance, be able to comply if you say, "Please bring me that book and put the teddy in your room".

Most of the commands you give your child will be non-negotiable, and you will expect her to carry them out. But at times your child won't want to do what you ask, perhaps because she is busy with another activity or because she thinks your instructions are uninteresting or unimportant. That's why it helps to give her an explanation. She won't fully understand the reasons, but doing so will encourage her to think beyond her own immediate wishes. So, for example, if you ask your child to stop making so much noise, point out to her that you want her to stop because you are getting a headache. Explanations help your child realise why you are asking her to behave in a particular way.

In addition, point out the emotional consequences of her following your instructions; you could tell her, for example, that you'll feel good if she puts her toys away neatly, or that Daddy will be sad if she breaks his favourite pen. Linking the instruction to an emotional outcome in this way makes your instruction more significant for your child, and she is therefore more likely to respond positively to it.

Questions

Starting at four years, when she will have enough language and sufficient intellectual skill to frame a question, your child will begin asking you things. Although somewhere between four and six years of age is usually the peak time for constantly asking questions, its only at about five years old that she starts to think through both the kind of problem she is trying to solve, and the kinds of question she wants to ask, before putting a question into words. But even before then, children typically think about choices, weigh up the possibilities and ask questions about them. For instance, offered the chance to go to the shop with Dad, or stay at home with Mum, your child may ask whether Dad might buy a treat or Mum will play a game. The answer to the question might determine whether going shopping or staying home looks like the better choice. Your child is considering the future possibilities for each scenario and imagining how each might feel before deciding whether to go or stay. This requires a fairly high level of abstract thought.

Questions come in all sizes. Big ones might relate to birth and death ("Where do babies come from?" or "Is Grandma in heaven?"). Others may be "What if…?" type questions ("What if the pool is closed?"), and others may start "Why…?", as in connection with behaviour ("Why did you turn the tv off?"), or about situations or events ("Why is this apple green? Why can't we go there?"). It is important not to deter your child from asking questions and to answer with honesty, even if all you can say is "I don't know". You may find your child's questions irritating, but answering them helps her extend her vocabulary and knowledge. And, for your child, questions are a great way to start a conversation.

Questions also arise from your child's natural curiosity about her environment and the things that go on in it. For a young child, learning about the world is important and, as you'll come to realise, it is a lot easier for your child to ask a question than for you to provide a good answer. Although occasionally you child may ask questions that you are unable to answer or she may not properly understand your answer, you should take your child's questions seriously and answer as best you can. For questions that don't have easy answers (e.g. "Why did Grandma die?"), only provide information that is appropriate for your child at her current age ("She was very sick and the doctor couldn't make her better" …).

The ability to ask questions comes from being able to make complex sentences, as well as to think in abstract terms. Your child may ask some questions because she has doesn't understand the things happening around her and needs more information to make sense of things. You can help your child to develop both her thinking and style of questioning by asking her "What if…?" and "How does…" questions. This helps your child to develop different styles of interaction as well as to explore the world in an abstract way. You should try to encourage your child to ask about the way something works, rather than allow her to break it open to try to find out.

In terms of expanding your child's thinking, it is better and more challenging to ask open-ended questions that can be expanded upon than closed questions, which have yes or no answers (so "Why do you like vanilla ice cream?" is better than "Do you like vanilla ice cream?"). If you are planning an excursion to a museum, for instance, you should say "What shall we do when we get there?" – which can lead to many possible answers rather than asking "Shall we see the dinosaurs first?" — the answer to which is "yes" or "no". Where a question is 'closed', your child won't be encouraged to suggest other possibilities that exist.

Concentration

Over time, your child will be able to function in much more complex ways. From around age three, she'll be able to stick with an activity for longer, becoming less distracted by external events and better able to focus on the task in hand, even if it is a bit difficult. If she does gets stuck, she will be more able to frame a question that will help her to deal with the problem and to come up with different solutions; if, for

example, she is working on a jigsaw, she's better able to choose appropriately shaped and sized pieces.

Your child's use of trial and error (as a way of exploring things) becomes increasingly sophisticated and she will use a great deal of persistence in trying to understand objects and make them work. So most activities, even though they may still be quite simple, commonly last much longer than when she was younger. Moreover, left alone, your child will find new ways to stretch and entertain herself. At the same time, her play becomes more imaginative and complicated; she may act out roles such as being a doctor or fireman, or create complicated scenarios involving model toys or animals.

Curiosity

Your child is a natural learner. She instinctively tries to make sense of everything she sees, hears and touches. This natural curiosity — her desire to discover the undiscovered — drives her to learn more at every opportunity. Everything she sees represents a new and exciting opportunity to explore and learn more. And this intrinsic motivation to reach new heights continues throughout her childhood.

You will need to keep a close eye on your child because she will want to open every box, empty out every container or search every cupboard. She's not purposely being bad, she just wants to find out how things work. By the time she reaches school age, her curiosity will be channelled and more controlled, and new learning opportunities should be the means to satisfy her eagerness to acquire more knowledge.

A thirst for learning

Even before she starts school, your child may show an interest in reading and numbers. Let her interest and ability guide you. If she seems ready, you can help teach her letters and numbers. A lot of reading and counting occurs naturally throughout your child's daily routine so she will start to recognise the names of shops that you frequently visit and may count items that you put in your trolley. Praise her when she demonstrates these early learning skills — she thrives under your approval. The information she acquires through her natural thirst for learning will give her a good start to formal schooling.

Do not, however, be tempted to advance your child too quickly. All children need a normal childhood and your child can become stressed if a lot of pressure is put on her to achieve. By all means, feed her interests but make sure you don't overstimulate her; it's important to just let her express her creativity in play.

Self-perception

Throughout childhood the way your child perceives herself changes. Around three years of age, your child's self-perception is so strong that it usually overshadows consideration of others. Your child may demonstrate through bad behaviour that she refuses to accept that what you want is more important than what she wants.

Between three and four years of age, your child will know a lot about herself, for instance, that she is a girl (or a boy), her name and age. She can list these things for you, when asked.

By the time she is five or six years old, your child will be able to describe herself reasonably accurately; she has a sense of who she is and how she relates to the people around her.

As part of self-perception, your child needs to hone her ability to think about and distinguish between feelings, to recognise them as discrete emotions and then use them to direct her behaviour. This is covered further in the next section.

How to help your child

Understanding herself — what's she's good at and what she finds difficult — will be your child's greatest key to success. One way of getting her to learn about her abilities is to help her set and meet her goals. Goals can be big ('I want to be rich!') or small ('I want an extra biscuit'). They can be for things she wants to do today ('I want to go swimming') or in the future ('I want to learn karate or to go to the seaside on holiday'). The key thing is that they are for specific things your child really cares about, and are realistic but challenging.

Where possible, faciliate your child's goals. You can't make her rich but you can encourage her to save any pocket or birthday money and watch it accumulate, and she could have an extra biscuit if she completes a task, for example. Bear in mind her choice for your summer holiday. Have your child set goals and review them regularly.

Bear in mind, too, that your child watches how you react to situations and manage your emotions. You also may be inadvertently teaching your child ideas that can affect her self image. Do you have 'food issues' or express a belief that girls shouldn't be boisterous or that boys shouldn't be caring?

The emergence of personality and the growth of emotions

The unique individual that is your child — a result of both her genes and environment — will not be fully known until she is much older, but during the preschool years, certain aspects of her temperament will become more constant and more obvious to you. These both impact on and are affected by her emotional responses and will have a lot to do with how she develops socially (see also page 119).

Temperament

By the time she is four compared to two, your child is more likely to be more patient, more articulate, will have started to develop insight into the feelings of others and has learned the art of reasoning. However, she is also likely to be quarrelsome at times and to fight with her friends as they all try to exert their independence.

By the age of five, individual personality traits will be apparent. You may notice that compared to her peers, your child is more fearful, or more extroverted or more caring. Personality is not static so these early traits are not completely reliable hints to her mature personality. In fact, as children get older, they begin to change at an accelerated rate. Different surroundings and experiences affect even inherited traits, so that a child can change and accommodate to things as they change around her. You may be surprised if your boisterous and booming toddler becomes a quiet and hardworking school child.

Learning to understand and accept the temperament of your child is an important stage in nurturing her personality and helping her to fit in with her environment. If, for example, your child is reluctant to go to parties or to a friend's house to play, you can develop strategies to prepare her and give her the confidence to cope with the situation. The important thing is to focus on her strengths.

Take a step back and look at who your child is. If your child is 'strong-willed', for example, set her challenging tasks or give her complicated toys. She has perseverance, after all, and is able to manipulate and analyse. If you deal with her temperament in a positive way, she will thrive.

Bear in mind, too, that while it is helpful to acknowledge particular features of your child's temperament, it is not a good idea to label her as having a particular personality trait. Your child's personality is still developing, and hearing herself described in a certain way may upset her and also may make her live up to the description. In addition, if you believe you you've mapped out your child's character, you may become blinkered and be too rigid in how you manage her.

Gender identity

Over the preschool years, your child will develop her sense of 'boyness' or 'girlness'. This psychological phenomenon is distinct from a sexual preference and usually depends on body shape. At age two your child may have told you that she is a girl, but it's not until around age six, that she'll comprehend that she was never a boy and will always be a girl (toddlers believe that a person's gender is changeable and depends on what he or she does or wears).

What causes gender differences is unproven though experts cite 'nature' or 'nurture' or both. Those in favour of nature, claim there are in-built differences in human infants from almost the time they are conceived. For example, proponents are convinced that boys demonstrate 'maleness' due to their higher levels of testosterone, the hormone that

'TYPICAL' BOY AND GIRL PRESCHOOLERS

Though each child is an individual and there are wide differences in behaviour among children of the same sex, experts agree that there are some useful generalities.

Boys walk, talk, feed and dress themselves and toilet train later than girls. At an early age, they are more interested in things and more likely to show and feel frustration. At age four, they are more muscular than girls so they enjoy more active, aggressive and vigorous play. They are keen to be dominant and to have their own way. The right side of the brain develops more quickly in boys, leading to a greater grasp of space. This they explore through movement games such as climbing and chasing, and measuring activities including driving cars through space or shooting darts across it.

Girls walk and acquire self-help skills early and they talk a lot more than boys of the same age. From a young age, they are more interested in people than boys and more willing to follow the bidding of others. At age four, the left side of the brain, which is associated with language, becomes more active, and girls spend even more time talking — to parents, playmates and toys. This enables them to build relationships at home and at playgroup. They also are more practised in using fine muscle skills such as those for drawing and painting.

is linked to aggression and activity, which starts to affect body cells in pregnancy. Girls are more nurturing and caring because of the physiological processes involved in a woman's ability to bear children. Experts who favour nurture or environment, however, claim that gender differences are more likely the result of parents treating boys and girls differently — for example, it's been proved that parents find aggression in their sons more acceptable than in their daughters and conversely, fear and sadness less acceptable in their sons than their daughters. In one famous experiment, infants dressed in pink were handled more gently and delicately by adults whereas those in blue were bounced around — even though the actual gender of the child was unknown.

Almost certainly, however, both factors contribute to a child's gender identity and while there is little you can do about pre-existing genetic factors, it is important that you offer your preschooler, no matter her gender, a wide variety of play opportunities and experiences that support the development of many skills. (Parents generally show more interest in their child's play if it is gender-appropriate [boys playing with soldiers and cars, girls with dolls and tea sets]).

Children learn about their sexual identity by watching and copying adults around them. Your preschooler is susceptible not only to your behavior and attitudes re gender but also to those of friends and relations and on television and in other media. Even if you and your partner both work and share household responsibilities equally and make an effort to police any examples of gender identity in your actions or speech, your child may persist in acting out a conventional gender role — your daughter walking around in high-heeled shoes and wearing make-up, your son brandishing a sword.

Preference for one's gender begins early. From the time babies first show interest in other people, girls and boys both prefer others of their own sex and from 18 months of age, they choose different toys and activities. By age four, girls and boys spend three times as many hours playing with either all-girl or all-boy groups, and at age six, eleven times as much with their same gender.

In order to explore what it is to be male and female, and thus to learn more about herself, it's natural that your preschooler engages in gender games. You may try and eschew sex-stereotypical toys and activities like dressing fashion dolls and using light sabres to play at intergalactic war, but your child may prefer such activities above all others. Moreover, in order to differentiate girls from boys, you may often hear your preschooler use gender stereotypes in her speech — (to her mother on rummaging through the toolbox "You can't use a hammer, only Dad can!" or "Of course I know how to kick a football, I'm a boy".

Some children, however, do go against gender type: your son may be shy and gentle or your daughter fierce and adventurous. Don't be concerned, therefore, if your son wants to wear high heels or your daughter plays 'shoot-em-up'; there is no evidence that playing with gender-opposing toys or engaging in gender-opposing activities will have any lasting impact whatsoever.

Sex play

Preschoolers are very interested in their bodies and as they get older, are also curious about those of others. As a toddler, you may have found your child touching her genitals and, as she gets older, you may catch her engaged in other sex play such as touching another child's genitals; or she may rub up against you in a suggestive way. It's important to recognise that such behaviour is commonplace and normal but you may feel uncomfortable about it, particularly if it stirs sexual feelings on your own part. In such instances, rather than a reprimand or punishment, it's best to try interesting your child in another activity or addressing her interest more directly by answering any particular questions she may have about sex and sexual behaviour. Talk to your child about what behaviour you find allowable — touching herself but not anyone else — and don't leave her alone for too long with other children without supervision. Make sure, too, she learns to respect your privacy; if you close your door, she should know to knock first.

Your preschooler will have questions about where babies come from, male and female genitals and sexual activities — even if she doesn't voice them. If she does, it's best to give simple and succinct answers and to provide further information when or if an additional question is asked rather than engage in extended explanations. While your answers will depend on your comfort level, you may decide that the whole truth isn't necessary at this stage, especially if you think your child isn't able to comprehend what you mean. For example, should your child walk in on you during love making and demand to know what you are doing, you might answer "Just giving daddy a cuddle"or "Something that mummies and daddies do" rather than explain the mechanics of the situation.

The development of emotions

Recognising emotions both in herself and others will enable your child to express them and to understand why she and others feel the way they do. This can help her to deal with difficult situations and to react more appropriately and effectively as she gets older. Instead of falling into a sulk when some treat is refused, she may be able to 'negotiate' a more favourable settlement if she learns to keep her emotions in check.

6 questions your child might ask

1 **"Where do babies come from?"** Your child may want to know how a baby gets in and out of the mother's tummy or may refer to what she expects to be the answer — "What supermarket did you buy me in"or "Do I have seeds for making a baby?"

2 **"What are you doing/what's that noise?"** If you are caught making love, your child will be curious about what's happening..

3 **"What's this?"** Anything she comes across that is related to sex and sexual activity from male and female genitals, to condoms and birth control pills.

4 **"Can I see ...?"** Your preschooler may ask to see (or even touch) your or your partner's genitals.

5 **"Why does my penis or vagina ...?"** Your child will be curious about how her genitals 'behave'.

6 **"Why don't I...?"** Your child may identify her gender as either male or female but want to know why she doesn't display mature characteristics like pubic hair or breasts.

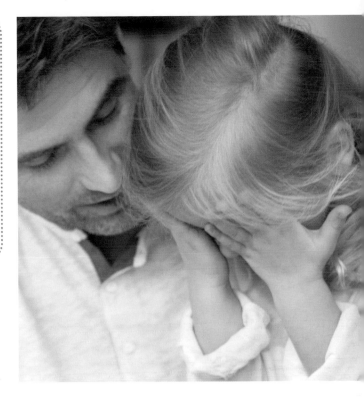

Unfortunately the 'terrible twos' don't always cease on your child's third birthday and your young preschooler may still struggle with strong emotions. Some three year olds are extremely confident but others are fearful and insecure. Extremes of emotions, though both positive and negative now — loving certain things to excess, greatly disliking others — characterise many a four year old but at five years, your child should be generally positive in her outlook, calm and serene, with the maturity to take most troubles in her stride.

Your child's emotional needs

Although every child is different, all have the same fundamental emotional needs; the challenge for you as a parent is to recognise those needs and to find ways of meeting them. Dominating the preschool years is the emotional need to feel loved and valued unconditionally; your child needs to feel that you care deeply for her no matter what she does and that you accept her as a worthwhile individual.

Also vital is her need to feel safe and secure; she needs to feel relaxed and happy when she is at home, in your company, and to feel that you can protect her from all dangers. She also needs to achieve; she thrives on success, has to learn to cope with failure and seeks your approval when she improves.

Finally, there is also her need to have friends and to be popular, to become independent and to cope with the ups and downs of everyday life.

Rather than looking at each of these in isolation as if they are items on a list to be checked off one at a time, the best way to understand and meet your preschooler's emotional needs is by asking two questions. Is she happy and settled? Is she making progress? If the answer to both questions is "Yes", then you can be confident you are meeting her emotional needs through your effective parenting, even if you haven't particularly planned it that way. If the answer to both is "No", then it is likely her emotional needs are not being met (although her lack of progress could be due to a developmental problem rather than an unfilled emotional need).

How to help your child

A healthy attachment to your preschooler is vital (see also page 119) as it is mainly through this two-way connection that her emotional needs will be met. Therefore, maintaining a strong bond between you should always be your top priority. One way to do so is through communication. If you encourage your preschooler to voice her feelings to you instead of keeping them locked up, her openness will go a

7 signs your child may be stressed

1 He has poor eating habits and appetite loss.

2 His sleeping patterns are disrupted at night, with an increased frequency of nightmares.

3 He displays increased aggression towards other children and adults.

4 His behaviour is withdrawn when previously he was outgoing.

5 His concentration and attention has dropped.

6 He has a lowered ability to tolerate frustration.

7 He exhibits regressive behaviour (thumbsucking, toiletting accidents).

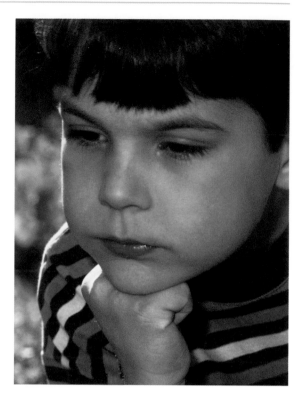

long way to stopping emotional problems from building up. When she is troubled by something, she'll tell you, and that will ease her anxieties. Good communication with you also makes her feel loved and valued.

But meeting your preschooler's emotional needs also involves helping her cope when things go wrong, for example, when she isn't successful, or when she has a disagreement with her best friend, or when someone in nursery laughs at the way she is dressed. Resilience is her ability to recover or bounce back when things don't go her way; it is her ability to cope when the odds are stacked against her. Some children are, by nature, more resilient than others. And some children tend to buckle under stress.

You can help boost your child's resilience by showing empathy and understanding when she is troubled. That will make her emotionally stronger. When she does tell you the difficulty she faces, it's important that you don't make her feel she is at fault or that she has to struggle to cope. Instead, suggest

ways to turn the situation around — inviting her best friend over for a play date may enable both children to put the matter behind them.

Remind your preschooler of incidents in the past that she found challenging and yet managed to cope with and chat with her about what she did then that worked. In other words, help her learn from her past experiences. That way she will discover solutions herself without you having to solve the problem for her. And when she loses her confidence and expresses negative comments about herself, point out her strengths by reminding her of all the things she is good at. Working with your child using these strategies also confirms to her that she is important to you and that you think she is wonderful, which further adds to her resilience.

You also need to take her feelings seriously. She may only be a young child, but her feelings are as important to her as yours are to you. Of course her world is less complex than yours and her worries and concerns are much simpler, but they are very real to her all the same. So don't trivialise her when she tells you she is upset about something, don't be annoyed with her if she appears to cry unnecessarily and listen to what she tells you when she is unhappy. As well as helping her express herself, that approach also makes her feel special. You know she is special to you because she is your child, and you know she is terrific. Yets he needs you to demonstrate that so that she feels special. Tell her how much you love her and why you think she's such a great child; she has heard you say this many times before but she can never hear it enough.

Give her plenty of attention when ever you can. It's not just about spending time with her. What matters is that when you are with your preschooler, you focus your attention on her, whether playing with her, reading her a story or chatting together. She feels very contented when you show interest in all aspects of her life. Comforting her when she is upset also helps. In most instances, all you need to do is put your arms around her, give her a gentle hug, and tell her that everything will be all right — that usually will be sufficient to drive her unhappiness away. Once she has calmed down, talk with her to find out what is causing her distress, and then try to find a way to solve the problem.

Do your best to avoid negative comparisons with other children — whether your child's friends or siblings. You may be tempted to encourage her to improve by pointing out how another child behaves better, or achieves more, than her. You hope that by giving the other child as an example, she'll try to copy him or her. But that strategy rarely works. Comparisons with friends or siblings typically makes a young child feel even less secure and can cause a rift between your children, or between your preschooler and her friend. Instead, focus on your child's strengths. Emphasise her good qualities. Your child's confidence is fragile and easily rocked. That's why it is good to tell her why her friends like her, or why you enjoy her company — this makes your child feel more positive about herself.

Taking an interest in her achievements has the same effect. Even though you may find it hard to get excited every time your child completes a jigsaw, particularly if she does so regularly, it is an achievement to her and she wants evidence of your interest and approval.

Moods

Every preschooler experiences a range of moods — happiness, sadness, anger, jealousy, irritability, sullenness and aggression — throughout a typical day. Part of growing up involves learning how to manage these different emotions so that your child maintains balance and stability in her life. As your child gets older and has an increasing awareness of those around her and her own feelings, her moods may become more complex. Although most young children are predominantly happy and content, there may be times when your child will feel irritable.

Often, such moods will be short-lasting and may be related to tiredness, boredom, hunger or thirst but, in some cases, your preschooler's mood of discontentment may have an underlying cause that needs to be addressed. It is up to you to recognise

REGRESSION

This is a healthy psychological strategy that your child sometimes uses involuntarily to protect his emotionally during times of stress, but it is also his way of letting you know that he's not coping well. Your child may resort to behaviour, language or mannerisms associated with an earlier developmental stage because it can make him feel safer. For instance, if you and your partner have frequent arguments, your fully toilet trained child may start to have 'accidents' if he's around when you do so. Likewise, if a new baby arrives in the famil, your preschooler may start to suck his thumb and talk in a baby voice. In this instance, regression enables him to compete with the new baby for attention.

through words, rather than behaviour. That's not always easy for a preschooler because her language skills are still under-developed, and it's a lot easier for her to hit someone than to tell him or her how frustrated or angry she feels. Nevertheless, encourage your child to describe her emotions rather than to act on them. Tell her that you want to know what she feels inside, explain that you will help her put her emotions into words, and be patient as she slowly learns to express herself through spoken language instead of physical actions.

Try to create a listening environment at home, one in which your child is able to say what she's feeling and thinking in the full knowledge that she will be listened to. Have discussions about other people's emotions too. Ask her to think about the feelings of her friends and her siblings when she plays with them. This will go a long way to helping her gain control over her moods. Psychologists claim that girls and boys have the same potential for managing moods, it's just that their strengths lie in different areas (see box, page 105). You might not be able to change what moods your preschooler goes through but you can influence the impact these moods have on her behaviour.

Grumpy phases

You can sometimes feel that nothing you say or do is right when your preschooler contradicts you at every turn. This does not mean that you are doing anything wrong, just that your child is going through an irritable phase. Often this will coincide with times of change, when she is feeling unsettled. Tiredness may also be a factor. Sometimes, though, children go through such phases for no apparent reason, and the mood will lift as suddenly as it began. Like adults, children can seem to get out of bed on the wrong side for no apparent reason. If your child is in a grumpy mood, keep smiling and be positive, encouraging her to get on with her day.

Irritability in the short term may be related to being hungry. It may also be that your child has had a poor night's sleep and needs to rest for an hour or two. However, irritability may also indicate that she has something on her mind. Talking to your child

these moods, and to provide help and support whenever it is needed.

A moody child, who tends to let negative feelings dominate, can be difficult to live with. Her friends will soon drift away because they find her unpredictable, and the child herself will spend more time being miserable than enjoying herself.

In contrast, a child who is aware of her varying moods, who is reasonably capable of controlling them, and who is also sensitive to the varying feelings of those around her, is more likely to have a strong sense of wellbeing and contentment. Your preschooler's level of emotional management and understanding is a combination of the sensitivity she was born with, the skills that she learns while growing up, and the interaction between these abilities.

How to help your child

You can, however teach your child to deal with her moods more effectively. Possibly the most useful strategy is to encourage her to express her feelings generally about what she has been doing at child care and maybe asking her specific questions about friends at nursery may uncover something to explain her mood.

Managing anger and aggression

Dealing with anger will be challenging for your preschooler. Having passed through the intense tantrum stage of the toddler years, she is now expected to make more of an effort both to curb her anger and to express her aggression in ways that are neither frightening nor harmful to others. She needs to take more responsibility for managing her rage instead of relying on you to calm her down as she did when she was younger. She's old enough now to realise that extreme outbursts of anger and aggression are unacceptable and avoidable.

 5 strategies for dealing with anger

It's important that you give your child practical techniques to deal with his anger and/or displacement activities when he feels tense and irritable; suggest that he try the following:

1 Your child could come to you the moment his anger starts to rise.

2 He could walk away from the situation that is fuelling his temper.

3 He could watch a dvd until he calms down.

4 He could pound a large lump of modelling clay.

5 He could engage in activities such as running about in the garden, kicking a ball as hard as he can, hitting a ball with a wooden bat, pedalling a toy up and down the path, and making a swing go back and forward at a fast speed.

How to help your child

Be open with your child about what you expect; tell her that now she's 'a big girl' she must stop behaving like a younger child. Explain that you are very unhappy when she loses her temper and that you expect her to try harder to control it the next time. Let her know that there is nothing wrong in feeling angry, but that there is something wrong in expressing her anger forcefully. As well as that, teach her practical strategies for controlling her temper, techniques that she can use whenever she feels her blood starting to boil (see box).

Make a list of any options; ask her for some suggestions as well, and then let her choose which methods she should use whenever she starts to feel angry. Practise these with your preschooler in role-play so that she knows what to do when the real thing arrives. In addition, suggest that she voices her anger as soon as it arises, instead of bottling up until she explodes. Explain that it is better for her to say "I'm getting angry because I can't finish this jigsaw" than it is for her to say nothing, simmer for several minutes, and then throw the jigsaw on the floor in fury.

You can also help your child gain control over her anger by showing her alternative and acceptable ways of expressing her fury that don't hurt anyone. These displacement activities are not always practical (for instance, running around outside when bedtime is approaching or when it rains) but there may be times when you can use this approach effectively. Direct her towards this activity when you see her start to become riled.

Anger and aggression management strategies might not work at first, no matter how often you practise them together. Don't worry, though, your child will improve with time and experience. When you see her temper ignite, remind her what to do to keep control. Give your preschooler a big hug and lots of praise when you see her control a potential surge of anger. She'll be as delighted as you with her success in anger management.

Jealousy and rivalry

Unlike anger, which usually has an outward expression and generally dissipates quickly, jealousy is typically internalised and lasts for a long time. That makes it an altogether more challenging mood for your child to manage. Jealousy is an unpleasant feeling — a mixture of resentment, fear, insecurity, possessiveness and suspicion — and it is always very destructive. At best it makes your preschooler unhappy and dissatisfied, and at worst it makes her behave nastily.

Your child can be jealous of others her own age, whether in her family or not, when she thinks she is treated less favourably than them. She can also be envious of possessions, and she may even be envious when she sees you giving your attention to her older brother or younger sister. This form is rivalry is natural. But your preschooler has to learn to keep her jealousy under control or she will feel miserable all the time and will be permanently convinced that she always gets a raw deal compared to everyone else.

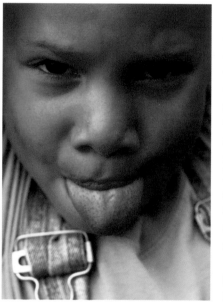

To help her master this powerful emotion, avoid making her feel guilty about being jealous. Remarks such as "You should be ashamed of being jealous of your brother" or "Only horrible children get jealous" simply encourages her to hide her true feelings from you. It also is likely to produce a poor self-image, as she will begin to see herself in negative terms. Instead, let your preschooler know you understand what it is like to be jealous of someone else. There is no harm in admitting to her that you also feel jealous at times, as long as you add that you don't let these feelings upset you or spoil your enjoyment. She'll be relieved to know that she can discuss and share this with you.

Encourage her to talk about her jealousy, instead of acting on it. That's better than suggesting she

pretends these feelings don't exist —denial won't make them go away. Ask her to explain to you why she feels jealous, and try to identify reasons why she shouldn't feel this way, for instance, because she has more toys than she thinks, or because you spend more time with her than she realises. When your pre-schooler learns how to manage her moods effectively, she'll find life so much more enjoyable.

Fears and insecurities

Every preschooler is afraid sometimes. While some fears can actually be good for your child — if she's afraid of strangers, for instance, then she won't go off into a car with someone she doesn't know — most fears cause inconvenience. Fears at the preschooler stage are perfectly normal, and fortunately, most disappear spontaneously without requiring any special help.

Many preschooler fears are in response to objects or events. For instance, there is the fear of small animals and insects. Small animals can be more frightening to a young child than large animals, maybe because they can move so fast and unpredictably — your young child feels she has no control over them and so she may be very afraid when she realises that a normally-caged gerbil or hamster, for example, has become free.

Then there is a fear of the dark. In darkness, your preschooler's imagination can run riot — in a matter of moments, she can become totally convinced that a wicked person is hiding in the blackness that surrounds her at night and she'll scream out to you in terror.

You may also discover that loud peals of thunder cause your child to hide under the table or duvet. She will be terrified of the noise, even though thunder cannot physically touch or harm her. Like many other fears, this is totally irrational yet extremely powerful.

Other preschool fears arise in response to emotions and relationships. For example, your preschooler wants to achieve, but if she is afraid of failure — perhaps someone laughs at her when she drops a ball — she might be afraid to try anything new in case the challenge proves too difficult for her. She may flatly refuse to go onto the climbing frame because she knows her pals can reach the top rung and she is afraid she won't manage this.

Sometimes a child fears losing her parents' love. If she is regularly made to feel rejected by her parents, she can to start to fear that she will lose their love entirely, and is very anxious in everything she does.

How to help your child

You should try in the first place to prevent your child from developing fears (although bear in mind that she may acquire fears despite all your efforts). Advanced preparation helps. If you know that she has to face a stressful episode in the near future (for example, she has to have a travel vaccination jab),

then give her notice. Tell her what to expect about the procedure, and point out that you will be with her at all times. Remind her of the times she had one in the past and coped well. And remain calm yourself. Any fear you have will quickly spread to your child. So if you are anxious about the challenge she faces, don't show it otherwise her fear will intensify. Have a calm and relaxed outward manner, and try to avoid suggesting in any way that she should be worried about what lies ahead.

If your child does develop a real fear, do what you can to help her beat it. Most important of all, treat her with respect. Her fear could seem trivial to you, but it is very real to her. She's not behaving this way just for fun, so don't treat her in a way which might suggest you think she is being silly. Give her lots of reassurance. As far as your frightened preschooler is concerned, the object of her fear is insurmountable but she will gain emotional strength from your confidence in her. Certainly, you should make sure that she doesn't arrange her life so that

4 reasons why a preschooler is more prone to fears

1   **He has a very vivid imagination**. That's why, for example, your preschooler argues vehemently that the shadow cast across his bedroom wall is actually a monster with special powers. His limitless imagination means that he can be extremely frightened about something that you regard as trivial.

2   **Fantasy and reality can merge sometimes in your child's mind during play**. This means, for instance, that an exciting play episode can suddenly become very intense and real for him, and a bad dream can seem as if it is really happening.

3   **He has an imperfect understanding of his environment**. Although he comprehends a lot about the world around him, there is lots he

still doesn't fully grasp. He doesn't know that flies do not gobble-up people, that he can't be washed down the drain in your bathroom sink, or that a small bird will not carry him off somewhere. Of course he will learn these things in due course, but in the meantime, his limited understanding leads him to believe that anything is possible.

4   **His sense of danger becomes more developed**. He is now more aware of the risk of physical injury and hurt from, say, falling over, bites from small animals and jabs from the doctor. His heightened sensitivity to these hazards can become transformed into specific fears.

secure children because almost every child uses a comforter sometimes. In fact, research has shown that a child who uses a comforter before she reaches school age typically has better relationships with other children once she is in school and is less likely to be shy, lacking in self-confidence and even to experience fewer nightmares. It's as though having a comforter could actually be good for your child.

Maybe it's the familiarity that appeals to her. Your child likes her object's instantly recognisable feel, smell and even taste. She knows exactly what it will be like to hold, and this provides her with reassurance and comfort. If she has a comfort object from the time when she was very young, its attraction for her probably lies in that link. A child is likely to have fond memories of her early years and is happy to use a comforter associated with that period. A comforter probably provides feelings of security and safety, when she doesn't have her mum and dad right beside her; it makes her ready to face the world independently, without them by her side. It's similar to being armed with a good-luck charm when you have to deal with a situation that makes you nervous, say, a job interview. This is what your child is doing, though in her case she prefers a comforter to a lucky mascot. The comforter helps her beat anxiety.

There is nothing intrinsically wrong with a preschooler using a comforter. However, you may be uncomfortable about seeing your child trail an old cuddly toy around with her wherever she goes. Don't worry, she will probably grow out of it by the time she's five. The main advantage of a comforter during the preschool years is that it helps a child to relax; it is virtually guaranteed to induce positive feelings, and that can only be good for her. Knowing that she has her comforter clutched firmly in her hand may be sufficient for her to deal competently with any crisis. For instance, allowing her to take her comforter on holiday means that she will be able to sleep happily in a strange bedroom. Or allowing her to take her favourite cuddly toy when visiting the doctor will ensure that she cooperates during the consultation.

FANTASY PLAY

Young children are blessed with vivid imaginations, which they use to explore and come to terms with a wide range of emotions. An imaginary companion, for example, can help a child to experiment with 'forbidden feelings' and experiences, so it's a good idea to encourage these imaginary friends, even supplying a few props for the 'friend' to play with.

Sometimes, however, a make-believe world becomes a little too real, and your child will become upset or frightened by some element of the situation or play — a scary jack o' lantern, an overly jolly Father Christmas or an accident to an imaginary friend. Imaginative play is important to your child's development, so don't belittle or make fun of these incidents. Instead, try to join in and solve the problem — let your child draw a smiley face on a Halloween pumpkin that you carve — but let him continue to manage his fantasy play as he'd like.

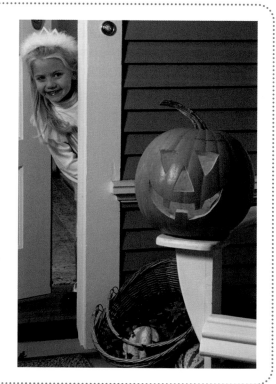

The main disadvantage of a comforter, though, is that it can be a nuisance, especially if your child becomes too attached to it. You'll already be aware of this if you've ever had to deal with her refusal to go out the front door until she has found the item. It doesn't matter a jot to her that you are ready and waiting to go and that everyone else is also ready. If she can't find her comforter, then everyone has to look for it. She'll probably be miserable the whole outing if she has to leave it behind.

Then there's the image created by a child who has a comforter with her. A baby with a cuddly toy is cute, while a five year old clinging desperately to a grubby old teddy gives an entirely different impression. She may look immature and babyish. Although she isn't bothered by this, you might be, especially if you think that her peers will tease her.

Hygiene is also an important issue. Old cot blankets and stuffed toys get dirty and harbour germs. Part of the attraction for her is the comforter's well-worn texture, so your preschooler won't thank you for cleaning it — she may even be furious because washing gives the comforter a different feel, smell and taste.

6 questions to assess the importance of your child's comfort habit

1 **Has the habit just started or has it continued without a break since early childhood?** If he has been biting his nails since he was a toddler and has just continued with the habit until now, then this is a habit, nothing more. However, if he never bit his nails during early childhood then suddenly started at the age of four or five, this could be a sign of an underlying worry.

2 **When does he use his comforter?** Some children cuddle their old teddy in private when they are highly relaxed, for instance, while watching television at home in the evening, or while reading a book in bed at night. The use of a comforter is more concerning when a child insists on using it even in public, say, at nursery in front of his peers.

3 **Are there any other areas of his development that cause you concern?** If his comfort habit is a sign of a deeper anxiety, you may be concerned about other aspects of his development too. For example, he might also be more irritable than usual, or sleep badly during the night. Usually, signs of stress affect more than one area of your child's progress and development.

4 **How resistant to change is his comfort habit?** In many instances, though not all, a comfort habit can be a sign of a deep worry when it is highly resistant to change. This is particularly true when the habit starts suddenly. If your preschooler persists despite lots of discouragement and support from you to help him stop, there may be something more to it.

5 **How long has he been doing this?** Preschoolers often drop comfort habits as quickly as they pick them up. One day, for instance, he insists on twiddling his hair all the time and yet the next day he doesn't touch it at all. The habit is often more significant psychologically if it lasts for more than a month or so without change.

6 **What effect has this on his life?** A normal comfort habit will have little impact on your child's life yet if you find that, say, he insists on sucking his thumb while walking along the street, getting dressed and eating, and that he becomes very distressed when you tell him to stop, that is a likely indication that he is worrying about something.

Preschoolers can also have comfort habits instead of comfort items. Typical comfort habits include: hair-twiddling (while concentrating hard on something or while relaxing during TV watching), which, if it goes on too long, may thin her hair in that area; thumb sucking (this is an extension of sucking a dummy in earlier years), which if it persists, may make the skin on her thumb rough or broken and her teeth damaged; genital rubbing (masturbation in childhood is comforting, not sexual — so don't overreact with embarrassment, shock or disgust) and nail biting (she nibbles away at her fingernails or at the skin surrounding her fingernails), which if it persists can cause unsightly skin blemishes and possibly infection.

Breaking the habit

Almost certainly, your preschooler will grow out of her comforter or comfort habit spontaneously by the time she starts school, whether or not you do anything about it. Yet there's no harm in helping drop the habit earlier if you want. Whenever you decide that the moment has arrived for your child to give up her comfort habit, avoid making it a battle of wills. She'll only become more determined to persist if you start fighting with her about it. The more that her comforter gains in importance for you and for her, the more she will hold on to it, determined to resist all attempts at change. So take a positive approach. Tell her "You look like a big girl when you go to nursery without your blanket" instead of "I'm really angry at you taking that stupid blanket with you everywhere"; or "I'm really proud of you when you watch tv without sucking your thumb" instead of "You look silly with your fingers stuck in your mouth all the time"; or "Your sister is very happy with you when play with her without holding your teddy" instead of "Your sister doesn't have her teddy all the time and I wish you were more like her."

It's not easy for anyone, child or adult, to break a habit, so your approach to discouraging her use of comforters should be supportive, encouraging and steady. Don't go for the 'cold turkey' strategy, which involves the immediate and complete withdrawal of the object or habit. That's far too demanding. She won't be able to break her habit that quickly. Better to suggest that she tries to avoid using the comforter for a specific amount of time (for ten minutes at first), then gradually extend this period. Her ability to survive without the comforter will increase slowly.

Likewise, don't use punitive measures. For instance, resist the temptation to paint her thumb with a commercial foul-tasting-but-harmless liquid to stop her thumb sucking habit — the chances are she'll just get used to the taste or suck a different finger instead. Instead, say "No" and then gently but firmly remove her thumb from her mouth.

The fact is that she does enjoy the comfort habit and she may not see any reason to change things at the moment. So expect some resistance when you ask her to stop. Persist with your discouragement anyway. Your preschooler will be more willing to give up her comforter or comfort habit when she feels that this change in behaviour brings her some benefit. That's why you need to tell her how happy you are with her new behaviour. Other ways of rewarding her for not using the comforter include pointing out that she looks like a 'big girl' now, reminding her that her friends will not laugh at her any more and maybe giving her a special treat because she has tried so hard. You can do this even when she only stops the comfort habit for a few moments.

When it's extreme

Some preschoolers continue to use their comforter, or continue with their comfort habit, long after most of their peers have given these up. If yours does this, you may worry this is a sign of a deep emotional problem. The chances are she'll be ready to give it up soon, but in the meantime, you need to establish its importance (see box, page 115).

Daydreaming

If your child is a daydreamer, with her head in the clouds, always thinking about something else other than the task she is supposed to be completing, you'll know how frustrating it is to try to get her focused. No matter how hard you try, she always seems to end up distracted in her own world, deep in thought, dreaming about other things. If, for example, you ask her why she hasn't tidied her toys away, which you asked her to do ten minutes ago, she'll probably reply. "Sorry, I forget. I'll do it soon." Even when she does make an effort to sort things out, the final result is not as organised as you had hoped for because her mind wandered on to something else soon after she started.

Daydreaming is a harmless activity for your preschooler, and it provides her with a rich fantasy world. When daydreaming, she can invent anybody she likes and have any conversation she wants. One of the marvellous features of this psychological phenomenon is that your child is totally in control of what happens in her daydream; she decides what goes on, who is there, and what they say to each other. She doesn't have that sort of control in most other aspects of her everyday life, so it's hardly surprising she enjoys daydreaming so often. However, you may worry that she could be learning so much more if she was more attentive to the world around her.

A child might even develop daydreaming to the point where she has a daydream friend — a character that she creates in her mind whom she treats as real. She may, for example, set the table for two, sit in one of the chairs, and then proceed to chat to the empty seat as though she can actually see someone there. She might even pour her imaginary friend a cup of juice and offer her a biscuit. Similarly, she might be furious with you if you don't make room for her friend during story time, or if you close the door to the room before her friend has crossed the threshold. Don't worry; your preschooler knows her imaginary friend does not exist.

4 steps to ensure your child's attention

1 **Reduce distractions where possible.**

2 **Use your child's name** to preface what you are going to say — say nothing more until you are sure he is looking at you.

3 **Keep saying his name** until he turns to face you.

4 **Once you have his full attention,** give him the instruction or information. If he looks away while you talk to him, or appears to slip into a daydream, remind him to continue looking at you. Don't give the instruction until you are absolutely satisfied that you have his full concentration. This ensures that he hasn't allowed his mind to wander on to other things.

There are many potential psychological benefits from this type of daydreaming. Most obviously, the friend does exactly what she's told to do. Your child doesn't have a problem about deciding what toy to play with next, or what game they should play together; her imaginary friend obliges without argument or challenge and livens up an otherwise dull and boring day.

A daydream friend can also boost your preschooler's confidence. For instance, if she is afraid to climb the ladder that leads to the top of the slide she can turn to her fictitious pal for emotional support. The friend can offer her encouragement and reassurance, giving her that extra push needed to spur her on to greater achievements. In addition, an imaginary friend lets her vent her anger without any repercussions. That's why you might see your preschooler severely reprimanding an empty space for naughty behaviour — just like you did to her a few moments ago. She gets rid of her frustration by taking it out on her imaginary companion.

As with all types of daydreaming, you need to set limits on her use of the imaginary friend, particularly if your child makes excessive demands on behalf of her friend (for instance, always wanting to have a seat at the table for her) and this may become tiresome. Be prepared to say that her imaginary friend doesn't need to be with her every minute of the day.

Discouraging daydreaming, improving attention

You might worry that your daydreaming preschooler has a serious problem with her attention and concentration, and that her frequent forays into the world of imagination signify an underlying disorder. Or you may worry that she needs to daydream because she is unhappy with her real world. Neither of these possibilities is likely, however (unless the frequency of daydreaming is so extreme that your child appears totally disconnected with the world around her). In most instances, daydreaming is a harmless childhood activity — your child knows the daydream is not real.

Even so, you may want to gently discourage the practice and to help her become more attentive to the world around her There are several strategies you can use for this purpose. For a start, remove distractions when trying to grab your preschooler's attention or when asking her to follow an instruction. For instance, there no point in asking her to tidy her toys when she's already watching tv — although she'll nod in agreement, she won't have absorbed what you asked her to do. Instead, mute the sound or switch the television off altogether before speaking to her. The same applies when she plays with her friends. Wait for a suitable moment before you say anything, probably when she and her friends are quieter, then break into their conversation. You won't succeed in catching your child's attention simply by trying to talk over their conversation — the louder you talk, the louder they will talk.

If your preschooler seems to daydream so easily that your instructions are rarely followed, make sure that you catch her full attention before telling her what to do. Then ask her to repeat the instruction back to you — this is a good way to get her focused on the task in hand, and it also helps her memory. If she can't repeat your instruction accurately, tell her again. Repeat this process until you are sure she has listened accurately.

Social development

Egocentrism, the belief that the world and those around you exist solely for your comfort and entertainment is universal in toddlers and is demonstrated by a refusal to share, take turns or refuse to wait for a parent to do something for them. Gradually, the realisation comes that the world does not revolve around this one, small person and that the feelings of others need to be taken into consideration. Developing an understanding of the perspective of others may come earlier if a child has siblings or if she spends time with groups of children, perhaps at child care.

By the time she's three, your child should show that she understands another person's situation rather than relating it to her own experience, for example, by seeking out your help if she sees a younger sibling cry.

Around four years of age, she will be able to consider conflicting emotions before responding — pleasure, if her younger brother is reprimanded for taking her toys but sympathy when he bursts into tears. Your child will also be more able to wait for things to happen as she gains more of an understanding of what is going on around her and that not everything that happens relates to her.

At five years, your child should be able to appreciate the needs and wishes of others, although this does not necessarily mean she will put the needs of others before her own. A preschooler of this age becomes concerned about her siblings and friends and will take care of a younger brother or sister, perhaps holding hands protectively when they enter a roomful of children or an unfamiliar place.

Ensuring the bonds of attachment

The relationship you have with your preschooler strongly influences all other relationships in her life. Therefore, the strength of attachment she has to you (and your partner) — that is the two-way emotional connection between you and your child — is extremely important. By now, of course, the bond between you will be solidly formed. Your preschooler feels close to you, is happy and relaxed in your company, shares her thoughts and feelings with you, and likes to cuddle you — these are the hallmarks of a strong parent-child attachment. However, even at this age, there is lots you can do to continue promoting a healthy psychological connection.

Perhaps most important of all is to continue appropriate loving physical contact with her, such as cuddling, hugging and kissing, holding her hands when you are out together, stroking her cheek or hair gently, and even patting her on the back when she has behaved well. Those warm, loving gestures make her feel loved, valued, safe and secure. Some parents mistakenly think this sort of contact with a child is 'babyish', and that by the time she is four or five years old, these physical demonstrations of love should stop. That's a pity, because having an appropriate physical dimension to your relationship

Your child and his friends

3 years old

This is the start of cooperative play and very often your child will share a toy — or offer something else in its place — but you will have to intervene from time to time to make clear his wishes or to 'settle' differences. He will, however, still spend lots of time playing by himself or alongside other children. Your child generally prefers being with one other child, who he will consider a 'special' friend but occasionally he will play with more children. Overall, he can spend about three hours a day playing with others. Over the course of this year, your child will play more often as part of a group and there may be lots of cooperation, and often clowning and fooling around. Friendships will become intense and your child may prefer others with a similar temperament and/or energy level. Some children may be excluded from group play. It's not unusual for playtimes to end in tears and bad behaviour.

4 years old

Other children are now a source of pleasure and exciting activities; your child prefers other children over adults and can spend hours playing with them. Playtime generally goes smoothly with cooperating, sharing and turn taking but you may need to settle disputes and may have to coax your child to accept a new playmate. Your child should enjoy being part of a group and will be better at expressing what she wants to happen and be more tolerant of others' infractions of game rules. She might have a special friend, but in any event, wants to be liked by other children. A leader or a follower? Over the course of the year, some children issue orders and find that others carry them out. Or, your child may become very strongly attached — even for a short while — to another child, possibly of the opposite sex, and take her lead from her or him.

5 years old

Your child now is an accomplished playmate, particularly with one or two children of his own age, and can be left unsupervised for longer periods, which is useful as play with others will take up more of your child's time from now on (though not as much as when he's at school). A five year old, however, still enjoys being with his family the most. You can plan on him spending a good part of his day with friends. He also will play with both girls and boys (something that will change as he gets older).

things along and hopefully make for a more harmonious atmosphere (see box, page 120).

Sharing a parent

As well as having to learn to share toys and other possessions, children have to learn to share their parents with others, whether this be other adults or a younger sibling, or even chores that need doing. Your child needs to understand that she cannot always be the focus of attention of her parents, who may want to spend time with others or who have their own activities to fit into the day. Provided she has your company, it is good for your child to learn how to amuse herself. No parent can be a playmate every minute of the day.

A child, particularly a first child, may find it hard to let you visit others or to do your everyday tasks rather than playing. If you experience this, try to involve her in your activities: If you are dusting, give her a cloth; if you are doing the laundry, let her help

you put the clothes in the machine; if you are writing a shopping list, ask her to make her own list by scribbling, or if she is older, by drawing the things you need. If this isn't feasible, don't stall her repeatedly; explain what you are going to do and when you will be able to play with her. Make sure you keep your promises: If you say you will play with her when you have finished the laundry, try your best to do it. And, when you do play with her, give her quality time. When you do something together, make her the focus of your attention.

Empathy and kindness

You may feel you face an uphill struggle when trying to teach your child to be caring and thoughtful about others, but you'll find this task much easier than you expect; you just need to find ways to harness her instinct for kindness. Empathy develops over time, although it may be apparent early on (a young baby may cry if she sees her mother do so).

When your preschooler sees other children or adults are upset, her natural reaction is to try to comfort them. She intuitively wants to ease their distress, even when she doesn't understand why they are unhappy or what practical help they might need. That's also why your child is generally very caring towards a younger brother or sister. She will be prepared to stand up for her siblings and won't allow them to come to any harm if she has anything to do with it. These acts of kindness and empathy happen spontaneously. It is as though a young child intuitively knows when to be caring towards others, when to help them, and when best to offer emotional support.

Despite these natural tendencies towards kindness, however, there are lots of incidents of anti-social behaviour amongst preschoolers every day. There are a number of explanations to account for this. First, your child has many basic instincts (as well as the instinct to be kind to others), and these instincts compete with another. For instance, her need to satisfy her hunger might be more powerful than her instinct to be caring — so she pushes her friend out the way in order to grab the sweets.

Second, your preschooler is influenced by the behaviour of those around her, especially by you and your partner. If she sees you bicker with each other about washing the dishes, or fight over the choice of television programmes, the chances are she'll do the same when she is in a similar situation.

Third, your child's natural impulse to be kind and empathic may be suppressed by the influence of television. Most contemporary role models in children's television programmes are admired for their strength, physical abilities and capacity to beat an opponent. Even though these fictional characters show occasional acts of kindness, such actions may go unnoticed in the eyes of your young viewer who may be more interested in adventure than she is in sociable behaviour.

How to help your child

As well as setting a good example yourself (after all, you can't reasonably expect your preschooler to behave in a kind way if you behave uncaringly or unkindly in front of her), make a point of praising any kindness that she demonstrates: there will be many times when your preschooler is considerate to friends or family. When that happens, tell her how pleased you are with what she's done. Make a big fuss of her for being so caring; your positive reaction will encourage her to behave kindly on other occasions.

You could also consider buying her a pet to look after. This needn't be a dog or a cat, just a small pet such as a goldfish or a hamster. The basic responsibility of feeding a small pet teaches your child to think about the needs of others. However, you'll need to supervise when she looks after the pet, but let her know that she is in charge.

Explain to your preschooler that her behaviour also has practical consequences. For instance, tell her clearly "When you helped your friend, she felt better" or "If everyone was unkind, nobody would help you." Statements like these help your child understand the wider implication of her empathic, kind behaviour. She begins to realise that kindness affects her as much as it affects others.

And give her opportunities to be kind to others. For instance, she can have responsibility for basic household chores, such as tidying the toys each night or helping set the cutlery on the table for the family meal. Giving your preschooler duties like these teaches her to think about others and encourages her to be kind towards them.

You can also involve her in charity. Whatever amount of money she gets to spend, for instance, for birthday presents, suggest that she gives a share of her money to charity. This is a very practical form of kindness that provides her with direct involvement. Make sure that she physically puts the coins into the charity collection — that makes it very real for her.

As well as positive encouragement of empathy and kindness, have zero tolerance for anti-social, uncaring behaviour. Don't let incidents of unkindness from your child go by unnoticed, even though they may be relatively minor. A strict non-accepting attitude at home lets your child see that you expect kindness and empathy at all times.

Manners

Preschool children often lack manners. It's quite likely that you have spoken to your child about this on a number of occasions, and yet your pleas for politeness seem to fall on deaf ears. It's as if learning good manners is a hard job for a young child because somehow she has managed to build up a whole repertoire of bad manners, such as sneezing without covering up her nose and mouth, touching other people's things without asking their permission, talking loudly (or even shouting) in public as if nobody can hear what she says, forgetting to say "please" or "thank you", and making unacceptable noises from one body orifice or another.

Her lack of manners can be frustrating whether it's her behaving dreadfully the moment you have a visitor or not showing any interest when given a gift. Worse still, her nose-picking during mealtimes sickens you and can be a very effective appetite-suppressant! Manners matter, as far as you are concerned, and you would like to see her awareness of them improve.

In most instances, though, your preschooler's poor display of manners is totally unintentional; she doesn't deliberately set out to have bad manners, she simply doesn't think enough about politeness because she's too busy thinking about something else, like what's on television or the latest toy that you bought her earlier today. Or maybe she isn't fully aware of the impact her behaviour has on others around her.

Sometimes, however, her lack of manners may be designed to have an effect. For instance, there was the time she made an insulting comment about the size of another child's nose and then she and her pal howled with delight as they collapsed in a heap of giggles. On that occasion, she intended to be rude because she thought that was funny. Then there was the time she belched loudly while sitting with her friends and then they all rolled around in fits of laughter. Yet these occasions are much less frequent than you probably suspect.

Good manners and politeness have to be learned; they are not inborn and they rarely develop spontaneously. By the time she is a preschooler, your child can begin to understand the idea of 'good' and 'bad' manners, however, and from then on the slow learning process gets underway. She won't learn good manners overnight.

Barriers to manners

When teaching manners to your child, expect to meet resistance for a number of reasons. First, the reality is that while adults like good manners, children often prefer bad manners, which is why she and her friends laugh when one of them is rude. All it takes is for your child or one of her pals to break wind loudly, and before you know it they all double up with delight. Most children — and if truth be told, many adults — get a good laugh out of those situations. They find them extremely funny.

Second, your preschooler has already discovered that bad manners usually generate a strong reaction from you. While you give mild praise when she behaves politely, or perhaps not even mention it all, she gets your full attention the moment she speaks rudely to a shop assistant. She knows that if you are too busy to spend time with her, she can change all that by making a rude comment or noise, which is loud enough for you to hear.

Last, good manners require effort, and sometimes your preschooler just can't be bothered. It's easier for her to sit and say nothing when you give her a snack than it is to thank you for it; and it's easier to say nothing when she is with her peers and to think only of herself, than it is to make polite conversation.

That's why you need to explain to your preschooler why manners matter. Keep your discussions about good manners very practical, spelling out the positive benefits to her personally. For instance, point out that behaving politely will make her more popular with her peers. Tell her that although a display of bad manners will make her pals laugh at first, nobody wants to play with a child who constantly picks her nose or makes rude noises and smells. In the long run, good manners help your child to make friends more easily. And the same applies with adults. Her mum and dad, aunts and uncles, nursery teachers and other grown-ups in her life always will think more favourably of her when she is polite.

Teaching manners

Use positive language when teaching good manners. No child likes to be told all the time that she is doing this or that wrong, or that people are irritated by her behaviour. Think how you would feel if she said to you "I think the way you eat your food is terrible" or "I'm fed up having to constantly remind you to cover your nose and mouth when you sneeze." Your self-esteem would drop and you'd be thoroughly miserable — it's no different with her. You should say "You are a such neat child, and that's why I am surprised the way you eat isn't as tidy as it could be. Maybe you just need to eat a little more slowly" or "I know you can sneeze politely because I've seen you do it sometimes. Maybe you just need to remind yourself to do that every time." It's amazing how much more responsive your preschooler will be to constructive comments than to negative ones. Embedding your observations about her manners in some form of praise, and offering an alternative course of action to improve her behaviour, encourages your child to listen to you.

She also needs to understand the purpose of good manners. Although it is obvious to you, for example, that she should always say "please" and "thank you", it may not be obvious to her. Take nothing for granted and give a full explanation each time. Likewise, be patient when she asks questions about manners, for instance, "Why is it good manners to do that?", each time you try to teach her a new aspect of politeness. You'll find that some manners are hard to explain (for instance, can you really provide her with a good reason why she should ask permission to leave the table when she has finished her meal?).

Have realistic expectations. Don't try to teach her too many good manners at once — she'll feel totally overwhelmed. Instead, pick one aspect of good manners to start with, perhaps one that is easier to learn, for instance, saying "please" when she asks for something. Talk about that with your preschooler, explaining that you are much more likely to give her what she wants when she asks politely; then shower her with praise when she eventually does what you told her.

Set an example of good manners yourself. After all, it's not fair to expect her to cover her mouth when coughing if she sees you splutter all over the place with your mouth unguarded. Your good manners provide a role model for her to follow. Likewise, never laugh at her bad manners, even though it may be highly amusing. For example, you might struggle to stop from chuckling when you hear your child's sweet voice telling her grandmother, say, "Get off your lazy bottom and get me a biscuit". If you do laugh at such behaviour, your preschooler may take this as encouragement to do the same again in the future.

Yet it's a matter of balance. You don't need to react every single time your child's manners fall below the standards you have set. Sometimes she just forgets what to do or say, it's as simple as that. Everybody makes mistakes sometimes, even you! You can safely ignore occasional lapses in politeness. The most effective way to teach your child manners is to praise her when she shows good manners rather than to reprimand her when they are bad. Highlight what she does right, not what she does wrong.

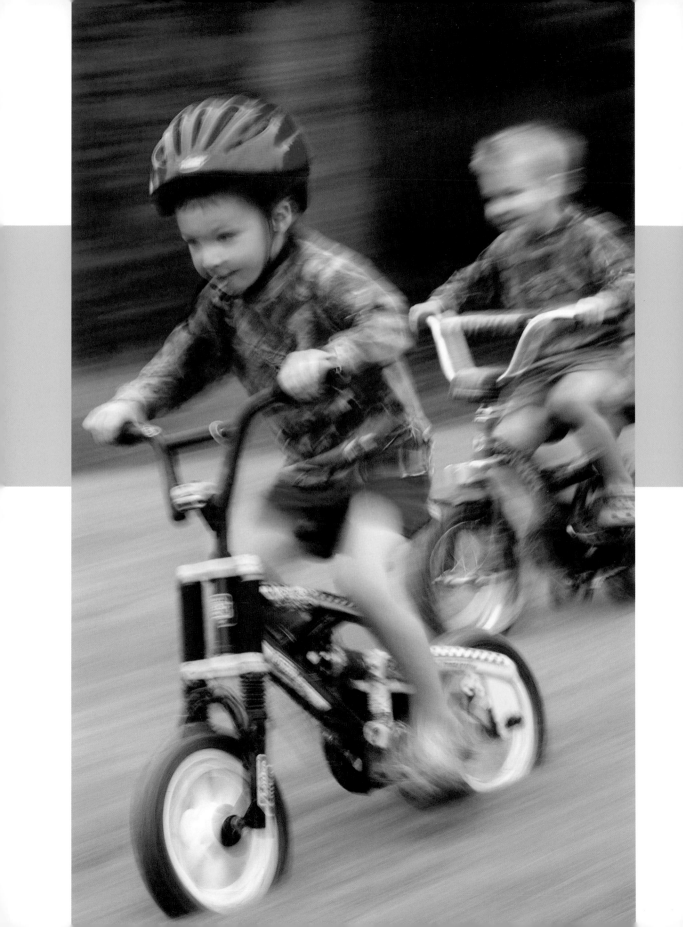

CHAPTER 4
PARENTAL CHALLENGES

In addition to age-old situations like managing bad behaviour, including lying, bullying and tantrums, and encouraging your child to be independent and making sure he is ready for school, today's parents have to deal with the influence of the internet, computer games and mobile phones. While it's important that your child benefits from what modernity can contribute, it's also vital that, like all previous children, he be an acceptable member of the community. Your role in ensuring that he knows what good behaviour is and is able to act accordingly, is paramount.

Managing bad behaviour

A loving families discipline isn't about controlling your preschooler or about forcing him to conform to your rules. It's about helping him to think about others, to think about the effect of his behaviour on those around, and to gain self-control over his urges and desires. Discipline is about your child gradually taking more and more responsibility for his own behaviour rather than you having responsibility for that on his behalf. In fact, the actual origin of the word 'discipline' comes from the Latin word which means 'learning'; in other words, your child learns through discipline. That's why you should approach discipline with him as though you are trying to create a system that enables him to learn rules so that he can behave properly, rather than a system that coerces him into behaving properly.

Establishing rules

Parents differ in their approaches to disciplining their preschoolers; some are stricter, some are more flexible, some explain more, and some use punishment more than others. You have to decide which style of discipline is best for your family. At this age, however, your child's understanding and reasoning has developed to the point where you can justifiably expect him to follow rules — for most of the time. He realises that there are other people in the family who have feelings and ideas, and that living in a family involves thinking about mum and dad, and about his brothers and sisters as well as about himself.

This doesn't mean that he'll willingly follow the standards you have set without ever putting up a challenge. Young children are by nature

egocentric (in other words, they tend to think of themselves first) and it is only through encouragement and experience that they begin to consider others. Your preschooler's responsiveness towards family discipline (for example "You must tidy your toys when you finished playing with them" or "You must take a turn putting the plates on the table for dinner") develops gradually. As his natural instinct is to think that a rule applies to everyone else but him, you'll need to help him accept that rule applies to him too. The first step is to make your preschooler aware of the rules. Although they may be obvious to you, they might not be so obvious to him. For instance, you probably have the rule that the lounge should be tidied when visitors are due, and this seems self-evident. Yet your child might not see it that way. As far as he is concerned, leaving the room in a mess could be perfectly acceptable. So make your family rules explicit. Your child's willingness to follow them can only develop when he knows what they are. Keep repeating the rules until you are sure he understands them.

Consistency is also important. There will be times when you bend the rules, for example, you might tolerate your child's grumpy behaviour more when you know he is unwell, or you might let him stay up later than usual when it's a special occasion. Most times, though, it's best to stick consistently to your family rules as this will help your child adjust to them.

As an adult, you are able to transfer a rule from one situation to another. You know, for example, that the rule about your child not hitting another child means he isn't allowed to hit anyone at all. It is a general rule that should be followed at all times. Yet your young child might not realise that. For instance, he might think the rule means he can't hit his friends in nursery but that it's still okay for him to hit his big brother. That's why you need to give him very specific and practical explanations. For instance, instead of saying "It's not nice to hit people" he'll understand more easily if you say "Don't hit anyone, not your friends, not your parents, not your brother or sister, and not your cousins. If you do, I'll still love you but I'll be very annoyed with you." A clear and unambiguous description will be easier for him to grasp.

There is no doubt your young child is more likely to adhere to your discipline at home when he sees everyone else in his family do the same. You can hardly expect him to follow the rule "No feet are allowed on the furniture" when he sees you resting your feet on the coffee table.

Rewards and punishments

Make a big fuss of your preschooler when he does follow your rules — he loves praise and approval. This is much more effective than continually reprimanding him for something he has done wrong. Always use more rewards than punishments: positive discipline that gives attention to what your child does appropriately is much more motivating than negative discipline that focuses on what your child does inappropriately. So give him a cuddle or a special treat (see box on rewards, page 132) when, say, he helps his brother without prompting from you. In addition to rewarding your child spontaneously when he regularly demonstrates desired behaviour, you can, together with your child, plan a reward in advance in order to achieve a desired behaviour ("If you keep your toys tidy for the next few days, you can have ...."). But bear in mind that your preschooler will be unable to wait for too long to receive his reward.

No matter how well your preschooler conforms to the standards set by your loving family discipline, there are likely to be times when he breaks a rule and you decide to punish him. However, be careful to avoid empty threats. If you warn your child that

such-and-such will happen if he misbehaves once more, follow that through. If you don't, he will quickly learn that you don't mean what you say and he'll soon start to ignore your threats. That's why you need to make sure that any punishment you use is fair (that it's deserved), that it is reasonable (that it's not extreme but proportional to the infraction) and that it's enforceable (that you can actually carry it out). Never, ever, threaten to leave your child and

FAMILY COUNCILS

Many families, and particularly those with older or step-children, find that regular meetings are ideal for sharing information and sorting out problems. While some families do this casually — over the dinner table, for example — others favour a more formal regular meeting involving specific topics, such as the weekly schedule, forthcoming outings or 'rule' changes. Four year olds and up should be able to enjoy and contribute to such gatherings and may even take a turn as leader.

For such events to be successful, make sure:

♦ Everyone gets a turn to speak and is listened to;

♦ Pleasant and positive suggestions are encouraged while negativity and criticism are not;

♦ Agreement on what need's solving — a sum for pocket money, a holiday destination, a new bedtime hour;

♦ Review suggestions made in the previous week(s) to see how they turned out;

♦ Limit the amount of time for the meeting; a preschooler may not be able to sit still for more than 15–30 minutes.

♦ A good time is had by all. Use the occasion for praising your child's behaviour in the past week and sharing her accomplishments.

walk away. Not only will this be extremely distressing to him but you almost certainly will have to eat your words!

Tell your preschooler what the punishment will be if he doesn't do what he's told. Give him advance warning, for example, "If you do that once more, I will take that toy away from you for the rest of today." If he ignores your warning and proceeds to repeat exactly what you asked him not to, say "I told you if you did that again I would take your toy away. You did that again, so I'm going to take it away now. I love you but you have misbehaved." That establishes a clear link between his behaviour and the subsequent punishment. Don't change your mind about punishing him just because he bursts into tears once he realises what trouble he's in — of course you can cuddle and soothe him because he's upset at the thought of being punished — but in most instances you still should do exactly as you warned. Bear in mind too that discipline loses its impact when there is a big time lag between the misbehaviour and the punishment because your preschooler might not remember why he is being punished. For instance, reprimanding your child in front of his father when dad comes home in the evening because of his misbehaviour just after dad left the house in the morning is too big a time gap —punishment should come as soon as possible after the misbehaviour.

Think closely about the way you manage your preschooler during a typical week; if you realise that you give out more punishments than rewards, or

4 types of rewards

1 **Stickers and stamps**. Gold and other coloured stars or appropriate picture or word stickers or stamps ('Well Done') can be their own rewards or collected in a book for yet a further reward..

2 **Items your child likes**. Toys, books, garments, art supplies, athletic equipment and the occasional edible treat (ice cream cone or soda).

3 **Special activities.** A trip to the movies, a day out at a fun fair or adventure park, a visit to a toy shop or creative activity centre, a sleepover at the grandparents, an outing to a football or rugby match, visiting the zoo, aquarium, museum or planetarium.

4 **Special privileges**. Choosing a dvd or television programme for the family to watch, selecting a restaurant for dining out, having a friend over to play or deciding what should be served for dinner.

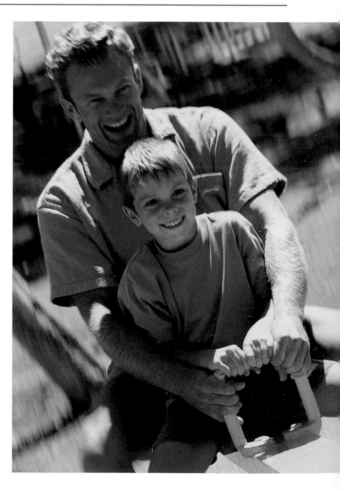

you just feel that you punish your preschooler too often, swing the balance in the other direction. An excess of punishments creates a negative downward spiral that makes both you and him miserable. Use rewards and punishments that are meaningful to your child, not those that are meaningful to you. It comes down to knowing him well and recognising what he likes and dislikes.

Time-out

This procedure can be used for any young child as part of a strategy to improve his behaviour. It involves sending a child to a specified place, such as a chair, with no entertaining distractions (generally not his bedroom) for a period of time — generally one minute for each year of age. Before using time-out, you need to explain that you will tell your child what he needs to do or stop doing something to avoid the time-out and that you will give him a warning before you institute it so that he has a chance to change his behaviour. Time-out needs to be used in conjunction with positive reinforcement of desired behaviours, and should only be used when your child understands the reason; it should not be used for non-specific 'bad behaviour'.

Spoiling

Saying "No" to your preschooler at times is part of a loving family discipline. Telling him "No, you can't have that, do that or touch that" or setting limits and sticking to them consistently helps your child learn that he has to follow your expected standards of behaviour. In contrast, if you give him everything he asks for, allow him to do whatever he wants, and permit him to think only of himself, he will become spoiled. In the short term, giving into him will make you happy because you won't have the challenge of setting limits (you avoid confrontations with him and you have fun buying him lots of presents) and him happy too (because he does what he wants and he gets a steady stream of new toys and clothes). In the long term, however, spoiling will make you both unhappy. Your preschooler will become totally uncooperative and demanding, which will make your life more stressful, and he'll feel dissatisfied for

much of the time. Not only that, his peers won't want to play with him as he won't want to share, take turns or play by the rules of a game.

Parents who spoil their child usually do this out of love but so too do parents who practise an inconsistent discipline without rules and limits. So when you find that your friends or relatives start to tell you that you spoil your child, stop for a moment and think about the way you manage him. Consider the potential negative effects that spoiling could have on him, and remind yourself that spoiling him isn't the only way to express your love for him.

Whether or not you continue to spoil your preschooler is up to you, but if you to decide to change towards a more balanced, consistent discipline, you won't find it too difficult. Remind yourself each day that setting rules and limits is in his best interests, as that helps him to gain control over his feelings and to think about others. Start to say "No" to him. Expect him to be furious with you — after all, he likes the way things are at the moment — but hold your ground and don't give in even if he rages at you. Start to ask him to make choices instead of agreeing to all his demands, for example, "I love you but I'm only going to buy you one of these three toys. Which one would you like?" Give him minor responsibilities for others, such as helping his brother put away his clothes or taking a piece of cake over to his friend. As your preschooler gradually adapts to your new expectations, tell him how pleased you are with his behaviour — positive reinforcement is always effective.

Lying

Virtually every child is capable of lying sometimes. It's a normal part of development. A three year old might insist that the crayon marks on his bedroom wall were drawn by someone else, even though they weren't there an hour before and he's the only one who's been in the room during that time. Even the

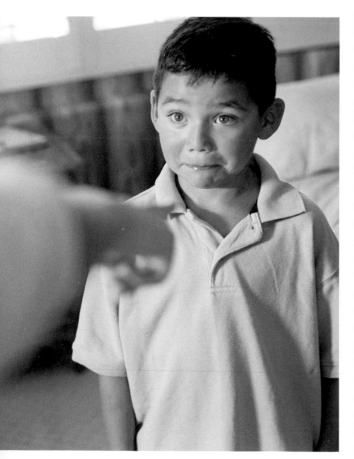

most honest child can distort the truth, especially when faced with a furious adult questioner. However, you will want to discourage lying right from the start because honesty is a key part of every relationship. It's very difficult to trust a child who lies regularly. And if lying becomes a habit during the preschool stage, it may become even more frequent as your child grows older.

From the age of three onwards, you can be confident that your preschooler knows the difference between right and wrong and that he also knows that lying is unacceptable; so if he lies to you, there is usually an important reason. Whatever the type of lie your child tells you, make sure he understands that it is wrong to lie and that you always want him to tell the truth.

Your reaction on discovering that your child is lying will heavily influence what he says in response to your follow-up questions. In a classic study, children were led individually into a large room that had a hamster in a cage in one corner, and a pile of enticing toys in the other. The researcher told the children that unless the hamster was watched constantly, it might escape and run away, and she asked them to use a rolled-up newspaper to keep the hamster in the box. The researcher then left the room. As you would expect, the lure of the toys soon became too strong to resist, and each child inevitably moved towards them, turning his back on the hamster. At that precise moment the researcher, who was observing through a one-way mirror, tripped a switch causing the hamster to disappear down a hidden trap door. When the child returned to the cage he was stunned to see that his charge had vanished. He was even more stunned when the researcher stormed back into the room, demanding to know where her precious hamster had gone! The results of the study established three important principles about children's lies. First, every child will tell a lie to avoid discovery if he feels threatened enough; second, a child who is very scared to own up will try to maintain his lie even under severe questioning; third, a child who feels he is not listened to when he tries to explain why he lied will conclude there is no point telling the truth.

Dealing with lies

Prevention is better than cure, when it comes to lying. It is better to raise your child in a way that discourages lying before it happens than to punish him after you've discovered he is lying to you. Have clear rules about lying, for instance, "Don't tell lies to me or to anyone" is easy for your preschooler to understand, whereas "Telling lies isn't a very nice thing to do" is too vague. Another preventative strategy is to explain to him that his behaviour has consequences. A young child doesn't always fully grasp that his actions can affect other. Explain to him that "Telling lies makes me sad" or "If you tell lies, none of your friends will like you."

No matter how hard you try to discourage your preschooler from lying to you, however, there may be times when he's not entirely honest. Once you have discovered that he has lied, speak to him openly about what he has done, letting him know that you are sure he lied to you. Listen to his explanation. His justification for the lie will not be acceptable to you but let him give you his side of the story anyway. Respond calmly and seriously. You may be hurt, troubled and possibly embarrassed by your child's lie, but don't over-react. Leave him in no doubt that you are unhappy with what he has done, though do bear in mind that if your reaction is too extreme then he will try even harder to hide the truth from you the next time. It's also important to recognise that your preschooler has probably lied out of his self-preservation instinct, and not because he wants to upset you. So don't be pessimistic. The fact that he lied to you on this occasion doesn't mean he will grow up to be a persistent liar.

By all means punish your child for lying, but don't make it too severe or he will feel like he is a victim. You could put him to bed early that night, give him a strong reprimand or stop him from playing with his favourite toy for a short while.

The best time to punish your child for lying is immediately after you have discovered the lie and have heard his side of the story. Any later and the punishment will have less impact. Immediate punishment also means that the incident can be brought to an early close. While you want your child to know that you totally disapprove of his behaviour when he has lied to you, you also want him to know you are not rejecting him. He'll learn

4 reasons why a preschooler might lie

1 **She might lie in order to protect herself.** Your child knows when she has broken a rule and she may deliberately lie to you in order to protect herself from your anger or punishment. She is aware this is wrong but she lies to you anyway in the hope of avoiding discovery.

2 **She might lie to protect a friend.** Friendships are very important at this age. Your preschooler may try to cover up for her friend's mistake either by giving a distorted account of events or by taking the blame herself. She feels this is sufficient justification for her lie.

3 **She might even lie because she thinks that telling you what you want to hear** (even though it is untrue) will make you happy. That's why she tells you she has tidied her room, even though it's still in a mess, because she knows you would be pleased if her clothes and toys really had been put away.

4 **She might lie as a result of peer pressure.** If she and a group of friends are caught doing something they should not be doing, then she may lie along with her peers because she does not want to break ranks. She may be afraid of group rejection if she tells the truth.

matter with him. You may need to persist before he opens up to you.

Responding to bullying

You feel so frustrated watching your child suffer this way. His life should be stimulating not terrifying, satisfying not depressing. And to you the solution is obvious — he just needs to ignore the bullies until they go away and annoy someone else. But it's not that easy for a playground or classroom victim. The continual rejection and bullying by a small group of peers (or maybe by only one child) can gradually wear down your child's self-esteem. Feelings of powerlessness will steadily replace his feelings of empowerment, and he will perceive himself as trapped, unable to do anything that can alter the daily grind in school.

That's why you should always treat complaints of bullying seriously. Bear in mind that it takes a great deal of courage for your child to admit to you that he is being bullied; he will be terrified in case the bully finds out he has spoken to you.

Reassure your child that you will keep the matter entirely confidential. Listen to his complaints, don't

make him feel silly or babyish, and let him know that you understand the problems he faces. He'll starts to feel more confident already, just from knowing you are there to support him

Then give him some practical advice. Persuade him to walk away discretely whenever the bully moves towards him. Too often this type of avoidance-strategy is mistakenly construed by the victim as an act of cowardice when, in fact, it is really quite sensible. When your child does move out of the line of fire, he should do this slowly without running. Encourage him to show as little reaction as possible to the bully's threats. Teasing and bullying will, probably stop eventually if the victim displays indifference to the actions against him. Ignoring verbal and physical threats is difficult, but it can be done successfully. Practise this with your child through role play at home.

Never tell your child to fight back. Tempting as it may be to encourage him to retaliate, that strategy has a number of drawbacks. First, he may end up with a severe beating. Second, if you advocate aggression, then your child may think this is a suitable way to deal with all sorts of problems in his life. Instead, advise him to stay with a crowd of other children, especially in free-play situations either inside the school building or outside in the playground. Bullies usually pick on children who are isolated, therefore, a child standing alone is easily identified as potential target. Being with a crowd reduces the likelihood he will be bullied. And help him develop positive body language. Your child probably looks afraid, because he anticipates the bully's attack. Teach him to stand so that he looks assertive and confident. For instance, he should walk with his shoulders held back, his back upright and his eyes looking directly in front of him, not towards the ground. He should also try to have a relaxed facial expression, perhaps with a smile.

Ultimately, however, you will have to speak to your child's play group leader or adult in charge about the problem. All institutions have an anti-bullying policy and there should be an established approach for tackling and eliminating bullying. Make an appointment to discuss your concerns in confidence. Staff may not have noticed and therefore you should bring it to their attention, but make it clear that your child should not be publicly identified as the child who complained. Ask the leader about the group's anti-bullying strategy and what he or she proposes to do to halt the bullying. If you already know the bully's parents well, you could consider having a confidential chat with them about their child's behaviour, though it may best be left to the staff to handle this.

My child is the bully

You'd feel terrible if someone accused your child of bullying and your first instinct might be to dismiss such a suggestion out of hand. Yet repeated claims by children, parents or teachers could force you to consider the possibility more seriously. If you suspect your child is a bully or if someone suggests he is, weigh up the evidence carefully. The accusation could be accurate. Think through some of the possible factors that could be influencing your child's behaviour. Tell him that you are aware of the situation and that you want it to stop. Even if he denies the accusation, continue to explain why you

dislike all forms of bullying. This chat alone may be sufficient. Encourage your child to think of the victim. He may never have thought about the impact of bullying on the victim — he might simply see the whole thing as a joke. So explain to him how terrible the other child feels when he bullies him. Then make a point of discussing his behaviour with him regularly. It is not a mater of policing your child, rather it is about letting him know you care. Your positive attention alone might reduce his need to bully others.

Disruptive behaviour

Virtually all children go through disruptive phases. Disruptiveness is related to temperament, parenting style and environment. Many, but not all, children tend to fall into one of three broad and loosely defined categories: easy, slow to warm up or shy, or difficult or challenging. These labels are a useful shorthand, but none can offer a complete picture of a child. Also, particular patterns of behaviour often predominate at different stages. Many parents find it more useful to think about their child in terms of nine temperamental traits (see page 142).

Consistency is very important for a child, both in respect to his daily routine and discipline and in support and involvement in his activities. In addition, providing your child with plenty of encouragement will help foster a positive environment both in the home and away. If you are inconsistent with discipline, are not supportive and/or positive and do not participate in your child's activities, it will negatively affect his behaviour.

If you allow him to watch aggressive behaviour on tv or videos, or participate in aggressive games, this will also encourage your child to become more disruptive.

How to help your child

Aggression, attention seeking and lack of empathy are temperamental characteristics associated with disruptive behaviour. Even before he started talking, your child communicated feelings he wasn't able to put into words through his behaviour. So if your child becomes being disruptive, this is likely to be

Disciplining your child

3 years old

Although whiney when in a bad mood, your child essentially loves to please, so gentleness should be your guiding principle in procuring better behaviour. She will be easily distracted by making a game of something, an activity or even a simple 'bribe'. It will be possible for her to have her way sometimes, particularly when it's of no great consequence, and it's important not to make every issue one in which you always have to prevail. Use different strategies: give her choices, avoid rushing her, warn her of imminent changes (countdowns) and, if necessary, use time-outs.

years old

Your child will respond well to simple rules and routines and clear boundaries enforced with incentives (rewards and privileges) and withholding them. Strong limits are necessary to protect him from out-of-bounds tendencies, but you should anticipate the probability of unacceptable behaviour. Try not to react emotionally to any attention-seeking behaviour. Whispering to your child may be more effective than shouting, as it will both calm him and catch his attention. Many harmless actions can be ignored and it's best to avoid confrontation and to use humour and suggestion rather than demands. As your child may be troubled by particular issues, it's best to talk about them when things calm down to prevent bad behaviour in future. Don't forget to praise and compliment him when he behaves well.

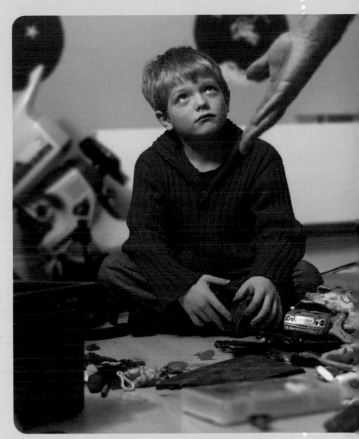

5 years old

Your child won't always be successful at being good so ensure you don't put temptation in her way. Remind her frequently about what is and is not acceptable behaviour and what is expected of her — but don't expect too much too soon. Keep your remarks simple and to the point. Don't get into a lengthy discussion about why her actions are unacceptable. Taking away privileges or favourite toys (for longer than previously) may be your best options. If you must reprimand her, do so calmly and using a matter-of fact tone. Time-outs may still be effective. Your child is sufficiently mature for natural consequences (not putting on one's gloves in winter means fingers get cold) to impart their own lessons.

ASPECTS OF TEMPERAMENT

Activity level: How much physical activity, restlessness or fidgeting your child demonstrates in daily activities (and which may also affect sleep).

- Rhythmicity or regularity: Whether or not your child follows a regular pattern for basic physical functions such as appetite, sleep and bowel habits.
- Approach and withdrawal: The way your child initially responds to a new stimulus (rapid and bold or slow and hesitant), whether it be people, situations, places, foods or changes in routines.
- Adaptability: The degree of ease or difficulty with which your child adjusts to change or a new situation, and how well she can modify her reaction.
- Intensity: The energy level with which your child responds to a situation, whether positive or negative.
- Mood: The degree of pleasantness or unfriendliness in your child's words and behaviour.
- Attention span: The ability to concentrate or stay with a task, with or without distraction.
- Distractibility: The ease with which your child can be distracted from a task by environmental (usually visual or auditory) stimuli.
- Sensory threshold: The amount of stimulation needed for your child to respond. Some children respond to the slightest stimulation, others require more.

why he hit you. You need to try and understand the triggers for various situations and predict in advance when fireworks may arise. Other things you can do to manage a difficult child include:

- Keeping your child active, with plenty of outdoor activities;
- Praising him whenever he is being calm and helpful, or is playing quietly;
- Giving him some special time each day when he can choose the activity;
- Making sure that he knows the rules about relationships, e.g. politeness and consideration (not easy for a preschooler); teaching problem-solving skills can never start too young;
- Explaining in advance what will happen if he is disruptive (does he know what this means?);
- Ignoring behaviour that is boisterous and energetic but not hurtful or harmful;
- Setting a limit on time spent watching tv or dvds or using the computer or digital devices;
- Making clear 'unacceptable' behaviour — e.g. fighting, hurting a sibling or damaging toys;
- Using time-out if he oversteps the limits (see page 133);
- Avoiding parental conflict or change in the family structure.

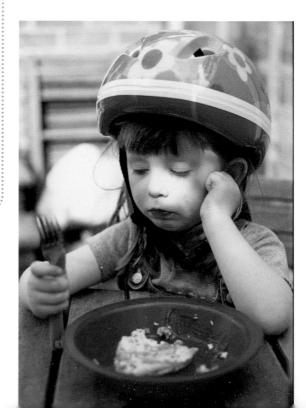

the result of feelings such as anger, fear, anxiety or frustration. You should, therefore, defuse a difficult situation by commenting on the emotion rather than the behaviour. Talk about why he may be angry, worried, anxious or frustrated rather than

Tantrums

All kids engage in tantrums to release strong feelings of anger and resentment although the severity of the tantrum often has no correlation with the enormity of what is withheld or denied. (There is, however, a correlation between severity and lack of sleep: tired children tantrum more often and the tantrums are much more intense and harder to stop.) When not allowed to have his way, your child may suddenly start screaming. He may lie down on the floor and beat his fists and feet against the ground or may bang his head repeatedly against a wall, throw objects around the room or begin hitting or biting.

The best way to deal with a tantrum is to prevent it from ever occurring. Once started, however, it is too late to give in or try other techniques. At this point, if at home, the most effective way to end the tantrum is to ignore your child, conveying the attitude that you couldn't care less. "You can do this all you want, but I'm not going to be upset by it." Ignoring your child includes walking away from him, not looking at him, singing a song and/or not responding to his pleas. If you are concerned that your child may hurt himself, pick him up and convey him to a safer place but try hard not to look at or respond to him.

If a tantrum occurs in a public place, pick your child up and immediately head for home. While many of the others present have had a similar experience with their own children and are probably thinking to themselves, "I feel so sorry for that mother/father. I remember how embarrassed I felt

---

WHEN TO EXPECT BAD BEHAVIOUR

◆ Your child is hungry..
◆ You or your child is tired or don't feel well.
◆ You are in a hurry and try to rush your child.
◆ You are stressed maybe because everyone needs you at once.
◆ Daily routines are disrupted.
◆ At the end of a long day.
◆ It's important that she behaves well.
◆ Everyone is watching.

ACTIVE OR HYPERACTIVE?

It is essential not to label a child who just shows normal childhood behaviour as hyperactive. Your child is unlikely to be suffering from hyperactivity, if she is, for example, just exuberant or full of energy and is sometimes disobedient, defiant or naughty. Neither is she hyperactive just because she gets fidgety while you are having a long conversation with another adult, refuses to sit still for long, such as when at the table, or is restless on a long journey.

Most children get aggressive or have temper tantrums occasionally, as well as become active when it is time for bed or in a new place such as a supermarket. Boredom is guaranteed to make the most placid child act up in some way, which is not necessarily a sign of hyperactivity.

A noisy or uninhibited child is not the same as a hyperactive one, nor is one that wakes up full of energy at six in the morning.

Finally, a child who is having behaviour problems because she is suffering from stress for any reason should not be labelled hyperactive.

---

when my daughter did this", they certainly don't want their meal, movie or other good time ruined by your screaming child.

It also will be stressful for you if your child is disruptive in playgroup or nursery as well as at home. In such a case, it is important to maintain close relationships with his carers. Bullying (see page 136) is frequently a factor and can be very distressing and if it's your child who is being bullied, he may not admit to it, so you may need to tease out the information gradually.

If you are concerned about your child's behaviour and need some advice, consult your doctor, who will be able to talk to your child and look for factors that may be involved.

Parenting and the internet

The moment you have a problem with your child, a parenting challenge that you have to face, or a question about his progress and development, you don't want to wait for a solution. Whether it's how to manage a tantrum, how to stop him sucking his thumb, or how many words he should be speaking by now, you want an immediate answer to your question. And that's where the internet comes in. No need to wait till grandma visits, no need to keep ringing your friend till she is available — one click and you have all the information you need. But it's not that simple. How do you know the advice is sound? What do you do when you read different opinions on the same topic? Does it matter if the advice is for a child who isn't the same age as yours?

Using internet parenting positively

All parents respond to information and advice about their child in their own way, depending on the problem and the personalities involved. Each parent-

child relationship is unique, just as each parent and each child is unique. That's why when it comes to parenting advice, one size does not fit all. What works for another parent and child might not work for you and your child. Yet that doesn't mean there is no role for parenting by internet. In fact, you can use it positively in several ways. For a start, the internet is a great way to extend your knowledge base. Whatever parenting question runs through your mind, someone else has almost certainly thought of it before and posted facts and figures about it on the web. Thus, you can learn a great deal about the background, frequency and causes of your parenting concern. This is especially true when it comes to specific problems, such Asperger's syndrome, ADHD, dyspraxia or slow speech development.

And parenting on the internet can also help you consider alternative perspectives. It's so easy to get locked into a particular mind-set when dealing with your child because of the pressure you are under. Simply reading another person's take on the same issue can open your mind to alternative explanations and strategies for managing your child. For instance, some websites suggest managing a child's fussy eating habits by focusing on the food itself (advising small portions, correct temperature, pleasant texture) while others suggest that the parents' attention to their child during mealtimes is what matters most.

Many parents gain reassurance from discovering that plenty of others have had, or are having, the same difficulty as them. Even if you think you would handle the same parenting challenge differently, it can be helpful to read about another parent's experience.

...avoiding the pitfalls

But all is not completely rosy in the digital garden. For instance, exercise caution when you read parenting advice. While a great deal of web-based information is accurate, helpful and appropriately detailed, parenting websites are not moderated — in

USING THE INTERNET

ADVANTAGES
- Instant access to parenting information and advice;
- Very diverse range of parenting resources and opinions;
- Nobody judges your parenting skills;
- Private contact, without involving friends or family;
- Confirmation that others share this parenting difficulty.

DISADVANTAGES
- Quality and source of advice isn't guaranteed;
- Not tailored to suit your individual child;
- You can get overloaded with too much information;
- You don't share your concerns with other parents;
- Parenting websites only tell you first steps, there is no continuity.

other words, anybody can create a parenting website and write anything he or she wants. Don't believe everything you read on the internet. Instead, look for common themes across different parenting websites. Whatever the problem you are facing with your child, for example that he is wetting his bed, compare the parenting information and advice across at least half a dozen different sites. That's not a guarantee of accuracy, but there is more likelihood that the information on a parenting page is suitable if you see the same advice on several websites.

In addition, to be safe, use parenting websites with a good reputation. Parenting sites that are, for example, connected with parenting magazines or parenting organisations take their responsibilities seriously. They typically offer mainstream advice that is tested and reliable, although that doesn't mean it will be right for you and your child specifically.

There is a danger that when you look at too many parenting websites, you might start to think you can't deal with any child problem on your own. That's quite a typical reaction. It's very easy to lose sight of your own skills as a parent, once you start relying too much on internet advice. By all means, use the web for another parenting opinion but have confidence in your own judgment; a parenting website will never be able to raise your child for you!

Making it work

There are some rules you should follow to help you get the most out of parenting by the internet. First, never try to implement parenting advice that makes you feel uncomfortable. If the strategy suggested for managing your child's challenging behaviour doesn't feel right for you, then leave it alone. Anyway, you won't be able to implement advice in which you don't have confidence.

Second, run information from parenting websites past a friend or relative. No matter how much you like a particular website or web page, there's no harm in having a chat about it with someone you know personally. Listen to this person's opinion, even if you initially don't agree with it. Advice from the virtual world can seem different when discussed in depth in the real world.

Third, don't doubt your own judgment. In the end, raising your child is your responsibility and you should try to have confidence in your own parenting instincts. Bear in mind that before the internet was created, parents used to rely almost totally on their own ideas and opinions.

Fourth, look for research-based parenting advice. Some very sensible parenting suggestions derive from personal experience. However, parenting advice that's based on solid professional research is more likely to be reliable. So check out the evidence that the website draws on to support its suggestions.

Last, resist peer pressure. Some websites have lots of positive reviews from parents. While comments from other users should not be ignored, you can't be sure they are genuine. And even if they are, bear in mind that what worked for lots of other parents and children might not be effective for you and yours.

TV viewing

The chances are that your preschooler spends time most days watching tv, either because he enjoys specific programmes or because you find that tv watching is a useful activity that keeps him fully occupied while you have time to do something else.

Television allows your preschooler access to experiences that would otherwise be unobtainable. He can 'visit' other parts of the world, 'travel' alongside animals, birds and fish, and have safe adventures, all without removing his bottom from the seat!

There are also benefits when it comes to developing his thinking skills. For example, a short period of television watching during the day (around ten minutes) helps promote his concentration. A child who is able to sit still for that short amount of time will steadily improve his concentration and this will help him learn once he starts preschool and school itself. In addition, many quality preschool programmes help the development of colour and shape recognition, naming everyday objects and elementary counting. Viewing these, therefore, can enhance your preschooler's learning skills. So there's nothing wrong with letting him watch some tv…except that you should also be aware of some of the potential pitfalls of your child's viewing habits.

When It's too much
You want your child to become an active discoverer, to seek out information when he wants and to inquire about things which arouses his curiosity. However, if he spends too much time passively watching television, he might, for instance, be less willing to search for a particular book in the library because he is so used to telly programmes doing all the work for him. There's also the risk that he may not watch the programmes you want him to. Leave him alone in front of the television and you could return a few minutes later to find he has been viewing something aimed at an adult audience.

Every child is different and so there is no 'ideal' amount of television time, although most experts would recommend that a preschooler watches no more than two hours of television in total in any one day. Some would say it should be much less, perhaps not at all.

Be prepared to use the off button, particularly if you notice signs that he's watching too much (see opposite). Of course, he will probably protest that this is unfair or that he will miss his favourite programme, but keep it switched off if you feel he has had enough for today. (Hide the remote control from him if necessary, until he calms down.) Think seriously about the amount of time he watches tv.

Decide on the maximum amount you will allow during one day, the sorts of programmes you want him to watch, and the spread of viewing time (for instance, one hour when he comes home from daycare, or half an hour at lunch and half an hour in the evening before bedtime). Then stick to these limits, no matter how much your preschooler complains. He'll soon adjust to your plan.

Pester power
The attraction of telly adverts may be so strong for your preschooler that you hear his endless cries of "Mum, I want that" or "Buy me that, dad." Pester power can be very strong and draining. The problem is that tv adverts can transform your preschooler into a consumer addict whose sole concern is the acquisition of as many material good as he can get his hands on. It's as though he believes that persuading you to buy him something he saw advertised on tv is the only major goal in life worth pursuing and that everything else takes second place.

TV adverts boost your preschooler's pester power in two ways. First, there is his natural tendency to desire what he sees. Television commercials present toys and games in a very favourable and imaginative way so that a young viewer's attention is grabbed instantly. You can hardly blame your child for being lured by them. At this age, he is not sophisticated enough to realise commercials can be misleading, that they can exaggerate, and that the product may not live up to his expectations; he is completely enticed by adverts.

Second, adverts influence the other children he mixes with. So it's no surprise when he comes home from nursery one day asking for a new set of trainers with a particular brand name. To you, his existing pair of trainers are perfect, but to your child they are not the ones he really wants because all his pals have a different brand after seeing them advertised on tv.

Yet there is lots you can do to reduce the impact of pester power. When your child asks you for something that he saw advertised on the telly, your initial response should be to ask him why he wants it. Although this strategy seems obvious enough, you may be tempted instead to give an automatic knee-jerk reaction — either saying "Yes" because you want your preschooler to be happy or "No" because you are fed up with his endless demands.

Instead of giving such a definite reply one way or the other, ask your child to justify his request. Why does he want this toy? How is it different from the ones that he has already? Does he know any other child who owns this toy and who thinks it is good? This forces him to think about his demand and gives you a starting point for discussion — it also lets him see that there is more to getting a new toy than just asking you for it. Even if he is able to justify his request, try to reach a compromise. You might tell him, for instance, that he can't have the game advertised on television because you bought him a new toy last week. Listing all the recent

5 ways to tell its time to switch off

You can tell if your child has been watching too much TV by seeing if she:

1 Is restless and has a bored expression on her face, even though she doesn't ask you to switch the television off;

2 Has been watching for a while and complains that she has a headache and that she feels sick;

3 Watches her favourite dvd again and again, even though there are plenty of other children's television programmes available;

4 Has been put in front of the television so that you can have a break, but she constantly wanders off seeking your attention;

5 No longer enjoys playing with her toys, and complains that she'd rather watch television than play games.

goal independently to boost a child's belief in his own abilities. He will feel good about himself knowing that he did it on his own.

Independence also helps your child's learning. In many instances, he learns more effectively by doing things for himself than with your help. For example, once he eventually completes a jigsaw puzzle on his own, he'll still remember the solution weeks later.

Safety concerns

When he was a baby and totally dependent on you, you probably dreamt of the moment when your child would be able to do things by himself, when he could stand on his own two feet without needing you to be by his side all the time. You probably longed for the freedom that his independence would give you. But now that this moment has actually

arrived, you may be suddenly suddenly afraid for your child.

One the main reason why parents are anxious about encouraging their preschooler's independence is concerns about safety. After all, his sense of danger is not fully developed. He still may do all the sorts of things he's not supposed to, like sticking his fingers into electric sockets, spilling cups of hot water, or running on to the road when there is traffic. Your child has to learn to deal with these hazards independently, so that he can look after himself when you are not with him, but that takes time. Right now, you probably place your concern for his safety before your concern for his independence.

Naturally, you want your child to be safe and well, and to avoid upset and injury if at all possible. Sheltering him from life's knocks is a vital part of your job as a parent, and is one of the many ways you express your love for your child. But the line between reasonable safety precautions and over-protectiveness can become blurred. Bear in mind that your preschooler needs freedom to extend his skills, so that he learns how to manage more by himself — that simply won't happen if you remove all possibility of risk by keeping him wrapped up in cotton wool at the very age he needs to interact more indepedently with his surroundings.

However, you do need to be very careful about leaving your preschooler to explore on his own, no matter how independent you want him to be. You should always try to be in a position to keep an eye on him so that you can steer him away from everyday dangers. That doesn't mean you should be over-protective, but it does mean you need to show sensible caution so that he remains safe and well.

Safety should always come first. That being said, your child is unlikely to thank you for thwarting his independence in this way, even though you do so in his best interests. Instead, he is likely to be annoyed with you because he can't do what he wants. So explain your reasoning to him. He'll understand eventually.

Helping your child

When it comes to boosting your preschooler's self-reliance, work together with him and keep it fun. Gaining independence requires your child to take a leap in the dark, to risk trying to achieve something that he can't already do. He may be afraid of failure, or that he won't be as capable as his friends or siblings. So give your preschooler lots of reassurance that he can succeed. If he thinks you take a genuine interest in him, his motivation to become independent will be higher. And remind him of the benefits. Spell these out to him clearly. For instance, "If you put your toys away neatly, then you'll be able to find them more easily" or "If you help to set the table, you'll be making mum's life easier." Your child understands practical examples like these, which adds further incentive for him.

It's also important not to expect too much too soon — encourage small steps to greater independence, a little at a time. This enables you to pull in the reins, if he doesn't seem able to cope. What may seem a simple and obvious task to you (for example, pulling on his jumper) may seem monumental to a poorly coordinated preschooler. He needs time to master each part of the task properly before he can move on to the next one.

Have very clear and specific targets. For instance, "I want you to put this jumper on by yourself" is clearer than simply telling him "I want you to try getting dressed on your own." Tell your child what you expect him to achieve. Then break it down into lots of little stages. For instance, first he gets the jumper out the drawer or cupboard; then he lays it flat on the bed; then he puts in one arm; then he puts in the other, and so on.

And the rate each child learns this is individual; if you've known another child who found it easy to self dress early, this doesn't mean your child will reach that stage at the same time. But you need to praise your child's successes. The more times he achieves each small step in his attempt to become independent, the more enthusiasm he will have for further progress. Reassure him when he's upset by failure and encourage him to try again until he masters it. Eventually, he will.

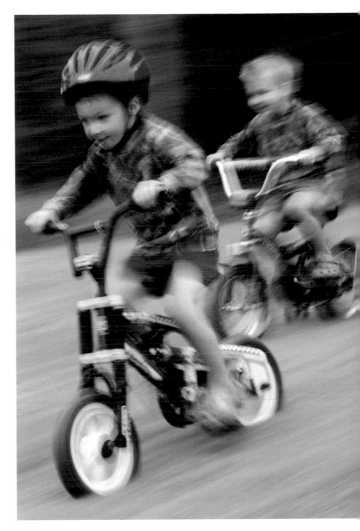

If you are not sure what to expect of your child in terms of independence at each age and stage, have a chat with other parents about what they have experienced or expect of their children; you don't have to follow what they permit exactly but you may find what they say helpful and interesting. You'll also find the information in chapter 3, Developmental changes, helpful.

CHAPTER 5
FAMILY MATTERS

Having a secure family life is vital for preschoolers. Mum's input has been taken for granted for years but now more dads are becoming the stay-at-home parent. Help may also be on hand from grandparents and if nurtured, the extended family. Protecting your child from unnecessary worries is vital when there are financial worries, a new baby is expected, a move is anticipated or illness, separation or death occurs. And what's a parent to do if adopting a preschooler or when living with a child with special needs?.

When dad is the caregiver

Our generation of families is more flexible than any previous, and more fathers than ever before are taking responsibility as prime caregiver for their preschool children. Sometimes this happens for unavoidable reasons (for instance, when dad is made redundant or is otherwise unable to find steady employment) or for financial reasons (for instance, if mum's income is higher than dad's) but more often than not, dad becomes the main caregiver through conscious choice; he wants to be the principal parent raising his child during her preschool years.

Yet this arrangement, which enables dad to become the main caregiver, is not simply a case of both parents switching roles, with family life going on exactly as it would if the parental roles were reversed. When the father is main caregiver during the preschool years, this has implications for everyone in the family and these should be thought through carefully. The more both parents are aware of the potential challenges in this arrangement, the more effective it will become. Even in families where both parents are the same gender, the decision about which one becomes the main caregiver has an impact on everyone involved.

Effect on your preschooler

No matter how strong the relationship is between a mother and her child, a preschooler usually has a special connection with his or her father. Psychologists studying the relationships between parents and their children have found significant differences between the father-child relationship and the mother-child one and, when dad is the main caregiver, these differences will influence your child's upbringing on a day-to-day basis. For example, although both parents like to play with their child as much as they can, dad is more likely to encourage boys and girls to take part in rough-and-tumble play, whereas mum is more likely to prefer sedate activities. Mums tend to play in a way that encourages a child's sensitivity, is nurturing and

brings the two of them in close physical contact; dads, on the other hand, tend to favour play and activities that are intellectually challenging for their children.

Mums and dads often have a different attitude towards their child's independence. Although both parents usually want their child to become self-reliant so that she can mix confidently with other children her own age, more mothers than fathers worry about leaving their child when she starts nursery or school, and more mothers than fathers expect their child to cry in that situation.

When dad is the main caregiver, your child will chat more with him and although your preschooler still talks away to mum, telling her lots of personal things — perhaps more than to dad — being able to talk to dad as well means your child has someone else to listen to and be advised by. In addition, your preschooler will typically be less challenging behaviourally with her father than with mum. Most preschoolers are less likely to push limits that are laid down by dad than by mum, and are probably more willing to accept discipline and rules from him.

The more time a preschooler spends with her father, the more she learns about relationships from him. The relationship both boys and girls have with their father often acts as the standard by which they judge the quality of relationships they will have with other male figures later on in life.

Effect on dad

The task of providing full-time care for a preschooler is demanding for any parent, mother or father, and the practical demands are the same irrespective of the main caregiver's gender. However, given that the majority of stay-at-home parents are women, despite changes in social and familial attitudes and opportunities, it is reasonable to assume the stay-at-home father has particular hurdles to get over during the preschool years. By far the major challenge is making child-care decisions on a daily basis. Even if mum is heavily involved in child-care issues despite her full-time employment, dad is the one that has to deal with everything as it arises from one moment to the next. That's why it's important for the stay-at-home father to have confidence in his own parenting skills, yet still be able to discuss and share child-care decisions as much as possible with his partner. Dad shouldn't assume all decisions are his sole remit, much in the same way as a stay-at-home mother wouldn't assume all the decisions were hers.

Another major challenge is the daily grind of coping with child-care and domestic chores. This can wear down the enthusiasm of the most determined stay-at-home father, particularly if previously mum was the one with responsibility for managing household chores — and the chances are, this burden may be shared more with the working parent than if mum was the one who stayed at home. So for someone who might have been accustomed to independence as a working man, the transformation into the main caregiver is likely to be daunting. On the plus side, a stay-at home father often attracts sympathy, admiration and plenty of offers of support and that all helps. On the negative side, however, he can also be on the receiving end of prejudice from those who consider that traditional parenting roles are best for raising children.

Then there is the self-doubt that often arises. A father who is the main caregiver is bound to have moments of uncertainty about his skills as a parent. The thought that he has the main responsibility for raising his preschooler can shake the foundations of his self-belief. Encouragement and praise from his partner can help boost dad's confidence. In reality, however, most dads actually do a very good job as the main caregiver.

Effect on mum

Even when it's decided that dad assumes the role of main caregiver after full discussion between both parents, and even when both are in full agreement with that decision, the chances are that mum will have at least a few twinges of guilt and regret — and

for many mothers working full-time, these feelings are much, much stronger. That doesn't mean a woman distrusts her partner's ability to raise their preschooler, nor does it mean she thinks her child will suffer psychologically in that home situation. It's just that guilt and regret may be an instinctive reaction, particularly if mum would rather be the stay-at-home parent and has swapped roles simply for practical or economic reasons.

One of the common fears a mother experiences when leaving her child in dad's care during the day

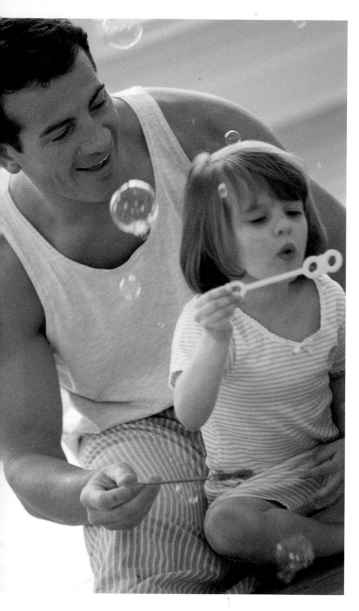

approach, and values those precious moments together with her child before and after the working day, the emotional attachment between them will remain strong. Of course, time management becomes extremely important. When dad is the main caregiver, mum needs to manage her non-working time effectively so that she spends as much non-working time in the company of her child as possible. Instead of worrying about how much time they are apart, she should enjoy the times they spend together, whether talking, playing or eating.

Every parent wants to be there for all the important 'firsts' in her preschooler's life, whether it's when she first names colours accurately, rides a bicycle with stabilisers or reaches the top of the climbing frame in the adventure playground. When these 'firsts' are missed, it is quite common to feel guilt. But a working mum shouldn't beat herself up about it. Aside from the fact that she'll eventually see her child do what she missed seeing the first time round, what matters most to a preschooler is that she is loved, valued and cared for by her parents. She won't mind that her mother missed a 'first', as long as mum shows excitement and interest later on when she hears about it.

A bright future

There is no reason to assume that your preschooler will lose out psychologically in any way whatsoever by her father taking on the job of main caregiver. In fact, she'll probably benefit in many of the ways already discussed. Nor will her relationship with her mother automatically suffer. Have confidence in both yourself and your partner as parents. There is ample evidence from research and from everyday life, which confirms preschoolers in this situation thrive normally.

is that the bond between her and her preschooler will weaken — but that is unlikely to happen. What matters is not the amount of time a mother and her child spend together but the quality of their relationship with each other. A preschooler who spends all day with a distracted mother who would much rather resume her career than be a stay-at-home mum, for instance, is less likely to bond than a child who spends only a few minutes at the start and the end of each day with her loving, attentive, caring mother. If a working mother has a positive

Making the most of grandparents

If you are fortunate to have a close, warm, loving relationship with your preschooler's grandparents, you'll already be aware of the potential benefits this special attachment can bring your child. Every loving bond in your child's life adds something distinctive, and makes its own unique contribution to her development. So a strong grandchild-grandparent connection is good for your child.

However, grandparents can give added value to you as well. For example, they can act as trustworthy, reliable and willing child-carers. You don't need to check out their credentials or ask for references before using them to look after your preschooler. They raised you or your partner and you have confidence in their ability to look after your child carefully and sensibly when required. This can be especially useful when you need to arrange childcare at very short notice. Of course, you can't expect your child's grandparents to be on call 24/7 — they have their own lives, schedules and possibly work commitments, so they may not be as available to support you with childcare arrangements as you might like. But your negotiating skills and the way you present your requests can make a difference. If grandparents are made to feel that the childcare they provide is special, they are more likely to help you when asked. On the other hand, if they think that they are your second choice or that you take their availability for granted, the chances are they won't be so responsive. A tactful and sensitive request such as "We'd love you to look after ... on Monday because she has such a good time with you" is better than saying "We need you to look after ... on Monday because we can't get anyone else."

Grandparents can also be a great source of advice. The reassuring comments from a grandparent who has raised several children of his or her own into adulthood can be very comforting for a parent who lacks self-confidence. Don't be afraid to seek such guidance. To approach your child's grandparents in this way is certainly not a sign of weakness — in fact, many people would argue that it's a smart parent who recognises his or her own weaknesses and then tries to do something about them.

Yet bringing grandparents on board the parenting team does need careful management. On the one hand you want advice and support, but on the other hand, you may end up feeling disempowered. Always keep in mind that grandparents want the best for you and your preschooler, and they also want to maintain a positive relationship with you. Tell yourself that they are not deliberately trying to undermine you, but that they are only trying to help.

That being said, unless you give the grandparents clear guidelines, they may spontaneously give you as much help as they think you need, so it's best to keep your requests specific in order to reduce ambiguity. For instance, if you tell grandparents "I can't cope, I need your help," this suggests you are struggling on all fronts so don't be surprised if they respond by trying to do everything for you — this is a normal, loving reaction. It's far better if you say something like "Can you take ... to the park this afternoon because I don't think I'll be home in time." It's a question of balance. As long as you don't become over-dependent on your child's grandparents, you'll maintain confidence in your own parenting skills.

Another way grandparents give added value is that they typically think their grandchildren are perfect. It is often said that parents 'love' their children but that grandparents are 'in love' with their grandchildren. In other words, they may be so totally infatuated that they can't see anything wrong in anything the children do. That means grandparents are likely to tolerate more from your children than you do, and will probably be very willing to help out when you feel stressed. Bear in mind, though, that this could result in your preschooler receiving mixed messages about discipline. She'll be very quick to pick up on differences between carers when it comes to rules and limits and you may even hear her indignantly announce "But grandma lets me do that when she looks after me." Tackle such assertions immediately and directly. Make it clear to your preschooler that when she is with you, you set the standards for her behaviour, no matter what she is allowed to do when she is with grandparents. And have a gentle word with the grandparents, too. If you express your concerns in a caring child-centred way ("I'm worried that she is getting confused over the mixed messages she gets about discipline") and not in a critical grandparent-centred way ("I'm worried that you are far too soft with her"), the chances are they will treat your worry seriously. Put all these ingredients together and you have a recipe for grandparents who have the potential to provide a rich source of support, advice and practical help. The challenge for you is to make the most of them.

Grandparents as carers

Consider childcare options for your preschooler very thoroughly before even mentioning this to your child's grandparents. You may decide that although the grandparents are available and could provide cost-effective (free) childcare, you would prefer your preschooler to have a more stimulating experience during the day while you are at work. If so, you'll find it easier to explain this to the grandparents if you haven't already told them that you were weighing up whether or not to ask their help with childcare. They won't be comfortable thinking that they were considered then rejected!

Some preschoolers are fortunate enough to have two sets of loving grandparents who are eager to provide some, or all, day care when one or both of you are at work. That could be wonderful for you as well, because you know your child is going to be well looked after during the day. If both sets of grandparents can offer excellent care, you truly are spoilt for choice!

Think carefully about each offer, though, and consider how realistic it is for each set or individual to look after your child. Bear in mind this is a very demanding task, physically and emotionally. If a grandparent has health problems, or is particularly frail, then caring for your preschooler may be too much for him or her. There are other practicalities too. Either you will have to take your child to and from her grandparents every day, or the grandparents will have to do the daily travelling. Consider what would be involved with each set.

The ideal option would be to split the childcare responsibility so that one set of grandparents cares for your preschooler two days a week and the other set three days; they can swap days on alternate weeks. That would keep everyone happy. But if childcare can't be split equally this way, explain the reasons for your optimal choice, and make it clear that it is for practical or health reasons only, not because you think one set of grandparents will provide better care for your child than the other (even if you do think that). Make sure that the grandparents who aren't picked as the ones to provide childcare are given lots of opportunity to see their grandchild at the weekends. This offer should go a long way to help ease any potential feelings of rejection.

Favouritism

It's very common for grandparents to form an especially strong emotional connection with their first grandchild. And when the next grandchild comes along (whether yours or your sibling's child), they will form a strong psychological bond with him too. But in some instances, the oldest grandchild becomes the grandparents' favourite; they have known her longer, think she's cute and smart, and she does more than her younger siblings. Favourites, however, are always divisive. Young children are quick to pick up on this, and no grandchild likes to think grandma prefers a sibling to her.

To head off a potential crisis, tell the grandparents how much you and your siblings appreciate their input with and affection for their grandchildren. Then tell them that you think perhaps they prefer the oldest, that you understand why they feel this way (because they are so close with her and because she is so bright and beautiful), but that you worry this could have a negative effect on the younger ones. Explain that no child wants her grandparents to prefer one grandchild over all the others and that ultimately, this leads to low self-esteem and a sense of rejection. All their grandchildren deserve their love. Be ready for them to try to convince you that you are wrong, that they don't have a favourite, and that even if they did, the grandchildren wouldn't be aware of it. Point out again that favouritism is always unfair on children, and is always destructive. Whether or not the grandparents agree with you — and expect them to be slightly upset by your observations — suggest that they need to take the matter of favouritism very seriously.

You can't make your child's grandparents feel differently; even if they admit to favouritism, they probably won't be able to change their emotions. Yet they can change how they act on their feelings. In other words, just because they have a favourite doesn't mean that they have to behave as if they have a favourite. Suggest, for example, that they spend the same amount on birthday presents for each of their grandchildren, that they take the same interest in all of them, that they praise all of their achievements and that they have loving physical contact with each one. In addition, suggest they make a special point of spending time with each child alone every visit, if possible, and even if only for a few minutes. Those practical steps will encourage each grandchild to feel that she is special to her grandparents.

Positive approach

It's up to you to keep the relationship with your child's grandparents positive. True, some grandparents are very forceful, totally convinced that they know best and may be overzealous in offering their opinions. But most are reasonable, loving relatives with the best interests of their children and grandchildren at heart.

Bear in mind that grandparents, like everyone else, like a pat on the back every now and again — they like their help to be recognised and to feel appreciated. The best way, of course, is to express your gratitude verbally. For instance, you might say "Thanks for helping me get ... to sleep this afternoon; I feel more confident about managing on my own with her tomorrow."

If you asked a grandparent for advice, give some feedback; if grandpaents know that you are coping better with the situation now, they are less likely to get involved subsequently. Therefore giving positive feedback avoids the potential for them to interfere and undermine you.

Make sure, too, your preschooler understands that you value her grandparents. If, for example, she hears you moan and take a sharp intake of breath when they arrive at your home, she'll start to adopt those negative attitudes as well. Keep all criticisms of her grandparents — and any disagreements with them — well away from your young child. Make her grandparents feel welcome in your house and let her see that you value them. In most instances, that special bond with grandparents adds something uniquely wonderful to a young child's life and to your life as well; as such, it should be welcomed and encouraged where possible. That's the best way to get the most out of grandparents.

Involving your extended family

You may have heard from your parents or grandparents how, when they were young, everyone (that is, grandparents, parents, aunts, uncles, cousins, nephews, nieces and grandchildren) usually lived in close proximity to each other, and it was common for many family members to live in the same city — even the same street. That network brought huge potential benefits, such as having a host of helping hands for parents to draw on for practical support and child-care advice. Parents never needed to feel they were alone when it came to managing their children. Grandparents in particular were viewed as having the wisdom derived from raising children from birth to adulthood and consequently were frequently called on for ideas and suggestion — this was made easier by the fact they lived nearby. Frequent contact with so many adults gave children a set of roles models for the children to respect, admire and learn from.

Of course, this close-knit extended family had its potential downside too. With so many people dropping in every hour of the day, parents hardly had a chance for any privacy. Rarely were they alone with their child for any length of time. The house always had to be kept clean and tidy to avoid criticism from uninvited visitors. Then there was the endless — often unsolicited — advice. Everyone had an opinion and they didn't need any encouragement to share their thoughts about child rearing with the parents. And if there were disagreements in the extended family, there was no way they could be ignored or allowed to simmer until everyone calmed down — disputes had to be dealt with as they arose because people saw so much of each other. However, most people then agreed the benefits of a warm, loving extended family outweighed the potential disadvantages.

But that traditional model of the extended family is rarely found today. We are much more mobile now, and rarely expect to live in the same location in which we grew up. Nowadays, it's likely you, your parents and siblings live in different parts of a city, if not in different cities altogether. And even if your family members live near each other, it is likely that the adults (including grandparents) all work and that you often have jobs with different hours, which decreases even further your contact, even though you use email, texts, phone calls and Skype. In theory, contact should be easier because you can now be in touch with your extended family any time of the day. Yet indirect contact isn't the same as speaking to someone who is right in front of you. It's harder to discuss a problem or concern about your preschooler through emails or text messages so you may come to rely on other sources of information, such as parenting books, magazines or websites. While these can be extremely useful when it comes to helping you decide the best course of action to take as a parent, their advice isn't geared specifically to you and your individual needs and background, as is that from your extended family.

Families usually shave shared values, which is why, if your child is to model and incorporate them into her way of living when she grows up, it's important that she have meaningful contact with her family so that these values can be fostered and nurtured. Unfotunately, however, because extended family gatherings are commonly infrequent and typically limited to recognised occasions such as over the festive season or for special birthdays or anniversaries, when they do occur, they can be stressful because all those attending don't know each other as well as they would if they had more regular contact with each other.

Rekindling family ties

When you think back to your own childhood, you may have a sense of loss, a fear that your child is missing out on something that should have been an important part of her childhood. You worry that she won't have the same rich family upbringing that you had when you were a child. While you can't force your extended family to live closer to each other, compel your parents to live beside you or even move

4 ways to create a wider support system

1. **Become a member of a religious congregation** and attend social gatherings there as well as services.

2. **Become close to another family,** and allow your child to spend time with them.

3. **Seek out groups in the community** such as family support programmes or even neighbourhood activity centres where your child can meet like-minded families.

4. **Ensure your child has godparents** or designate some close friends as special 'aunties' or 'uncles'.

closer to them possibly because of employment demands and opportunities, there are things you can do to strengthen your child's sense of family. Make sure she keeps in touch by calling or writing them (even if the letters or e-mails are only dictated to you), and encourage the exchange of photos.

Above all, maximise every family occasion to make sure your preschooler gets the most out them. For instance, talk to your child about the next planned family get-together well in advance. Try to develop her anticipation and excitement about the upcoming event and point out all the fun and excitement she'll have at that time. Mention the different people she'll meet, describe them positively (even if in reality you feel negative about them) and involve her in choosing a gift, if possible. All of these strategies make her feel connected to her extended family.

On the day of the gathering, dress your preschooler in her special clothes so that she feels this is a special occasion; remind her of all the fun she will have there, and set out in plenty of time. Once there, introduce her to everyone. Keep an eye on her as she starts to play with her cousins — she may be a little nervous

and need some reassurance from you at the start. Do your best to ensure she doesn't become too wild, excited or tired. If you think it is all getting a bit too much for her, settle her down to a quiet activity so that she can regain her emotional stability. When it's all over, ask her to tell you what she enjoyed most about the day, who she liked best and so on. In this way, your preschooler will develop an appreciation of her extended family.

Bear in mind that you can also take the initiative. Instead of waiting for the next formal date in the calendar to trigger a family get-together, arrange one sooner to take place in your family home. While that could be a lot of work for you, and not everyone might be able to come along, it's better than waiting a long time for your child to see her relatives once again. The more frequently she meets them all, the more she'll enjoy their company and the more she'll gain from having closer relationships.

Being a help around the home

3

4

5

3 years old

Your older toddler has sufficient kitchen skills so he can help to stir batters or use an eggbeater, fill and level off a measuring cup and assemble salad ingredients.

Around the house, he can help to load the dishwasher and washing machine and help put away utensils and clothes. He also can collect litter to throw into wastepaper baskets or newspapers to put in the recycling bin at home. He can gather up his toys and put them away according to type. He can hold a dustpan and help with your sweeping up.

Outdoors, your child can assist with planting seeds and plants, water plants with a small watering can and help sweep up leaves.

4 years old

Your child's kitchen skills now include setting the table, putting away groceries, making simple snacks — a ham slice on bread — decorating and cutting out biscuits.

Around the house, she can sort clothes by colour for the washing, pair socks, fold bath and face towels, help get things to care for younger siblings (fetch a nappy) and may be able to use a small broom effectively.

Outdoors, she can pull weeds (if shown which ones), take in toys or seat cushions when rain threatens and use a hose on plants and grass.

5 years old

Your preschooler's kitchen skills include making a simple meal — sandwich, crisps and fruit, producing simple baked goods from scratch (under supervision), pouring his own juice or water from a pitcher or carton and clearing the table of plates and utensils.

Around the house, he can dust and polish furniture, help make his bed (fluff duvet, put on a fitted sheet and pillowcase), sort and stack magazines, put stamps on the outgoing post, tidy his room, help feed family pets and amuse younger siblings.

Outdoors your child can pick and deadhead flowers (under supervision), put leaves into sacks, place household trash bags into bins, help wash the car and help unload groceries from the boot.

how this could be achieved, for instance, she can invite her friends over to visit her in the new home at weekends, she can call them after nursery during the week or they can phone her, and she can see and speak to them on Skype. She'll be pleased if you are able to tell her that her new room is big enough for a friend to sleep over. Explaining all these suggestions in detail — with the promise that you'll do all you can to help her keep in touch with her pals — reduces your child's potential anxiety about the change of family home. Let her see you take a note of her friends' phone numbers and contact details. It's also a good idea before the move for you to make a specific arrangement for her to meet with her best friend very soon after the move. She will look forward to this. Keeping these links with her past relationships — however tenuous — makes her feel more secure.

As soon as is practically possible after you have bought your new home, take your preschooler to see it. Point out all the advantages it has compared to your existing home, such as a larger garden, more rooms, closer proximity to shops and better play areas, and involve her in decisions about decorating and furnishing her bedroom. Ask her opinion about the colour of the paint and wallpaper. The more involved she feels in the transition to her new home, the easier it becomes for her.

The same applies to her new nursery, if the home move makes such a drastic change necessary. Expect her to be apprehensive about meeting the staff and her new peer group, so do this sooner rather than later. Once you have found your new home, but before you have moved, arrange to visit the new nursery with your child. Talk to her enthusiastically about it, telling her all the activities she'll enjoy there. You could arrange with the nursery that she visits several times before she starts, possibly mixing with the children for a few minutes each time. This enables your preschooler to build up her self-confidence and familiarity before leaving her current nursery, and helps the adjustment process.

Although you'll be extremely busy in the run up to moving home, try to find the time to make a special 'moving home' party for your child and her friends, a few weeks before removal day itself (don't call it a 'goodbye' party, as that has negative associations). Your older preschooler will particularly appreciate the opportunity to host this occasion for her friends. On the invitation, ask the children to bring a small memento such as a photograph or small toy, and at the party, your child and her pals should swap them with each other. Encourage her to store these precious keepsakes in a special box that she can easily access whenever she wants.

After the move

The move itself will be a hectic time for all of you, and your preschooler may still be upset despite all your preparations for the change. Spend time with her each day, talking to and reassuring her. The typical preschooler can be very fragile emotionally when under pressure and needs lots of love and attention during difficult phases. These chats with you allow her to express her worries and anxieties, rather than bottling them up inside. All the time, maintain a positive attitude about the relocation of your family home — this encourages your child to have an upbeat approach too.

Do what you promised about helping your older preschooler keep in touch with her old friends. She may need some prompting from you, not because she doesn't want to speak to them but because she is afraid they will have lost interest in her. Encourage her to pick up the phone, and ensure that she makes an arrangement to see them the first weekend following the move. At the same time, however, get her socially involved with children in her new area. Look for opportunities for her to form new friendships with your neighbours' children, and enrol her in your local preschool facility if you haven't already done so — this is probably the most effective way for your child to meet new peers.

Give her plenty of reassurance that these new children will like her as much as her old friends do. You'll probably find that in time, your child's new pals become more important to her than her former friends, largely because she spends much more time with them. New pals will gradually compensate for the loss of the old ones.

A new brother or sister

Suddenly finding that there's a new family member on the way can come as a shock to a young child. Most commonly, a younger brother or sister appears two years after a firstborn child — just the age-gap that research has shown most likely to result in tension, jealousy and resentment. It's no wonder that the typical older child becomes a handful when the second baby arrives in the family. And when you think about it from her point of view, such difficult behaviour is hardly surprising. After all, your first born is used to having you all to herself, and she wants that way of life to continue forever. She worries about having to share your time with someone else. She might also be afraid that you will love the new baby more than her, and that she will be less important to you, or even that you want a second child because she herself is not good enough for you or that you are having another baby just to punish her. In other words, she feels insecure.

Looked at this way, you can understand why she will be unsettled by the news that a new baby is on the way, as well as the actual arrival itself. And she can show her anxiety in different ways. She might become clingy, tearful and moaning, or aggressive, hostile and uncooperative. It's the change in her behaviour that tells you something is wrong. As a parent, you know that loving your second baby won't decrease your love for your older child — but she doesn't know that. She has to learn by experience, which takes time. In the meantime, she may feel jealousy and hostility towards you and the new baby.

However, if family life is to be as rewarding as possible for you and your children, it's vital that your children are strongly connected. You should try and create this connection before your second baby is born and continue from the birth itself (see page 180). What happens in the early days and months can set the tone for your children's relationship with each other throughout their lives, which is why it helps when their tie is positive right from the start.

of questions about what she has been doing since you last saw her. After a few minutes, introduce her to her younger sibling. Make sure the new arrival has a present lying beside him in the cot for his older sibling (one that you purchased previously and took into hospital with you or have at home) and arrange for your first child to have a present for your second baby. This exchange of gifts is stage-managed, yet it can help form an emotional bond between the two children right from their first meeting, and reduces the likelihood of tensions between them later on.

During the early days

Once that initial meeting is over, get your older child involved in some of the minor chores of baby care. She'll be full of self-importance when you ask her to bring you a clean nappy from the pile in the corner, or when you thank her for rubbing in some cream on the baby's legs after bath time. Basic, responsible tasks make her feel part of her brother's or sister's life.

The first few days when you are back home with your family after the birth of your second baby will normally be a very busy time, with visitors keen to see your new arrival. They can help your existing

child keep any feelings of jealousy in check by bringing a present for her as well as one for the baby. Wherever possible, ask your visitors to do this and do try to encourage them to spend a few moments with your older child before they go charging in to see the baby. True, the main purpose of their visit is to inspect the new arrival, but there is no harm in quietly asking them to spend a moment or two chatting to your older child first. And appoint your firstborn as tour guide. She'll love to be given the job of leading visitors into the baby's room, and will take great pride in explaining all about him. This particular role ensures she gets lots of attention, too, and emphasises that she is the 'big one' at home — you'll find that she responds very positively to your request.

It's also important for you to maintain your relationship with your first born at the same time as encouraging her to have a strong relationship with her new sibling(s). One of the best ways to do this is by making sure you spend some time alone with your older child every day, perhaps while your partner is bathing your second baby or when the youngest is sleeping. A few minutes individual attention from you every day will make her feel that she is still as special to you as she was before her sibling came along. If your first child can continue her usual daily routine without the baby's schedule interrupting, for instance, going to play group or visiting her friend, then so much the better.

It may also be a good idea for your child to spend more time with your partner and/or other relatives and friends. Generally speaking, fathers spend more time on parenting and household chores once a second baby arrives, but you don't have to wait until your second baby arrives to encourage your partner's participation (see also box page 188).

It also makes sense to have the grandparents on hand more, too. The more used your child is to being looked after by others, the better it will be for you once the new baby arrives. And, if you are planning to have a nanny or au pair, make sure he or she is familiar to your child before the new sibling arrives.

Two children at home

In the months and years that lie ahead, you'll have the delight of watching your first and second children grow up together. But that's not a passive process. How you manage them and contribute to their lives is the biggest single influence on the outcome of their development. Recognising and responding to their individual differences will be a key challenge for you — but if you achieve this, it will be highly rewarding for you and for them.

Even if your new baby is of the same gender, don't expect, however, that he or she will be similar in temperament, personality, likes and dislikes to the elder. If you're lucky enough to have an easy and relaxed preschooler who deals calmly with everything that comes her way, your new baby might be hard to settle and easily upset. You'll be surprised at times at how two children from the same family, with the same home environment and the same upbringing, can appear so entirely different from each other! And even when they appear to be initially similar, their different abilities and personalities may produce widely differing results later on. That's the nature of child and family development.

Aim for fairness

The most important thing when there is more than one child in the family, is to respond to each child as an individual. Aim for fairness in your parenting rather than equality.

Perceived lack of fairness is a common complaint of siblings; the cry of "She always gets more than me" is heard in most families at one time or another and it is one the main causes of sibling jealousy although there are other factors, too. In fact, sibling rivalry is so common in virtually every family that

---

4 ways a second baby changes your life

While having a second baby means that there's one more person to love and who loves you, it's also true that you will

1 **Be much more tired.** This is particularly true if your older child is active or if he regresses and if your baby is not yet sleeping through the night.

2 **Have less spare cash.** While you may be able to save money on some equipment and clothes, your second baby may end up costing you a lot more than your first— you may not be able to accommodate a new baby into your existing home as easily as you did the first and may have to stop working to care for both.

3 **Have a lot more work to do.** Looking after the needs of two children will take up most of your day. As well as seeing to your preschooler's daily care routines, providing activities and outings for him and tidying up after him, you will also have to manage feeding, dressing, caring for and changing a young baby.

4 **Have less time in which to do things.** Feeding, bathing and dressing two children takes a lot of time as does taking them places and sorting out their squabbles. Moreover if one child becomes sick, you have the extra burden of care.

Your child and his siblings

3 years old

As an older toddler, your child may be unpredictable with any brothers or sisters, particularly those close in age. Older siblings may boss him around while he will dislike younger ones getting a lot of attention or taking his toys or interfering with his games.

4 years old

Your child's developmental abilities mean she can hold her own more with older siblings, being more assertive with them and instigating disruptive behaviour while with younger ones, her desire to be 'sisterly' or 'brotherly', which she may evidence, can be thwarted by her jealousy so that she becomes nasty and even violent towards them.

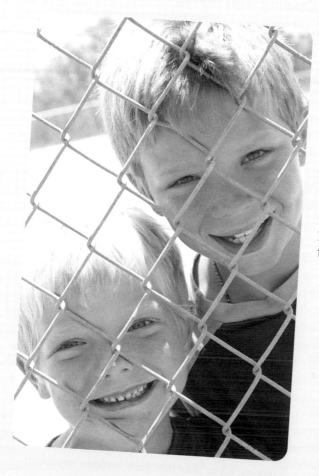

5 years old

Your preschooler feels more master of himself and extends his beneficence to his siblings, becoming less demanding and bossy. He can show much kindness and generosity to younger siblings while being able to share and take turns with older ones.

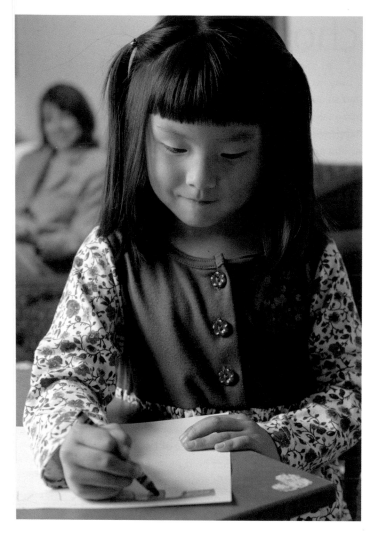

Some parents talk about "when you were adopted" instead of saying "when you were born", some tell their child that she is so special she was chosen to be part of the family, some have 'adoption day' celebrations as well as birthday parties, and some use photographs to explain the day their child arrived in the family. When discussions about adoption are out in the open early on, there is no embarrassment or strangeness about the topic.

Expect your preschooler to ask detailed questions about her adoption. Answer these honestly, calmly and at a level appropriate to her age and understanding. Give only enough details to satisfy her curiosity; avoid telling her too much all at once. There are many child-friendly books about adoption, pitched at children of different ages, and you might find one of these helpful in supporting your discussions. Chatting to other adoptive parents also helps you learn from their experiences.

When she is from a different background

Your adopted preschooler may face additional challenges if she comes from another country or is of a different race or ethnicity, because people can see immediately that she is not your natural child. They may start to ask you or her lots of questions about your child's origins and country of birth. That makes it even more important that your child understands her background from the earliest possible age.

While making it clear that she is your child, that you love her and that her place in your family is totally secure, try to develop her knowledge about her birth country (if it is not the one you live in), culture and parents. If available, show her pictures that show her before she came to be part of your family. And if no such photos are available, show her pictures of her native country. This helps strengthen her identity and self-confidence. With a good understanding of her past and origins, your preschooler will have a stronger understanding of who she is and where she comes from.

she would be shattered to hear this news from another person.

The majority of adoptive parents introduce the topic of adoption to their child when children are around the age of two years. Of course a child cannot possibly understand the implications of adoption at that age, but using the word 'adoption' starts to bring the concept of adoption into her consciousness. While you might choose to put off introducing the topic, if you still haven't told your child by the time she is four or five years old, don't delay any longer. Bear in mind that the older your child is, the more of a shock it will be and the more she will wonder why you did not tell her before.

When you already have a preschooler

Some parents who already have a preschooler adopt a baby, perhaps because they are unable to have a second child or they want to offer a loving home to a baby who wasn't born into such an opportunity. Whatever your reason for adopting, a singleton preschooler may resent a new arrival, not because her sibling is adopted but because your existing child is no longer the centre of attention. To be honest, your preschooler probably couldn't care at all about the baby's background — all he cares about is that your time, love and resources will now be split between two.

To make your adopted child's entry into your family as smooth as possible, tell your preschooler in advance about the new arrival. Talk positively from the start and tell her the new baby loves her already and thinks she is a terrific older sister. It's only natural your older child is anxious the first time she sees the new arrival, so do your best to ensure that you are not actually cuddling him the exact moment your preschooler first sees him. In addition, buy a gift for your older child and put it beside your new baby in his cot when your preschooler meets him. She'll be delighted that her new sibling bought her a special present; arrange that she has a gift to give to the baby too.

The more your older child is involved in the care of the baby, the more she'll feel connected with him. That's why you should try to give her minor responsibilities — asking her to fetch a clean nappy, for example. Hands-on jobs like that help form an emotional attachment between her and the new arrival. The first few days at home with your family after your adopted baby has arrived is a busy time, with visitors keen to see him. They can help your preschooler keep any feelings of jealousy in check by bringing a present for her as well as one for the baby. And give your child the job of bringing visitors into the baby's room. This particular role ensures she gets lots of attention and emphasises that she is the 'big one' at home. As a result, she will feel less threatened by the presence of the new arrival.

Although you will need to give your new baby loads of attention even if only feeding, changing and bathing him, try to introduce your preschooler to this idea gradually. Potential tension between her and the new baby will be greatly reduced if you manage some of these tasks when your older one is kept busy on some activity of her own. It's also important that you never compare your children. In anger, you may inadvertently compare your older child with your adopted baby, perhaps pointing out that her baby brother is much calmer than her. Such comparisons are always divisive, however, and usually create even greater tension between your preschooler and the baby. Last of all, treat your children as individuals. Each of them is unique with his or her own particular personality, likes and dislikes. Resentment between them is less likely when you allow that individuality to show through. Encourage their differences. Spend time alone with each of your children every day so that each feels special.

Sometimes parents adopt a child who is older than their existing one. In that situation, sibling rivalry can appear in both children, as each of them may be jealous of the attention the other gets from you. However, as long as each of them feels you love and care for him or her — and that you demonstrate this in practice by giving each of them their fair share of your time, attention and other resources — their relationship will become steadily more positive.

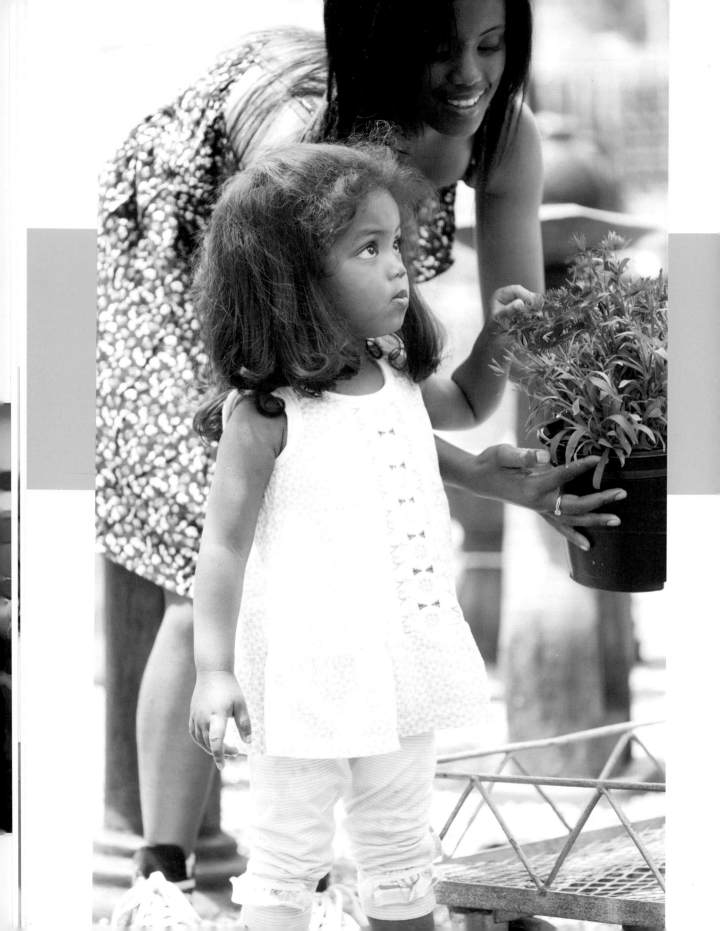

CHAPTER 6
YOUR CHILD'S WELLBEING

What do you need to know to keep your child in good health, to childproof your home, to care for your child if he is ill or has an accident? How can you recognise ill health and emergencies and keep your child safe when he is out and about? Here is the vital information you need to know in all such situations — and it's a good idea to become familiar with this chapter's contents before anything untoward happens.

Keeping your preschooler safe at home

Young children are naturally inquisitive, and fascinated by everything around them. It is your task as a parent to allow your child to explore his world as much as possible, but at the same time to keep him safe and well, and to teach him to become aware of likely hazards. These 'lessons' can help keep him safe as he grows up. Most children have accidents because they develop so quickly that parents can't keep up (how many times have you heard the phrase "I didn't know he could do that?") and have no sense of danger. You need to ensure your child doesn't have an accident because he exercises new-found skills unsafely.

You will already have had a good look at your home as your child developed from a baby who lay in his cot to a crawling, walking, and climbing toddler and put a number of safety measures in place. However, it's important to review any measures you have taken on a room-by-room basis every few months, to take account of any newly acquired skills. In addition, your preschooler will be involved in more and more adventurous activities outside his home — for example, learning to ride a scooter, pedal a bicycle, swim, try roller blades or even take part in group activities or sports — and there are important safely issues with each.

Supervising your child

The only way to be sure that your child is safe is to be aware of what he is doing at all times. The level of supervision your preschool child needs changes as he matures. Three- to four-year olds require constant supervision; four- to six-year olds may be able to play on their own but within earshot. For most younger children, supervision entails a parent or responsible adult being in the same room while they play, being aware of their activities, but not questioning everything they do; a few children,

BE ALERT!

PROTECTING YOUR CHILD FROM SEXUAL ABUSE

Sexual abuse of children is mainly done by people known to them — relatives, friends and neighbours. It can start at any age and generally begins with inappropriate touching progressing to other acts, though violence is rarely used. Children rarely report sexual abuse because their abusers generally resort to threats or claim they act out of love and most children are frightened or confused by what's happening to them and think that no one will believe them or that it is their fault. It's therefore important to be alert to signs of abuse and to recognise that it most often happens where there is little protection for the victim and there is someone who, because of other behaviour or circumstances (drinking, for example), lacks an inhibition against abuse.

Both physical signs and certain behaviour can signal abuse. Genital injuries or soreness, chronic urinary or vaginal infections and compulsive masturbation — particularly in inappropriate contexts — should be investigated by a professional as should any indication that your child has knowledge of sexual activities such as oral sex or penetration — whether spoken about or acted out. Less overt but still serious signs include frequent nightmares, a strong dislike of a particular person, and specific fears of being undressed or put to bed.

Since abuse is rarely committed by those outside one's circle of family and friends, telling your child to be wary of strangers (see 'stranger danger' page 213) may not be as important as being very clear about what is permitted behaviour and what is not. For example, it's not okay for anyone: to get into your child's bed; to ask your child to remove her knickers or show her genitals; or for your child to see another person's genitals or for another person to touch your child's genitals.

Public lavatories are a common site for abuse, so make sure you accompany your preschooler inside at all times and if this isn't possible, tell him she must never enter a cubicle with a stranger, no matter what is said.

however, may require much closer monitoring. Older children will need some independence, so it will be even more important to ensure that your preschooler's surroundings are safe when he plays on his own.

When you are out and about, at the playground, park or local leisure centre, for example, make sure the equipment is in good condition, and stay with your child at all times. Teach him safe playground practices like not walking behind swings, waiting to go down the slide until the last child gets off and then getting off quickly him self, and holding onto ladders and climbing frames with both hands. If he's leaning to ride a scooter or bike (or skates), make sure that it is well-serviced and that he is protected with a helmet and/or knee and elbow pads as

necessary (see also page 212). Bear in mind, however, that whatever precautions you take, no situation is ever completely hazard free. So familiarise yourself with the first-aid technques on pages 230–245 so that you can act quickly and confidently if an accident does occur.

Accident-proofing your home

Most accidents do happen in and around the home, but by eliminating as many of the obvious dangers as far as you can, and carefully supervising your child, you can reduce the risks.

Keep your home as uncluttered and clean as possible (easier said than done with young children) to protect your child from infections and food poisoning — but don't be over anxious. Contact with some bacteria and viruses help a child build up his immunity to disease. Store food safely and don't use items beyond the manufacturer's recommended best-by dates.

Make sure all keys (for the door, car, postbox and shed), are kept well out of your child's reach; this will not only stop him using them, but also prevents him picking them up and hiding them so you can't find them when they are most needed.

Hall, stairs and landing

Keep stairs and corridors clear of toys and other objects and make sure they are well lit. Never leave anything on the stairs; this will become a trip hazard. You will still need to keep stair gates on the top and bottom of the stairs. If your child likes his bedroom door open at night, it is worth putting another gate across his bedroom doorway in case he sleepwalks in the night.

- If you have rugs, make sure they have a non-slip backing and that the edges are not folded under; its all too easy to trip on them.
- Fit night lights on the landing. This is especially useful once your child is old enough to take himself to the bathroom at night.

Doors and windows

- Wedge doors open during the daytime, or fit door slam protectors to prevent a child's fingers becoming trapped as the door closes. Don't let your child play on doors — swinging on the handle, for example — as there's a risk of his fingers getting caught.
- Put a chain on the front door of your home so that your child can't open the door. Put the main lock as high as is safe and put the chain above it.
- If you have a bolt or lock on the bathroom door, put it towards the top of the door so that your child can't accidentally lock himself unto the bathroom.
- Make sure patio doors are made from toughened glass, as this glass does not break into sharp pieces if someone falls or something is thrown against it. You also can place stickers on the glass to ensure your child can see that the glass is there.

BE ALERT!

POISON SAFETY

Alcohol, make up, medicines, cleaning chemicals, washing powder, fertilisers and weedkiller are all poisonous to children.

- Keep all medications, cleaning equipment and garden chemicals out of reach of children — ideally in cupboards with a lock. Many chemical cleaners and medications have child-resistant tops but bear in mind that they only slow a child down, they are not childproof.
- Keep everything in its original container. Never, for example, put a poisonous substance into an old juice bottle. Keeping products in their original containers means your child won't make a mistake and think something is harmless and, if she does ingest something, you will know what it is and can let the medical specialists know.

- Put safety catches or locks on windows on the upper levels of your home so that the window only partially opens and your child can't open it and climb out. Don't put furniture under windows either, as children can use it to climb up to a window.
- If you have cord-operated blinds or curtains, or curtain tie backs, hook the strings or ties well out of reach of your child; any cord longer than 18cm presents a strangulation risk.

In the kitchen

You still need the protective devices you fitted when your child first became mobile such as cooker guards, child-proof cupboard locks and a short kettle flex, but now, your child may insist on 'helping' you in the kitchen. If so, give him safe tasks like stirring the cake mix or weighing ingredients; keep him well away from hot pans and knives.

- Make sure kitchen bins always have a firmly

fitting lid. Empty the main bin regularly. Always wrap sharp objects in paper and tape the parcel before putting it in the bin. If you have a number of recyling bins taking different contents, encourage your child to learn about what goes in each one, but discourage him from taking things out of them! Ideally keep all bins in a cupboard or out of your child's reach.

- Make sure your child is always sitting down when he has anything to eat or drink; there is a high risk of choking if he walks around with a snack or beverage.
- Keep all cleaning materials well out of his reach and buy products that have child-resistant tops.
- Don't carry hot drinks around yourself when there are young children running about the house. And don't leave them near the edge of a table or sideboard for your small child to reach up and grab.

BE ALERT!

ONLINE SAFETY

Children learn to use computers, tablets, smart phones and even interactive tvs from a very young age. While the internet can be a wonderful resource for you and them, it also can be a source of unwanted material, and children can accidentally download expensive or inappropriate games.

To prevent this you should:

- Talk to your child about any concerns you may have.
- Create a 'favourites' folder with your child's name on it and add some safe sites to it; that way she does not need to look anywhere else on the computer.
- Monitor your child's use of a computer. Keep the computer in the main living room where you can see what she is looking at; don't let your child have the computer in her bedroom.
- Install parental control software that lets you block your child's access to websites with adult material, track online activity and help protect your child from internet predators.
- Avoid ticking "remember password" panels, and don't let your child know your passwords.
  In addition, tell your child to:
- Let you know if she sees something that makes her feel uncomfortable.
- Not to give out passwords or personal details to anyone.
- Always check with you before downloading or installing software or requesting a new level of a game.

to complications. If you have a cat, you should wear gloves when gardening, and encourage your child to do the same if he helps you.

Contact with animal fur can cause allergies. If your child develops an allergy to fur, consider having a pet that does not shed its fur, a poodle for example. Keep pets out of bedrooms, just in case.

Teach your child not to approach animals he doesn't know well, even if it's a friend's pet. Always ask an owner if a dog is safe and if so how it likes to be stroked. Learn about animal body language yourself so that you can help your child: never approach a dog that has a stiff body posture; it is not comfortable — relaxed dogs are much safer. If a dog walks away or backs away from you, it does not want you close. When a dog is afraid it cowers and may hide under furniture. It might even put its ears flat back, show its teeth, snarl or growl.

Show your child how to handle pets; it may be some time before he completely understands, but it's worth starting young. Explain to him that he should never squeeze an animal, drop it, fall on it, pick it up too quickly, tease it, pull its tail or ears, disturb it if it is eating, sleeping or tending its young, or take a toy or bone away from a dog. He also should wash his hands after handling a pet, and never encourage a dog to the dinner table.

Plants, flowers and gardens

It's fairly common for young children to eat household plants or cut flowers, so make sure none

COMMON POISONOUS PLANTS

The following contain particular compounds that have been known to cause adverse reactions in people and animals.

Amaryllis	English Ivy
Anemone	Holly
Azalea	Hyacinth
Buttercup	Hydrangea
Calla lily	Iris
Chrysanthemums	Jerusalem Cherry
Cyclamen	Lily of the valley
Daffodil	Mistletoe
Delphinium	Philodendron
Dumb cane	Rhododendron
Poinsettia	Swiss-cheese plant

of yours are poisonous (see box). Put vases of cut flowers or pot plants well out of your child's reach so that he can't drink the plant water or pull them over (plant pots can be heavy and could cause a head injury). Check your garden, too. Remove plants that have poisonous leaves flowers or berries, or fence them off so your child is not tempted to pick or eat them. If you are unsure about the plants in your garden (you have just moved house, for example), contact the Royal Horticultural Society, they can provide lists of poisonous plants.

- Fix a childproof lock to each garden gate and put them as high as you can.
- Take great care around water. Swimming pools should have a fence that's at least 1.2m high with a self-locking, self-closing gate. Ponds and water features should also have a high fence around them, or better still be removed; wait until your child is much older before reinstalling one. Paddling pools should be emptied immediately after use and turned upside down.
- Lock the shed. A shed may be full of tools and chemials that are dangerous in a child's hands. If there are toys that your child uses in the garden, keep them in a separate shed.

Keeping your preschooler safe when out and about

You and your child can have fun exploring the world outside your home. You are his teacher not only about the things she will see and experience but also about keeping safe when away from home. It's important to make sure that the places you take her are as safe as they can be but also to supervise her at all times. Hold her hand when you are out walking. Make sure she is with you in shops. Teach her safe practices in the playground and if she's doing something sporty, ensure she has on the right protective gear. If you are travelling, make sure that you and she have all the right immunisations before you go (see page 217).

Cars and roads

It is essential to keep your child as safe as possible in and around cars. If you have a driveway and need to move your car, make sure your child is in the house under the supervision of an adult, or strap her into her car seat while you maneuvre the car. Always hold her hand when walking in a car park; other drivers can't always see small children.

If you are travelling in a car, the law states that all children under the age of 12, or shorter than 135cm must sit in a car seat — and that includes other people's children in your car or your child in someone else's car. Adult's seat belts are not safe for children, they sit too high on a child's chest and a child could be injured in a accident if he or she is wearing one. Your child can remain in a rear-facing seat until she weighs 18kg — this can be about the age of two years. After that she can sit in a forward–facing or booster seat.

Make sure that the car seat fits your car. Choose car seats that are easy to fit, especially if you have to move them from one car to another, for example when a childminder or grandparent looks after your child. Most cars have ISOfix attachments for car

seats, which is the safest way to secure the car seat. It is safer to put car seats on the back seats of the car; they can only be put on the front passenger seat if there is no airbag, or the airbag is switched off. Activate the child locks so that you child cannot open the doors while you are travelling; its amazing how many children try this.

If you are going abroad, some airlines let you take your child's car seat on to a plane and she can sit in it during the flight, then you can use it in a hire car. Alternatively, most car hire companies will provide car seats. However, always check the seat carefully before you put it in the hire car.

Trikes and bicycles

All children love ride-on toys and they are an excellent way to help them develop the essential important motor skills such as coordination (pedalling) and balance (on a scooter, balance bike

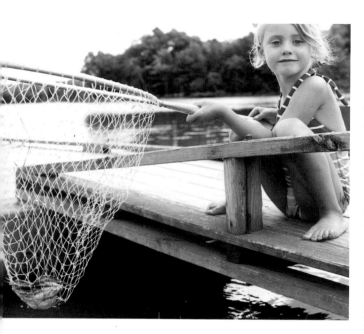

and fall. Before using, check that there are no dangerous materials, like broken glass or twisted metal on the ground.

The playground should be fenced off and dogs should not be allowed in the area. Swings, seesaws, and other equipment with moving parts should be located away from the rest of the playground. Swings should be limited to two per bay and toddler swings with bucket seats should have their own bay.

Always supervise your child in a playground and make sure she does not engage in unsafe behaviour. Young children can't gauge distance or foresee

Playgrounds and play centres

Whether indoors or in the park, children love playgrounds and climbing and sliding on the equipment is an excellent way for them to develop motor skills. Make sure the equipment is in good condition and clean before letting your child loose on it. Councils are responsible for checking that equipment is safe, and the law states that it must be checked annually. If you see any defective equipment always let the local authorities, or playcentre management know. The safest playgrounds have areas designated especially for younger children, that are away from those for more boisterous older ones. Younger children should not play on equipment designed for older kids because the equipment sizes and proportions won't be right for them, which can lead to injury.

Outdoor playground surfaces should be cushioned (wood chips or rubber for example, not tarmac, grass, soil or packed-earth), and should extend at least 1.8m beyond the equipment. No surfacing materials are considered safe if the combined height of playground equipment and the child (standing on the highest platform) is higher than 3.5m. Playground surfaces should be free of standing water and debris such as rocks, tree stumps, and tree roots, which could cause children to trip

TRAMPOLINES

Children love trampolines and they are a great way to work off excess energy but they are also the cause of a lot accidents, particularly in children under the age of six years.

◆ Choose a trampoline suitable for children under the age of six years;
◆ Consider models that have safety netting as part of the design, or purchase a safety cage when you buy the trampoline;
◆ If you have the space, dig a hole in the garden the size and depth of the trampoline so that it can be at ground level;
◆ Place the trampoline in an area clear from hazards such as trees, fences, washing lines, poles or other equipment. Ideally there should be a safe fall zone around the trampoline of at least 2.5 metres;
◆ Supervise your child at all times and never allow more than one person on the trampoline at the same time;
◆ Make sure your child only bounces in the middle of the trampoline — and never let him bounce out of the trampoline cage when he gets off.

dangerous situations and they often want to test their limits.

Indoor soft-play play centres should provide supervisors, but you should also be aware of your child's activities. Many of these centres are large and on several levels so it can be difficult to see your child all of the time. There should also be trained first aiders available in case of an accident. Surfaces should be mats made of safety-tested rubber or rubber-like materials. If the playcentre has a multi-story frame, the exposed support beams should be padded as well. Find out how often the play centre is cleaned; this is especially important if there is a ball-pit section in the play area.

Organised activities

There are many clubs and organisations that run team activities, such as football or gymnastics, for children as young as three years of age. Coaching children under the age of eight presents its own unique set of challenges primarily due to the children's developmental immaturity, short attention span and less developed muscles. If you take your child to one of these groups make sure that all the coaches are trained and understand the sport and the limitations of young children. They must also adhere to all child protection laws as well as health and safety guidelines — especially if some of the leaders are volunteers. There should always be trained first aiders present. If your child is injured make sure all symptoms have been resolved before returning to the activity; a child who sustains a head injury should not be allowed to return to the activity unless she has been checked by a doctor.

Check the playing surfaces the children are using: indoor flooring should be splinter-free, and field turf outside should be clear of hazards and animal faeces. Ensure that there is drinking water available; always make sure your child is well-hydrated before she starts playing.

Winter activities

Snow and ice don't signal a time to stay indoors and wait for spring. There are many activities that young childen enjoy: playing in the snow, throwing snowballs, sledging, ice skating, even skiing if you are near mountains. But as with everything it's important to stay safe.

- Your child needs to wrap up in sensible winter clothing to prevent hypothermia (see page 244); she'll need a warm jacket, gloves or mittens and a hat. Scarves can become caught in sledges, bicycle wheels and play ground equipment, so are not a good idea.
- If your child is skiing, skating or sledging, she should also wear a winter sports helmet; its all too easy to slip on ice and snow, which can result in a serious head injury (see page 241).
- If you take your child skiing, she will also need goggles or sunglasses and plenty of sunblock on her face. She can be burned by the sun light that reflects off the snow even on a dull day.
- If you take your child sledging choose a short gentle slope. Avoid slopes that end near ponds, trees, fences, or car parks, and make sure the hill

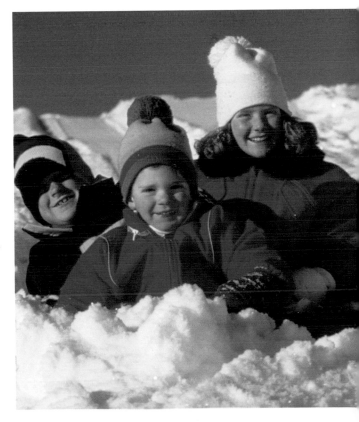

is free of obstacles. Choose places that are snowy rather than icy; icy slopes make for hard landings.

Sun safety

Everyone needs some sunshine as it's a main source of Vitamin D, which helps the body absorb the calcium needed for healthy bone growth; but you don't need that much. Young children especially should stay out of sun as much as possible as their skin is very delicate. There are dangers to too much sun. Sunlight emits invisible ultraviolet rays, which when they reach skin, can tan it but can also burn it.

There are three types of ultraviolet ray: UVA rays cause skin ageing and wrinkling and contribute to skin cancers, such as melanoma. UVB rays cause sunburn, cataracts and can affect the immune system and contribute to skin cancer. Melanoma, the most dangerous form of skin cancer, is thought to be associated with severe UVB sunburn that occurs before the age of 20. Most UVB rays are absorbed by the ozone layer that surrounds the Earth, but enough pass through to cause serious damage. UVC rays are the most dangerous but they don't reach Earth as they are blocked by the ozone layer. Skin produces melanin to protect it from UV rays, however, the fairer a person is, the less melanin there is in her skin, and therefore the risk of burning is greater.

If your child is out in the sun cover up as much of her skin as possible (sun-proof clothing is ideal) and always put a hat on her head. Put high sun protection factor sun cream, or sun block, on her skin and reapply at least every two hours (more often if its windy) and always immediately after swimming. She should stay out of the sun when it's at its peak — between 11am and 3pm.

Travel

Although the saying goes that "it's the journey that counts [rather than the destination]", travelling is not without hazards. On long journeys — whether by car, coach, train or plane — there's the boredom of being confined to one's seat for extended periods and (particularly if a sea trip) the possibility of motion sickness. Wherever you go, there's a chance of being exposed to different 'foreign' bugs. If it's not a self-catering holiday, you need to take precautions to reduce the risk of food poisoning or drinking dirty water.

Immunisation

Before you set off, make sure your child's immunisation programme is up-to-date (see page 218). Talk to your GP or local travel clinic to find out if you need any additional vaccinations for your destination. Do this well in advance of your trip as some of these vaccinations need to be given in two stages several weeks before you travel.

Trains

Encourage your child to sit down beside you, or on your lap. If she really wants to stand up, insist that she holds onto the hand rails as trains often stop and start suddenly. If she's not holding on there's a risk of injury. If you are on a longer journey you can explore the train but always hold her hand and don't let her wander off on her own.

Planes

Over the age of two years children need their own seat. If you are going to be driving at your destination, you may want to take your car seat on the plane for her to sit in (if this is possible). It is a good idea to encourage your child to use a lightweight buggy. which you should keep with you while in the airport, as there can be a lot of walking and a lot of people around.

Make sure too, that you have a supply of drinks and snacks with you in the event of your flight being delayed.

Preserving your child's health

It is very important that your child continues to be monitored throughout her early years. The healthcare team assigned to her when she was born (or your local surgery) will want to check on her from time to time, but as the person who is with her everyday, you are the one with the greatest responsibility for ensuring she gets the proper care or to notice if things are not as they should be. In terms of development, your child's genes and environment can influence the age at which key milestones are achieved but it's worth being aware of what these are and when they are usually achieved. But bear in mind that some children achieve them later than the 'norm', while others do so more quickly. If you are in any doubt, always talk to your health visitor or doctor.

For optimum health, your child must have a balanced diet to ensure she is getting the right nutrients, plenty to drink so she is well hydrated, lots of play and exercise, and finally, sufficient sleep.

Regular health checks

Your child should have already had developmental assessments from birth, and there will be another, at around age four, or before she starts school. Your health visitor or GP carries out the check-ups.

All aspects of your child's development — weight and height, posture, gross motor and fine motor skills, vision and hearing, speech and social interaction — should be assessed. Your child's height and weight will continue to be recorded in her child health book. However, at this stage it is height that's more important than weight as it is a better guide to growth rate. If there is any cause for concern you may be asked to measure your child at regular intervals over a period of six months.

Development, in particular of fine motor and language skills, relies heavily on normal visual and hearing skills, so it is imperative that any problems in these areas are picked up early and (treated appropriately) see below and page 262.

Immunisations

Vaccination is one of the greatest breakthroughs in modern medicine. No other medical intervention has done more to save lives and improve quality of life and it is vital that your child receives all her jabs. She should have had most of the immunisations she was due by the time she was two years old (see page 218) but there is a couple more to have at three years and four months, or soon after:

- MMR — the combined vaccine that protects against measles, mumps and rubella (German measles) given as a second dose
- DTaP/IPV — the vaccine that boosts your child's protection against four potentially serious childhood diseases (diphtheria, tetanus, pertussis [whooping cough] and polio).

After this, no more vaccinations are needed apart from annual flu protection until your child is around 12 years of age, unless you are travelling to countries where there is a risk of infectious diseases such as hepatitis, tuberculosis or yellow fever. Some travel vaccinations are not recommended for very young children so consult your GP before you book to travel as a family.

Some parents have been concerned about possible complications associated with the MMR vaccine, in particular whether it results in the development of autistic spectrum disorders (see page 194) and inflammatory bowel disease. The MMR vaccine does not cause autism and the fact that the MMR is given to children at or before 18 months, when the first signs of autism can appear, is coincidental rather than causative. However, not having the vaccination can lead to measles (a severe outbreak occurred in the UK in 2013), which can result in disability and/or death.

Going to the dentist

As well as ensuring daily brushing, it's important to take your child to your dentist for regular checkups. Most dentists recommend a check-up every six months from the time the front teeth erupt (12–18 months). At the initial visit the dentist will identify any dietary or dental problems; an early intervention can help prevent more complex procedures later on.

IMMUNISATION HISTORY

VACCINATION	PROTECTS AGAINST	WHEN GIVEN
5-in-1 DTaP/IPV/Hib vaccine	Diphtheria, tetanus, pertussis (whooping cough), polio, Haemophilus influenzae type b (Hib, a bacterial infection that can cause severe pneumonia or meningitis)	2 months 3 months 4 months 3 years and 4 months (preschool booster as 4-in-1 without Hib)
Pneumoccocal (PCV)	Bacterial pneumonia caused by *Streptococcus pneumoniae*	2 months 4 months 12–13 months
Meningoccal group C	Meningitis C	3 months 12–13 months (as Hib/Men C booster)
Hib booster	Haemophilus influenzae type b	12–13 months (as Hib/Men C booster)
MMR	Measles Mumps and rubella	12–13 months 3 years and 4 months
Rotavirus	The most common cause of severe diarrhoea among young children	2 months 3 months
Nasal flu	Influenza virus	2 years 3 years (then annually)

Visiting the dentist or hygienist is a good way for you and your child to learn about oral hygiene including the choice of tooth brush and tooth paste and effective brushing techniques. You'll also be given advice on a diet that promotes good dental health. At a check-up, your child will have her teeth cleaned and may be given fluoride treatment or have a supplement recommended.

Your dentist may recommend applying fissure sealants to the chewing surfaces of the back teeth, where decay occurs most often. These clear or coloured plastic coatings fill in the grooved and pitted surfaces of the teeth, which are hard to clean, and prevent food particles from getting caught, possibly causing cavities. They are quick and comfortable to apply, and can effectively protect teeth for many years.

Paediatric dental problems

If, however, your child develops a cavity in a tooth, it's important that it be filled. Primary, or 'baby,' teeth are important not only to help children speak clearly and chew naturally, but also to maintain the space for the permanent teeth. Although your child won't start losing her baby teeth until the age of six, her primary molars won't be lost until she's 10–12, and if a cavity is not treated, she can suffer pain, infection of the gums and jaws, impairment of her general health and premature loss of teeth. This last, can create orthodontic problems in the future.

Dental problems can start at an early age. Due to the amount of refined and hidden sugars in our food, according to the British Society of Paediatric Dentistry, 40% of all five year olds in the UK have experienced dental decay. Some parents erroneously believe that baby teeth do not have a nerve supply, and so do not need to be filled. The truth is that baby teeth being small have less space between the outer enamel and the nerve, and therefore decay does not need to progress far in the tooth before the nerve of the tooth is exposed causing an abscess. Treatment of a tooth with an abscess is far more challenging for a child than a simple filling. However, your dentist may decide to simply keep an eye on the decay if there is no pain and the tooth is

YOUR HEALTHCARE TEAM

The following people will help you monitor your child during the preschool years.

GENERAL PRACTITIONER

Your family doctor, or GP, will be your first port of call if your child is ill. He or she will advise you on measures to alleviate symptoms of illness and prescribe any necessary medication. Many GP practices have doctors with a special interest in child health, and may even run child health clinics where you can discuss any concerns.

PAEDIATRIC SPECIALISTS

If your GP feels your child needs additional medical assistance from a specialist, he or she will refer you to a doctor — generally at a hospital — with extra training in that particular aspect of children's, or paediatric health. These doctors specialise in anything from child development to heart disease. If you see a specialist, he or she will write to your doctor detailing the diagnosis and recommended treatment; you will be sent copies of all the letters.

HEALTH VISITOR

This is a nurse trained in child health and development. You will have been assigned a health visitor after your child's birth, and the same person can continue to advise you on all aspects of your child's care until she starts full-time school.

PAEDIATRIC DENTIST

This is a specially trained dentist capable of looking after the oral health — teeth, gums and mouth — of your child from infancy through to her teens.

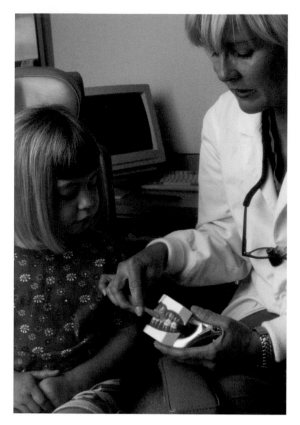

A reversible short-term hearing problem may be the case if your preschooler is:

- Not speaking by the age of 3;
- Speaking, but always mispronounces words;
- Struggling to keep up with conversations;
- Talks loudly and/or listens to the television on full volume;
- Does not turn towards a sound.

If your child has a cold, her hearing could be impaired because the tubes between her eardrum and nose become temporarily blocked with mucus, but an inability to hear can also be caused by glue ear (see page 267). If the problem persists, your doctor will refer your child for a hearing test either at the hospital or child health clinic. The tests may be repeated over a few months before any action is taken as the problem may clear up on its own.

Vision

At each developmental check, your child will be given simple tests to make sure her sight is developing normally as there are defects, such as long or short-sightedness, lazy eye (vision in one eye does not develop properly) and a squint (where eyes don't move together) that do not develop until later (see also page 269). Moreover, consult your GP If your child:

- Does not make eye contact with you;
- Has erratic eye movements;
- Is unusually clumsy (children with lazy eyes have difficulty judging how far away objects are).
- Does not turn towards a sound (children won't bother to look if they think they won't be able to see something).

Younger children are often unaware that they have a problem with their vision although as many as one in five children has an undiagnosed problem. A simple eye test may confirm that your child's eyes are normal. Young children will not be able to read letters off a chart or say which lenses are better, but an ophthalmologist can examine your child's eyes with a retinoscope to measure the eye's ability to focus. Some children need glasses, or in some situations, minor corrective surgery.

going to fall out naturally within six months.

Dental trauma is also common in children up to four years old, as this is the time they start to walk and have no fear. If your child is familiar with her dentist, she'll be less likely to be anxious or frightened should she need to be seen for an emergency visit. Because injuries to baby or primary teeth can potentially affect the development and health of the underlying permanent teeth, if your child displaces or fractures a tooth, it's important that she's promptly assessed by a dentist. This normally involves a thorough history, and detailed clinical and radiographic checks. Paediatric dentists are skilled in saving injured teeth.

Hearing and vision checks

If there is a family history of eye and ear problems, talk to your health visitor and or GP. You should be alert for signs that could indicate your preschooler has developed a problem.

When your child is ill

One of the most worrying aspects of being a parent is when your child is unwell. A young child may not be able to tell you what is wrong and it can be difficult to know whether to treat her at home, call your doctor or treat it is an emergency. Familiarising yourself with the signs of illness and the simple measures needed to relieve symptoms and knowing how to monitor your child (all described here) should help you gain the confidence to care for her.

Coughs and colds will be very common as your child grows up and it may help to bear in mind that her immature immune system becomes stronger as a result. Although she may be 'under the weather', as long as your child is still interested in playing, is eating and drinking, is alert and smiling at you, has a normal skin colour and looks well when her temperature comes down, any illness is probably not serious.

Nor should it worry you if your child has a fever and doesn't want to eat much. This is very common with infections that cause fever and as long as your child is drinking and urinating normally, that is fine; her appetite will return when she is better.

What you do need to do is treat any symptoms, such as fever, and monitor any change in your child's condition. If you are concerned, however, call your doctor and/or health visitor and he or she will let you know if your child needs to be seen.

What causes illness?

Viruses, bacteria and fungi are all 'germs' that can cause illness and infection. Most human illnesses are caused by viruses and bacteria, which are spread in droplets of moisture produced by infected individuals when they sneeze or cough. A viral disease is caused by a virus — an infectious agent that replicates inside the cells of a living being. Once a virus enters the body, the immune system normally develops antibodies that can fight it.

Bacteria are single-celled microorganisms that are often already present in the body. Many are helpful and harmless, but infectious or disease causing bacteria (known as pathogens) can make a person ill. Their infections can cause symptoms similar to viruses, but they can be 'killed' by antibiotics that break down the bacteria, curing the person and preventing the spread of the disease. Antibiotics kill bacteria by breaking down their cell walls, but they have no effect on a virus. Some bacteria are becoming antibiotic resistant due to overuse of the drugs, so doctors will not prescribe antibiotics unless they are certain there is a bacterial cause.

Fungi are simple parasitic life forms that can multiply through tiny spores that thrive in warm, damp conditions. Most are either harmless or beneficial to your health, but some cause disease. Spores can land on the skin or are breathed in so infections often start on the skin or in the lungs.

---

more **about**	Preventing spread of infection

Droplets in the air spread most infections. Teaching your child good hygiene habits from an early age can mean he suffers from fewer infectious illnesses.

Catch it _Make sure your child always has a tissue. If he wants to blows his nose or sneeze, encourage him to put a tissue in front of his mouth and nose first — to catch the droplets. You will need to do this for him at first._

Bin it _Tell your child to fold the tissue inwards and throw it away after he's used it._

Kill it _Have him wash his hands thoroughly to kill any remaining germs._

Fever

Normal body temperature for a child is 36–37°C (96.8–98°F). Anything above 38°C (100.4°F) indicates a fever. Fever occurs when the body's internal 'thermostat' raises the body temperature above its normal level, often as a response to an infection, illness or some other cause. You will know if your child has a fever simply by feeling her forehead with the back of your hand. But use a thermometer to get an accurate reading. If your child's fever is high, she may say she feels cold and shivery, or her skin may look flushed.

Body temperature varies naturally throughout the day. It is likely to be lower in the morning or after a rest and higher in the evening or if your child has been active. If your child is ill, check her temperature at regular intervals throughout the day. Don't take it if she's just eaten hot or cold food, had a drink or been running about as you will not get an accurate reading.

Treating a fever

To help bring a fever down, give your child infant or paediatric paracetamol or ibuprofen at the prescribed intervals, see below. Don't over- or under-dress her, keep the room warm, but not too hot, and

FEVERS AND MEDICAL ADVICE

Trust your instincts and call your GP if you are at all worried, but always seek medical advice if your child has a fever:

- ◆ Of 39°C (102.2°F) or higher (but if 40.6°C [105°F] or above, call an ambulance);
- ◆ Without an obvious cause, particularly if it lasts more than three consecutive days;
- ◆ Accompanied by a sore throat that lasts more than 24–48 hours;
- ◆ Accompanied by vomiting and/or diarrhoea lasting more than 24 hours, or 8 hours if he has not been able to hold down any fluids;
- ◆ And displays signs of dehydration, see page 223.
- ◆ And has pain when urinating;
- ◆ And a mild febrile seizure;
- ◆ And has recently returned from a trip abroad;
- ◆ And is breathing faster than normal, or continues to breathe fast even after his fever comes down.

---

*more **about*** | ### Paracetamol or ibuprofen

Paracetamol or ibuprofen can be used to reduce fever and treat any aches or pains. Give young children infant paracetamol or ibuprofen, which are available as a syrup or water-soluble tablets and can be used by children under the age of six. Your pharmacist can advise you. Try infant paracetamol first as it has fewer side effects; if it does not seem to be effective, then try infant ibuprofen. Never exceed the maximum dose. Paracetamol can be given every 4–6 hours. Ibuprofen has a longer interval between doses — 6–8 hours — so can be useful for controlling fever during the night. Don't give both medications at the same time unless a health professional has advised it.

Never give aspirin to children under 16 years old it can trigger a serious but rare disease called Reye's syndrome that can affect the brain and liver.

make sure it is well ventilated. If the atmosphere is very dry, hang a damp towel over the radiator to increase the humidity.

If your child's fever is particularly high, keep her as cool as you can. Dress your child in natural fibres (cotton is best) that allow heat to escape. Make sure her bedclothes are light, too, so that she does not overheat. If your child has a prolonged raised temperature, there is a risk that she could suffer a febrile seizure, see page 224,

Dehydration

If your child is unwell, she is more likely to become dehydrated, particularly if she has a raised temperature. She will lose fluids through sweating and if she has diarrhoea or vomits, she will lose even more. If she has a cough, a lack of fluid can make it worse.

Well children need at least 1.3 litres (2½ pints) of fluid a day (see page 40), and more in hot weather or when they have a fever. If your child is ill, make sure she always has a drink beside her. Make it fun: use a new or favourite beaker or 'a special one' that she's not normally allowed to have; try giving her a bendy straw. She may even want a beaker that she used when she was younger.

While water and unsweetened juice are healthier, it's okay to offer your child her favourite drinks, even if they are fizzy, if she prefers (but not diet drinks as these lack sugar). Encourage her to sip her drink regularly. If she won't drink, tempt her with some salty snacks first; these will replace some lost salts and make her thirsty.

How to monitor your child

When you are looking after a sick child, you need to take her temperature and check her pulse rate regularly and keep an eye on her breathing. Make a

TAKING A TEMPERATURE

With an aural thermometer

Place the thermometer in your child's ear until it 'beeps'— normally after only a few seconds. Don't use this type of thermometer if your child has an ear infection.

With a digital thermometer

Don't put a digital thermometer in your child's mouth until he is at least six years old. Sit your child on your lap. Raise his arm and place the end of the thermometer in his armpit. Lower the arm over the thermometer and hold it still until the thermometer beeps — about a minute. The reading given will be about 1°C below his actual body temperature.

- Measure out the medication exactly as directed;
- Never give medicines prescribed for one child to another child even if they both appear to have the same condition.
- Count out the tablets or load a spoon, syringe or dropper before you start. Put them (it) on a small clean plate ready to administer.

Liquid medicine

Sit your child or your lap or on a chair and give her the medicine.

If using a syringe, let her suck in the medicine while you press the plunger. Have a drink ready in case she does not like the taste.

Ear drops

Lay a young child on the bed on a towel, affected side uppermost. Sit an older child on your lap, facing away from you. Support your child's head, tilting it so that affected ear is uppermost. Pull the ear upwards and back slightly to straighten the ear canal and deliver the drops. Rub the base of the ear.

Eye drops

Sit down on a bed or sofa and lay your child down with her head in your lap. Pull her bottom eyelid down gently and drop the medication between the lid and ball of the eye. If your child resists, you may need help, or you can wrap a blanket around her arms and upper body.

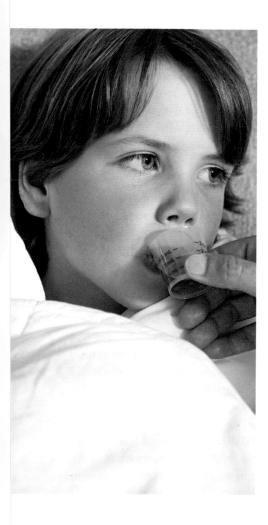

more*about*　　　　　　　　　　　　　　Medicines

If your doctor prescribes a drug for your child ask him or her:
- *What it's for;*
- *How much should be given and when;*
- *Whether it needs to be given before, with, or after food;*
- *What to do if you forget to give a dose — for example, should you double up next time or give the next dose as soon as you remember or after a certain time;*
- *How long to give the medication for. Is it all right to discontinue the medication if your child improves or is the medication an antibiotic, in which case it must be taken for a specific number of days and your child must finish the course even if he appears to have recovered;*
- *What are the side effects, and what to do if any appear;*
- *Will it affect any other medication, for example that given for another diagnosed condition or any over-the-counter medicines you may give the child;*
- *What to do if your child has not completely recovered after he has taken all the medication.*

The pharmacist will also be able to help and can advise on:
- *How long the medication can be kept;*
- *Where to store it; some medications need to be kept in a refrigerator, others need to be put in a cold, dry place.*

Nose drops

Sit your child on your lap and put your arm around his shoulder and support his forehead. Tilt him back slightly and administer the drops.

Nursing your child at home

When your child is unwell, it's best to relax your normal routine. Try not to show your anxiety and be ready to reassure her as she may be a little frightened, especially if she has been sick. At the beginning of an illness, a child may go off her food and want to sleep a bit more than usual. But she does not have to stay in bed, especially in the daytime. If she wants to be in bed, however, make sure you air the bed at least once a day and before she goes to sleep for the night.

A sick child often prefers to be in the same room as her parent. If this is the case with your child, make her comfortable on a sofa with her favourite bed covering. Put a table beside her and make sure she has a drink and a box of tissues ready to hand (and a bin for the used tissues). If she feels sick, leave a bowl within easy reach as well. Offer her snacks of her favourite food if she wants to eat something— small frequent meals are better than large portions which can be off-putting.

Occupying your child

Take your lead from your child. She may be happy to rest on the sofa in front of her favourite dvd — and may well fall asleep. When she is not resting, play some quiet games with her or read her stories. Children often regress when they are ill, and she may want to play with toys you thought she had outgrown or look at books that you haven't read for a while. You can break the rules to make her feel special; give her pens and paper or a tray of modelling clay and shape cutters to play with in bed. Keep her indoors when she is first ill, but as she improves, she will benefit from fresh air by playing outside (as long as it's not cold and wet). Don't let her run about too much as her temperature may go up again. If she is not infectious, you could invite a friend over for a short visit.

HOME MEDICAL KIT

Keep a set of commonly used medications at home. Check the contents regularly and make sure they have not passed their expiry date. Keep all medicines out of reach of your child and make sure they all have child-resistant lids.

- Paracetamol and/or ibuprofen — make sure it is appropriate for your child's age.
- Antihistamine to relieve mild allergic reactions — make sure it's appropriate for your child's age.
- Medicine syringe and stopper for medicine bottle or measuring spoon, depending on which one makes it easier to give medication to your child; your pharmacist may give syringes with prescribed medications.
- Thermometers, both digital and aural; check them regularly to make sure the batteries are working. If your child is prone to ear infections, you need to use a digital thermometer.
- Calamine lotion to soothe rashes.
- Cotton wool for applying creams.

Going to hospital

At some point in your child's life, she may have to be admitted to hospital. This can be very frightening for a parent, but also for your child. The admission may be unexpected, due to an accident or sudden illness, or it may be planned for a specific treatment, surgical procedure or to administer special medication. Your child may need to be admitted to hospital not necessarily because she is critically ill but because she needs treatment that can only be given in a hospital. However, you still may feel as if you suddenly have little or no control over your child and what is happening to her in the hospital. It will be a new and strange world for you and you may have to place your child's care in the trust of people you have never met before.

FIRST AID FOR MINOR INJURIES

INFECTED WOUNDS

If the wounding object was not clean or dirt was left in the wound or entered the body simply because the skin is broken, a wound can become infected: a day or so after an injury the area will begin to appear red and hot, becomes swollen and sore, or has a yellow discharge (pus). Clean around the injury with antiseptic wipes, cover the area with a sterile dressing and seek medical advice.

CUTS AND GRAZES
Young children frequently incur scrapes and cuts, which are rarely harmful although Infection is a risk whenever the skin is broken (see box, above).

What to do
Wash the injury under cold running water to flush out the dirt or if this distresses your child, use a bowl of tepid water. Dab the injury dry with a gauze pad wiping from the wound outwards and using a new piece of gauze

for each stroke. If there are tiny bits of dirt left in the wound, try brushing them off but seek medical advice if there is anything stuck in the wound as it may be plugging the bleeding and the wound could become infected if it is not removed — don't attempt to 'dig' it out yourself.

Press a clean pad on the wound to stop any bleeding. Cover with a plaster that has a pad larger than the injury.

BUMPS AND BRUISES
Bleeding just under the surface of the skin causes bruising that may appear to worsen for a few days after an injury.

What to do
To minimise swelling and reduce pain, sit your child down and raise and support the injury.

Apply a cold pack (see box, opposite page) against the injury for about 10 minutes. Seek medical advice if the pain persists.

SPRAINS AND STRAINS
If your child complains of pain or an inablity to use/put pressure on his hands or feet after running about or violent movement, he may have overstretched or torn a muscle, tendon or ligament.

What to do
Have your child rest the affected part (he should sit or lie down) and make sure to support it in a comfortable position. Apply a cold pack (see box opposite page) to help reduce pain and swelling and then apply a thick layer of padding firmly (but not so tight as to affect circulation) around the injured area. Keep the injury elevated.

Seek medical attention if your child is in severe pain or if he is unable to use the injured part.

NOSE BLEED
A forceful sneeze, a bang on the nose, or blowing his nose too vigorously or picking it can lead to bleeding. Seek medical attention

if your child loses a lot of blood or if he also has a head injury.

What to do

Sit your child down, tell him to lean forwards and pinch the soft part of his nose for about 10 minutes. Release the pressure and check the nose. If it is still bleeding, repeat the pinching for another 10 minutes. Give your child a bowl and tell him to spit out any blood in his mouth; if he swallows it could make him feel sick. Once the bleeding has stopped, clean his face with lukewarm water. Encourage your child to sit quietly for a short while, and ask him not to sniff or blow (or pick) his nose.

CAT SCRATCHES

A scratch or bite from a cat can result in minor bleeding, but may become infected with cat scratch disease.

What to do

Wash the area thoroughly and cover with an adhesive dressing. If cat scratch disease occurs, a blister or a small bump called an inoculation lesion (a wound at the site where the bacteria enter the body), will develop several days after the scratch or bite and may be mistaken for a bug bite or blister. Most commonly it is found on the arms, hands, head or scalp. The lesions are generally not painful. Within a couple of weeks the lymph nodes (glands) in the area nearest the scratch may become inflamed; for example, a scratch on the arm may result in swollen glands in the armpit. Your child may develop a slight fever and feel generally unwell. The symptoms generally last a few days but you should seek medical advice. Your doctor may prescribe antibiotics.

COLD PACK

A cold pack can minimise swelling and relieve pain. Either wrap a small bag of frozen peas in a tea towel (this is ideal as peas mould to the shape of the injury) or fill a plastic bag with some ice cubes and wrap in a tea towel.

FIRST AID IN AN EMERGENCY

As a parent you can make your home safe, but children still have accidents when you least expect it. Most injuries are relatively minor, but there can be more serious incidents, and it's important to know what to do. Enrolling on a first aid course can give you the confidence to deal with an incident, and in particular, help you identify when it's an emergency. It is can be reassuring to know that if you ring an ambulance (999) in an emergency, the operator will guide you through the essential steps.

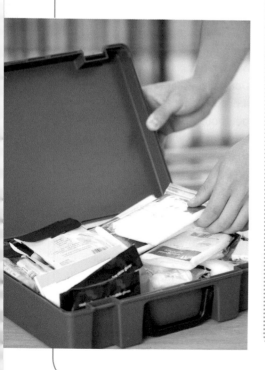

YOUR FIRST AID KIT

Keep a box of first aid equipment at home and one in the car — both should be out of your child's reach but readily accessible to you. Make sure that anyone who looks after your children, for example babysitters, knows where to find the box. Check it regularly and replace anything you use as soon as possible. Whether you are making up your own or buying a prepared kit, make sure it contains the following:

- Sterile wound dressings — these are dressings that have bandages attached.
- Sterile dressing pads.
- Selection of bandages: crêpe or self-adhesive bandages for supporting sprains and strains, stretchy open-weave bandages for securing dressings.
- Triangular bandage to use as a sling.
- Adhesive dressings— children love novelty coloured ones — but have some hypoallergenic plasters in case a victim is allergic to the other type.
- Blister plasters.
- Antiseptic wipes —ideally alcohol free for cleaning skin around a wound.
- Gauze wipes — for cleaning around a 'wet' wound, drying it, or to build up padding around a foreign object in a wound or as a dressing.
- Scissors and tweezers.
- Disposable, latex-free gloves.
- Anti-bacterial hand gel.
- Calamine lotion or antihistamine spray.
- Safety pins for securing bandages.
- Instant cold packs, especially for your car kit.
- Pocket mask to use for rescue breathing in poisoning situations.

WHAT TO DO IN AN EMERGENCY

Some first aid situations are potentially life threatening, and knowing what to do and when can save a life. Although it can be very frightening to find that your child has collapsed, or appears unconscious, it is important to stay calm and follow a clear plan of action.

First, make sure it is safe to approach your child (you cannot help your child if you become a casualty). If it isn't safe (there is a live cable, falling masonry or a fire, for example), stay back and call (or have someone else call) the emergency services immediately.

If it is clear to approach, treat your child where she is — only move her if her life is in danger as some injures can be made worse by incorrect handling.

Next, deal with potentially life-threatening priorities:

◆ Check for a response — is your child conscious or unconscious.

◆ Check to see if she is breathing normally.

◆ Look for, and treat, injuries that could affect the circulatory system, such as bleeding or burns (see pages 240, 241).

◆ Finally, assess her for other injuries. Listen carefully to your child, she may tell you where it hurts. Look for abnormalities, if she has broken a leg, the injured one may appear shorter than the other. Did you or anyone else see what happened, this could help you identify injuries. For example, if she fell down the stairs she may tell you that her leg hurts, but there is a risk that she has a spine or head injury.

IF YOUR CHILD APPEARS UNCONSCIOUS

What to do

1 Speak loudly and clearly to her — for example, ask her to "Open her eyes" and gently tap her shoulder.

If she responds, she is conscious, so attend to any injuries you find, see page 235. If your child does not respond, she is unconscious — shout for help and go to the next step.

2 Open her airway.

Place one hand on her forehead and tilt her head back, her mouth should fall open. Lift her chin by placing two fingertips on the point of her chin— make sure you don't press on her neck. Ask someone to call an ambulance.

3 Look, listen, and feel for breathing for no more than 10 seconds.

Place your ear as close as possible to your child's mouth and nose, look along her chest for signs of movement, and feel for breaths against your ear. If she is breathing, place her in the recovery position, see page 238. If she is not breathing, begin next step — rescue breathing and chest compressions (CPR/cardiopulmonary resuscitation) immediately.

4 Give rescue breaths.

Make sure the airway is still open. Check her mouth and pick out anything obvious near the front of the mouth; don't put your fingers in her mouth searching for obstructions as you may push the item further in. Then keeping the fingers of one hand on her chin, use your other hand to pinch the soft part of her nose. Take a breath, place your lips over hers and blow steadily until you see her chest rise — about a second. Remove your mouth and watch the chest fall. Repeat to give five breaths altogether.

5 Begin chest compressions

Kneel beside your child level with her chest and place the heel of one hand on the centre of her chest. Straighten your arm, lean over your child, and press down vertically, depressing her chest by about one-third of its depth. Release the pressure and let the chest come back up, but don't remove your hand. Repeat to give 30 compressions at a rate of 100 per minute.

6 Move back to your child's head and give two rescue breaths this time.

Then give another 30 chest compressions. If you are on your own, give CPR for one minute before calling for help. Continue CPR at 30 compressions followed by two breaths until help arrives or your child shows signs of recovery — opening her eyes, coughing, moving purposefully or breathing normally.

RECOVERY POSITION

If your child is unconscious but breathing, you must place her on her side in what is known as the recovery position. If you left her on her back, her tongue would fall back and block the air passages to her lungs, or if she vomits, fluid can collect in the back of her throat, also blocking the airway.

What to do

 Bend the arm nearest you at right angles to her body, and bring the furthest arm across her body so that her hand is against the side of her face nearest you. Bend her far knee, leaving her foot on the ground. Then pull your child's knee towards you until it is resting on the ground.

2 Adjust her head to make sure her airway stays open. Monitor her breathing and pulse — being alert to quality (fast or slow, shallow or deep) and any changes until help arrives.

CHOKING

Children often put things in their mouths to 'explore' them or can choke on a half-chewed piece of food. If a child is coughing but can still speak, there is only a mild obstruction and it's better to encourage your child to cough and clear the blockage herself. Intervene only when she can no longer speak, cough, or breathe.

What to do

1 Stand beside her and help her to bend forwards, supporting her upper body with one hand. With the heel of your hand, give her up to five blows on her back between her shoulder blades. Check her mouth and remove anything obvious, but don't sweep your finger round her mouth.

2 If the obstruction remains, give up to five abdominal thrusts. Stand behind your child and put your arms around her upper abdomen. Place one fist between her navel and breastbone and cover it with your other hand. Pull sharply upward and inward. Check her mouth again.

3 If your child is still choking, repeat steps 1 and 2 up to three times, then call an ambulance. Continue back blows and abdominal thrusts until emergency help arrives. If the child loses consciousness, treat as on page 237.

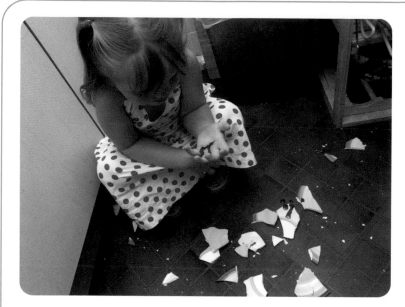

BLEEDING

Severe bleeding can be very distressing for you and your child, and if the blood loss is not stopped, vital body fluids will be lost from the circulation, which can result in a life-threatening condition called medical shock (see opposite page). If a wound is very large, stitches may be needed.

Ideally wear disposable gloves when treating your child.

PREVENTING INFECTION

Infection is a risk whenever the skin is broken. Ideally,

- Wash your hands or use sterile wipes or anti-bacterial foam to thoroughly clean them before and after giving first aid.
- Wear disposable gloves (latex free) to prevent cross-infection of germs.
- Check packaging of any dressing — if the wrapping is damaged it is not sterile.

What to do

1 Place a sterile pad over the wound and press firmly, or use your hands alone if no dressing is immediately available. Raise and support the injured part above the level of your child's heart to slow the blood flow to the area. Use a bandage to secure a dressing over the wound; the bandage should be tight enough to maintain pressure, but not so tight that it cuts off circulation to the limb beyond the injury. Call an ambulance. If the bleeding is very severe, treat as for shock.

2 If there is an object in the wound, do not try to remove it as it could be plugging more severe bleeding. Instead, apply pressure above and below the object then place pads around the object and bandage them.

BLOOD-STAINED DRESSING

If bleeding begins to show through a dressing, put another one on top. If bleeding comes through the second dressing, then the pressure is probably not being applied to the correct area — it needs to be right over the wound or source of bleeding. Take both dressings off and start again with a new dressing.

MEDICAL SHOCK

This is a serious condition that can result from severe blood loss (external or internal), burns, or allergic reaction (see page 244). The fluid part of the blood (plasma) carries nutrients and oxygen to the vital organs of the body. If significant amounts of fluid are lost from the circulatory system, organs such as the heart and brain won't receive essential supplies.

Signs of shock include pale, grey-blue, cold, sweaty skin; a rapid pulse that becomes weaker; and shallow, fast breathing. As more fluid is lost, your child will become restless, will yawn and sigh, be very thirsty, and eventually lose consciousness.

What to do

Ask someone to call an ambulance for you. Lay your child down on the floor on a blanket to protect her from the cold. Treat any obvious cause (bleeding or burns). Keep her head low, and raise her legs as high as you can and support them on cushions or a chair. Cover her with a blanket to keep her warm, but don't give her a hot-water bottle. Check her pulse and breathing while you wait for the ambulance.

BURNS

Burns are generally caused by flames or scalding, but some chemicals also burn. A burn is potentially serious and there is a high risk of infection.

A burn can affect just the surface of the skin (e.g. sunburn, in which case it is superficial); or there may be damage to some of the skin layers (partial thickness), or it can affect all of the skin layers (deep). Partial thickness burns will often have blisters, and are very painful. Deep burns, however, can be pain-free as nerves are damaged. Some burns can have areas of all three types.

Like bleeding, a burn can cause severe fluid loss from the body and result in medical shock, see above. Always seek medical advice if your child sustains a burn — if in any doubt about the severity, go straight to the hospital or call an ambulance.

What to do

Cool the damaged area straightaway by placing it under cold (but not icy) running water for at least 10 minutes: this stops the burning process and will help relieve the pain.

For a chemical burn, put on protective gloves and hold the area under cold running water to wash it off thoroughly. Make sure the contaminated water runs away from you and your child.

Remove any clothing from around the burn as the area will start to swell but don't touch anything that is stuck to the wound. Lay cling film along the injury (don't wrap it around a limb) to protect it, or for an injured hand or foot, put a clean plastic bag over it. Raising an affected limb can help reduce swelling and pain. Call an ambulance or take your child to hospital.

Never put lotions or ointments on a burn. If a blister appears as a result of a burn, don't put on an adhesive dressing, as the injury is likely to extend well beyond the blister.

HEAD INJURY

Your child may simply bump her head and have a small bruise and no other sign of injury. However, there is always a risk that a blow literally 'shakes' the brain inside the skull; your child may become temporarily dazed and have a headache but will recover completely (this is concussion) or

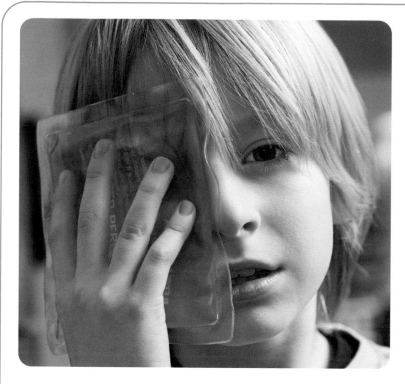

she may suffer a more serious injury called compression, in which bleeding occurs within the skull and presses on the brain, or she may even sustain a fracture.

Although symptoms of compression may not appear for hours or even days after an injury, if after a head injury, your child becomes disoriented, drowsy, and/or confused, develops a severe headache, a fever, weakness down one side of the body, and/or unequal sized pupils, take action immediately.

What to do

Sit your child down, quiet her and hold a cold pack against the bump — she may want to hold it. Reassure her and stay with her. If she does not recover completely within half an hour, seek medical advice. If she recovers initially, but later starts deteriorating, lay her down on the floor — not a chair as she could fall off — and call an ambulance.

DROWNING

A child can drown in only a few centimetres of water. If yours falls in the bath, remove her from the water immediately. If she falls in water outdoors, rescue her only if it safe for you to do so, otherwise call for help.

Keep her upright as you take her from the water. If the water or weather is cold, there is also a risk of hypothermia (see page 244). Any child rescued from water must be seen by a doctor.

What to do

As soon as your child is out of the water, lay her down and check to see if she is conscious and breathing. If she is unconscious but breathing normally, place her in the recovery position to ensure fluid can drain from her mouth (see page 238).

If she is not breathing, give five rescue breaths initially followed by 30 chest compressions, then two rescue breaths followed by 30 chest compressions (CPR). Continue CPR at a rate of 30:2 until help arrives or your child recovers (see page 237). If she regurgitates liquid while you are giving CPR, turn her onto her side briefly to allow fluid to drain, then restart CPR. If your child opens her eyes, coughs, moves purposefully, or breathes normally, place her in the recovery position. Call an ambulance even if she appears to have recovered completely.

POISONING

If you think your child has swallowed something poisonous, never try to make your child vomit it up. Some poisons burn the gullet on the way down and will burn again on the way back up.

What to do

If your child is conscious, try to find out what she ate or drank. Call an ambulance and give the control officer as much information as possible.

Save any clues you can find (pill bottles or plant berries, for example) and keep samples of vomit as it can help the medical team plan the treatment. If her lips are burnt, give her sips of milk to help soothe the burns.

If she is unconscious, treat as on page 236. You may need to wipe the poison from her mouth or use a mask for rescue breaths or try them mouth to nose.

BONE OR JOINT INJURY
Bones can be completely or partially broken in a fall (fracture). Alternatively, the bands of tissue that hold the joints together — tendons — can be stretched or torn, resulting in a sprained joint, or even a dislocated one. It can be very difficult to tell the difference between a break and severe sprain without an X-ray. If in doubt, treat as for a broken bone. If your child sustains a leg injury, don't move her. Make her comfortable where she is and call an ambulance.

What to do
Support the joints above and below the injured area. Use your hands initially, then rolled towels.

If your child has hurt her arm, wrap a folded towel around the injured area to prevent movement and take the child to hospital.

If your child has hurt her leg, suspect a break if the leg cannot bear weight. Support the joints above and below the injury — at

the knee and ankle for a lower leg — and place rolled blankets towels on either side of an injured upper leg. Call the emergency services..

If you suspect a sprain, see page 230 for the appropriate actions to take.

ELECTRICAL INJURY
Contact with domestic low-voltage electricity, or lightning can cause the heart to stop, and/or result in burns at the point where the electricity enters the body and where it exits.

INCOMPLETE FRACTURE

A young child's bones are much more pliable than an adult's. They have areas both of hard bone and 'softer' bone that allows for growth. As a result, an incomplete or 'greenstick' fracture may occur where only one side of the bone has broken and the other side is bent.

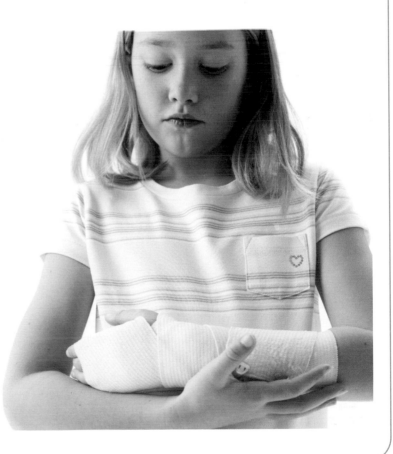

What to do

It is imperative to break the contact with the electricity before you touch your child. Ideally, switch off an appliance at the mains or if this is not possible, stand on a non-conducting surface such as a pile of newspapers, and using a wooden object (broom handle, long spoon), push the appliance away from your child.

If this is unsuccessful, remain standing on the newspapers, and loop a rope, clothes line or length of fabric around your child's feet and pull her away from the appliance.

If she is unconscious, treat as described on page 236.
If she is conscious, treat burns as described above.

Call an ambulance; a child with an electrical injury needs to be assessed by a doctor.

HEATSTROKE

Children don't have very effective heat control systems and a life-threatening condition known as heatstroke can occur if a child is exposed to very hot weather for a prolonged period. If the heat control system fails, the body cannot sweat and will be unable to lose heat.

If your child has a headache, is feeling dizzy and restless, has hot flushed skin, and her temperature is above 40°C (104°F) or if you lack a thermometer but your child

feels very hot when touched with the back of your hand, treat as below. Left untreated, your child will lose consciousness.

What to do

Act quickly. Ask someone to call an ambulance while you move your child into a cool, well-ventilated room. Remove as much of her clothing as possible and wrap her in a cold wet sheet, and keep the sheet cool by pouring more cold water onto it.

Leave the sheet in place until her temperature is down to 38°C (100.4°F). Replace the wet sheet with a dry one and fan her to keep her cool. Monitor her temperature, breathing, and pulse while you wait for the emergency services. If her temperature starts to rise again, restart the cooling process.

HYPOTHERMIA

Body temperature can also fall too low, for example, if your child is outside for long in poor weather conditions or falls into cold water, which can have serious consequences.

Suspect hypothermia if your child has cold, pale, dry skin and is shivering. If untreated, your child will become confused, her pulse will weaken and breathing will slow and be shallow until eventually she will lose consciousness.

What to do

It is very important to re-warm your child gradually. Get her inside and replace any wet clothes with dry ones. Wrap her up warmly, cover her head with a hat and put on gloves. Make sure the room is warm.

Never give your child a hot water bottle as this draws vital body heat to the surface away from where it is needed most. Give her warm drinks and high-energy foods such as chocolate. Stay with her until her temperature has returned to normal. Seek medical advice.

ALLERGIC REACTION

The body's immune system will react to something it perceives as a threat. Common causes of allergy include pollen (the fine powder released by trees, grass, or garden plants as part of their reproductive cycle), pet hairs (especially cats) wasp and bee stings, fungal or mould spores, latex and foods (especially nuts, eggs, cow's milk, wheat, soya, seafood and some fruit).

A reaction could be mild and result in a localised itchy rash, a runny nose and sneezing with reddened, watery eyes, or even abdominal pain or vomiting. Allergic reaction can also trigger an asthma attack (see page 256).

A reaction, however, can be far more severe and result in a generalised itchy rash, swelling of the mouth and throat, difficulty breathing, and even unconsciousness — a condition known as anaphylactic shock. If your child is diagnosed as having a severe allergy, you will be given a special autoinjector 'pen' containing adrenaline to administer if she comes in contact with the allergen.

What to do

Get rid of the source of the reaction, if possible. For example, remove a bee sting or take your child out of a room where nuts are present.

For a severe attack: If this is the first one, call an ambulance. Help your child into the position she finds most comfortable for breathing — often sitting up.

If your child has a known serious allergy, and she has an adrenaline auto injector pack, administer it as soon as possible. Take the lid off and press the injector into her thigh (see box). If the symptoms return, repeat the adrenaline injection every five minutes until help arrives.

For a mild attack: Talk to your pharmacist or seek medical advice. Keep your child away from likely sources such as pollen. A dose of paediatric antihistamine may help reduce the symptoms.

ADRENALINE AUTO INJECTORS

These are very straightforward to use. Take the lid off and hold the injector with your fist. Never put your thumb over one end because if you accidently hold the injector the wrong way up you could deliver the dose into yourself. Hold the injector against your child's thigh (over her clothes if necessary) and push hard for 10 seconds. Rub the injection site gently for up to 10 seconds to make sure the drug begins to circulate.

INFECTIOUS DISEASES

These are diseases caused by microorganisms — viruses or bacteria — and are easily passed from one person to another, although some are more contagious than others. Many, like diphtheria and even measles, are now relatively uncommon as a result of successful immunisation programmes. The diseases are generally spread through contact with the droplets of moisture released when an

DISEASE	SYMPTOMS
MEASLES A potentially serious and highly contagious viral infection. **Incubation** 8–14 days. A child is infectious from before the rash appears, to about day 5.	Initially there will be greyish-white (Koplik's) spots in the mouth and throat. After a few days, a red-brown spotty rash will appear; it usually starts behind the ears, and spreads around the head and neck before showing up on the legs and torso. It begins as groups of spots, but after three days the spots join together. Your child will also have a fever, cold-like symptoms, and reddened eyes that are sensitive to light.
MUMPS A viral illness, which is rarely serious in children **Incubation** 14–25 days, average is about 17 days.	Possible fever lasting about three days. Characteristic swelling of the parotid glands that sit either side of the face just below the ears; one or both sides may be affected. The swelling can cause pain, tenderness and difficulty swallowing.
RUBELLA (GERMAN MEASLES) A mild viral infection. **Incubation** 14–21 days. A child will be infectious from about a week before the rash appears.	A red-pink rash starts around the ears followed by tiny pink spots all over the body. Your child will have a fever and swollen glands in the neck and may have sore, red eyes. Up to a week before the rash appears she may have had a slight cold, cough or sore throat.

infected person coughs or sneezes. Many of the diseases have similar characteristics, such as rash and high fever and most are easily treatable. Some, however, can cause serious complications, so if in doubt, contact your doctor. Ring your doctor's surgery first as he or she may not want a child with a highly contagious illness to wait in the waiting area with other patients.

TREATMENT

POSSIBLE COMPLICATIONS

Symptoms normally last 7–10 days. For most children, medical treatment is not needed, but call your doctor for advice. Give your child infant paracetamol or ibuprofen to relieve the fever, and plenty of rest and fluids. Close the curtains if light hurts her eyes, and bathe them with damp cotton wool.

Diarrhoea and vomiting, conjunctivitis, ear infections and, more rarely, pneumonia. Hospital treatment may be needed for severe complications. Raised body temperature can cause febrile seizures (see page 224).

Call your doctor to let him or her know you suspect mumps; your child may need to be seen for the diagnosis to be confirmed. Give your child infant paracetamol or ibuprofen to relieve pain and fever and plenty of fluids. Offer soft foods if she finds swallowing difficult. Soothe glands with a cold compress.

Possible temporary one-sided hearing loss. Mumps can also lead to meningitis (see page 270) or inflammation of the brain (encephalitis). Older boys can suffer from inflamed testes, usually only on one side, but this rarely causes fertility problems.

Symptoms normally last 7–10 days. Call your doctor's surgery if you suspect rubella, but don't take your child to the doctor unless he or she asks to see her. Give infant paracetamol or ibuprofen to relieve the fever, and plenty of fluids. Keep your child away from playgroup or nursery. Alert your friends, especially anyone who is pregnant, and don't invite her over.

Inflammation of the brain (encephalitis) or joints may occur but these are rare. The main risk is to pregnant women, as contact with rubella infection can cause birth defects in an unborn baby.

DISEASE	SYMPTOMS
WHOOPING COUGH (PERTUSSIS) A highly contagious bacterial infection of the lungs and airways caused by the bacterium bordetella pertussis. If antibiotics (erythromycin) are prescribed, anyone who has been in contact with your child should be given a course as well to prevent the infection spreading.	A week of cold-like symptoms with a persistent, dry, irritating cough that generally progresses to intense bouts of coughing, which are followed by a distinctive 'whooping' noise on inhalation. Your child's face may be very red when coughing. The force of coughing can cause her to vomit and/or burst blood vessels in her nose (causing nosebleeds) and eyes (red spots appear on eyes).
DIPHTHERIA A highly contagious bacterial infection that affects the nose and throat or occasionally the skin.	Fever with temperature likely to be 38°C (100.4°F) or above, sore throat and breathing difficulties. Your child may also be exhausted, have a cough, complain of pain when swallowing and have foul-smelling nasal discharge. A grey-white membrane may form in her throat making breathing difficult. If her skin is affected instead of the throat, there will be pus-filled spots usually on her legs, feet and hands.
CHICKENPOX A common and usually mild viral disease caused by the varicella zoster virus. **Incubation** 17–21 days. A child is infectious until all her spots have crusted over.	Low fever and small red spots that usually start on the trunk and spread to the arms and legs. The spots develop into itchy blisters, which gradually crust over and form scabs that fall off. The spots take about five days to appear, then a few more days to form crusts. Some children have only a few spots while others are covered with them.
SCARLET FEVER A mild bacterial infection caused by streptococcus bacterium.	Often starts with a sore throat and fever. A widespread pink-red rash starts in one place but quickly spreads to other parts. The skin feels like sandpaper. Cheeks will be very flushed but the area around the mouth stays white. Your child's tongue may feel furry and be covered in red spots; it may peel after a few days, leaving the tongue sore.

TREATMENT

Seek medical advice. If whooping cough is diagnosed within three weeks of it beginning, your doctor may prescribe antibiotics — this stops your child from being infectious. In severe cases, your child may need to be admitted to hospital. Treat fever with infant paracetamol or ibuprofen and give plenty of fluids to prevent dehydration. Clear excess mucus or vomit during bouts of coughing so it cannot be inhaled. Keep your child away from playgroup or nursery for five days after she has completed the course of antibiotics.

Seek medical advice. Your child will need treatment in hospital in an isolation room — sometimes for up to six weeks. If there is a membrane in her throat, some or all of it will be removed surgically. Treatment will include antibiotics and an anti-toxin that neutralises the poisons produced by the bacteria. Anyone who has been in contact with your child will also be given a course of antibiotics.

Most children recover without medical treatment but if your child has impaired immunity, she will need intravenous antiviral medication in hospital. Relieve the itching by dabbing spots with calamine lotion. Treat fever with infant paracetamol or ibuprofen. Your child will normally recover completely within 10–14 days but seek medical advice if she is particularly unwell.

Seek medical advice; your doctor will prescribe a course of antibiotics. Rash will last about six days, then fade. If it is itchy, dab calamine lotion on the skin. Treat fever and a sore throat with infant paracetamol or ibuprofen and give plenty of fluids Most children recover 4–5 days after starting antibiotics. Skin on the hands and feet, may peel for up to six weeks after the rash has faded.

POSSIBLE COMPLICATIONS

Pneumonia, severe breathing difficulties, dehydration, weight loss because of excess vomiting, seizures, low blood pressure and possible kidney failure.

Permanent lung damage and possible respiratory failure; inflammation of the heart muscle (myocarditis); nervous system complications, which can affect the function of the diaphragm or bladder.

Possible bacterial infection of spots, more rarely inflammation of the brain (encephalitis).

Rarely ear infection, throat abscess, sinusitis or pneumonia may develop, but usually only if antibiotics are not given. If your child is sensitive to the Streptococcus bacteria, it can cause inflammation of the kidneys (nephritis) or of the joints and muscles (rheumatic fever), but this is very rare.

DISEASE	SYMPTOMS
FIFTH DISEASE (SLAPPED CHEEK SYNDROME) This is a contagious viral infection caused by the parvovirus B19. Children are only infectious before symptoms appear	Begins with fever where temperature may be 38°C (100.4°F) or higher, plus a headache and sore throat. This is followed 3–7 days later by a bright red rash on both cheeks, which spreads to the chest abdomen, arms and legs. Rash may last 4–5 weeks.
ROSEOLA INFANTUM Common viral illness (especially in very young children). **Incubation** 10-15 days	Sudden fever with temperature 40°C (104°F) or higher, which lasts 3–4 days, then returns to normal. Small pink spots appear as the fever subsides, usually first on the abdomen before spreading to face, arms and legs, and lasting 12–24 hours. Your child may have a sore throat and swollen glands in her neck.
HAND, FOOT AND MOUTH DISEASE A viral infection.	Fever with temperature around 38–39°C (100.4–102.2°F), and a rash of tiny red spots with darkish grey centres most noticeable on the back of the hands and feet. The spots can develop into painful blisters. There may also be blisters in the mouth, which makes eating painful.
TUBERCULOSIS (TB) A bacterial infection caused by mycobacterium tuberculosis. It mainly affects the lungs, and this type is highly infectious. It can affect the bones and nervous system, but this type is not infectious.	Persistent cough — lasting more than three weeks — that typically brings up blood-stained phlegm, weight loss, tiredness and fatigue with loss of appetite and high fever with night sweats.

TREATMENT

Treat fever with infant paracetamol or ibuprofen and give plenty of fluids. Soothe rash with calamine lotion. For most children this is a mild disease, which needs no special treatment. Your child can go to playgroup or nursery because as soon as the rash appears, she is no longer contagious.

No special treatment is required. Treat fever with infant paracetamol or ibuprofen, and don't let your child get too hot. Give her plenty to drink to keep her hydrated.

It is rarely serious, but can be very uncomfortable but usually clears up within 7–10 days. Treat fever with infant paracetamol or ibuprofen and give plenty of fluids — milk and water are best; avoid acidic drinks like fruit juice if your child's mouth is sore. Give her soft foods to eat. Don't break the blisters as the fluid is infectious. Blisters will usually dry up on their own within a week.

This condition is serious but usually curable with correct treatment. A chest X-ray and sputum and blood tests will be needed to confirm the diagnosis. An infected person will need at least a six-month course of antibiotics, possibly as long as 18 months if it is a variety that is resistant to antibiotics. Anyone who has been in contact with your child will need to be tested for the disease.

POSSIBLE COMPLICATIONS

Very rare. If a woman is pregnant she can pass it to her unborn baby, and there is a risk of anaemia and heart failure, which can cause miscarriage. Children with weakened immune systems can develop severe anaemia.

Raised temperature can cause febrile seizures (see page 224).

Very rare. Call your doctor if your child is unable to drink any fluids, shows signs of dehydration or is unusually tired.

TB spreads easily within a family who live in the same house. BCG vaccination can provide effective protection against TB and is recommended for groups of people who are at a higher risk of developing TB, and who have been in contact with someone with the disease.

RESPIRATORY ILLNESSES

The respiratory system is made up of the mouth and nose, throat and windpipe (trachea), which leads to the two lungs each of which is made up of lots of tubes. The larger tubes are called bronchi and they lead to smaller ones called bronchioles that end in tiny air sacs. Children have short passages between the different parts of the system, so infections can quickly pass from one organ to another.

COMMON COLDS

The common cold is a mild viral infection of the upper airways, which causes a runny and/or blocked nose, mild sore throat and sometimes a cough. There are hundreds of different cold-causing viruses and all children suffer from many colds every year while they build up their immune system. Children often develop colds even more frequently as soon as they start playgroup or nursery school as they are exposed to more children and viruses. Most colds last about a week and don't need medical treatment. A blocked nose, however, can be uncomfortable and prevent sleep.

What to do

Keep your child comfortable and treat the symptoms. Give infant paracetamol or ibuprofen for a fever. Encourage your child to blow her nose as often as possible with a tissue; assist her and make a game of it if it helps. Give her plenty to drink; dehydration can make a cough or a cold worse. Warm liquids such as lemon and honey or a herbal tea may help to relax her airways, loosen mucus and soothe a cough but avoid milky drinks as they can increase mucus production and overly sugary drinks as they can damage teeth. Commercial cold remedies and cough medicines will be of little help and are not recommended for young children.

If the atmosphere is very dry, use a humidifier or put a bowl of water in her room to increase the humidity, which will help to relieve a cough. Or, if the radiators are on, putting a wet towel on the radiator will release more water into the air. If your child is finding it difficult to sleep because of a blocked nose, try putting some decongestant drops on her pillow.

INFLUENZA

Also known as flu, this is another viral infection, similar to the common cold, but with more severe symptoms. Your child's temperature is likely to be high — 38-40°C (100-104°F), and she may say that she aches all over. She may feel alternately very hot and then very cold and shivery. She is likely to be lethargic and weak and may feel sick.

Flu can be very debilitating, and while antibiotics won't help since it's caused by a virus, it can

There are many different types of flu virus and from 2014 all children between the age of two and 17 will be offered an annual vaccination, which contains antibodies to the current most prevalent strains. Any child with a long-term health condition, such as asthma, must have the flu vaccination as the effects of the disease could worsen the illness.

leave a child weak and susceptible to other, more serious, bacterial infections that may need them.

What to do

Treat as you would a cold. Give infant paracetamol or ibuprofen for fever and plenty to drink to prevent dehydration. Your child will need to rest, but she does not need to stay in her bed; she may prefer to be on a sofa in the same room as you. Keep the room warm but not too hot, and well ventilated. Check her temperature regularly.

Seek medical advice if temperature stays high for more than 24 hours or your child develops a chesty cough, an earache or unpleasant nasal discharge.

SORE THROAT

A sore throat can be the result of a cold or flu virus, or a bacterial infection. Your child may tell you her throat is sore, or you may notice that she can't talk loudly or swallow easily. Look inside her mouth (you may need a torch); if

she has a sore throat the area at the back of her mouth will be red and inflamed and if there is a bacterial infection, there may be yellow or white spots on her

Tonsillitis

The tonsils are situated on either side of the back of the throat and are thought to act as a barrier against infection; for children, this is while their immune system is still developing. Tonsils prevent bacteria entering the body by trapping and killing them but they can become inflamed, causing a sore throat, and a child suffering from inflamed tonsils is likely to have a temperature of 38°C (100°F) or above.

Epiglottitis

The epiglottis is a flap of tissue that sits beneath the tongue at the back of the throat. Its main function is to close over the windpipe (trachea) while you're eating to prevent food from entering the airways. Infection is serious because the epiglottis can swell rapidly, blocking the air passages to the lungs. Symptoms will develop rapidly — a child will have a high temperature, severe sore throat, drool, and have difficulty swallowing and possibly breathing. If this is the case with your child, call an ambulance, as she needs hospital treatment. Do not put anything in her mouth or try to clear her throat. Sit her up to make breathing easier and keep her calm while waiting for help to arrive.

tonsils (tonsillitis). She is likely to have a cough, raised temperature and may complain of a headache.

What to do

Encourage your child to rest. Treat pain and fever with infant paracetamol or ibuprofen, and make sure she has plenty of liquids. Give her soft, mashed food if she is finding it hard to swallow. Seek medical advice if her throat is very sore and inflamed or if the symptoms don't improve after four days. There may be an infection and your doctor may prescribe a course of antibiotics if there is an infection.

SINUSITIS

The sinuses are small, air-filled cavities behind the cheekbones and forehead and a viral or bacterial infection can result in inflammation of the linings of the cavities or sinusitis. Symptoms include pain and tenderness of the face, a raised temperature and runny and/or blocked nose. It can develop on its own or be the result of a cold or flu, and can last a few days or several weeks.

What to do

Most cases will clear up without medical treatment but seek aid if your child is very uncomfortable or the pain persists. Give infant paracetamol or ibuprofen for pain and fever and plenty of fluids. Your child may be more comfortable lying down if pain is severe.

COUGHS AND CHEST INFECTIONS

A cough is a natural reflex action that clears the throat and lungs of irritants such as mucus, dust or even food. It can accompany a cold or flu and a child may cough simply because mucus is trickling down the back of her throat, or there can be an underlying infection in the chest. A cough can be dry with a hacking sound, or it can be what is called productive, in which mucus from

the lungs, or phlegm, is produced. Chest infections can be caused by either bacteria or viruses and vary from bronchitis, an infection of the upper airways, to the more serious pneumonia that affects tissue deep within the lungs.

What to do

If your child is coughing as the result of a cold, but she is eating and drinking normally, there is nothing to worry about. Give

infant paracetamol or ibuprofen to ease any fever. Proprietary cough medicines are not recommended for young children. Drinking warm liquids such as lemon and honey or a herbal tea may help relax the airways, loosen mucus and soothe a cough but avoid milky drinks, which can increase mucus production. If your child has a persistent cough, is off her food and has a fever and/or there is any sign of wheezing, take her to the

---

*more **about*** | Chest infections

Bronchitis

This is an infection of the upper airways. A child will have a productive cough that sounds 'wet'. She is likely to cough up yellowy-grey or green mucus. Like most respiratory tract infections, the cause can be viral or bacterial. Most cases will clear up without medical help, but if your child has a persistent cough, or the mucus is green, seek medical advice as antibiotics may be needed. There is a risk that bronchitis can develop into pneumonia.

Bronchiolitis

This is a viral infection of the lower respiratory tract that can be serious in babies, but rarely affects children over one year old.

Pneumonia

This is inflammation or swelling of the tissue in one or both of the lungs. The tiny air sacs within the lung fill up with fluid, making breathing difficult. A chest X-ray will confirm the diagnosis and your child will need to be treated in hospital. Pneumonia can be caused by a viral infection, in which case the treatment aims to relieve the symptoms; if the cause is bacterial, antibiotics will be given. Children are routinely vaccinated against streptococcus pneumoniae, the bacterium that most commonly causes the disease, as part of their immunisation programme (see page 218).

doctor. Likewise, see your doctor if the cough is worse at night and/or brought on by running about — this could be asthma (see below).

LARYNGITIS

This is an infection of the voice box or larynx. It is mostly caused by a viral infection and may follow a cold or sore throat. A child will have a fever and sore throat, but significantly will have difficulty speaking, sound very hoarse, or may not be able to talk at all. She will have a constant tickly cough.

What to do

Most cases of laryngitis clear within a week without medical treatment. Treat a fever with infant paracetamol or ibuprofen. Give plenty of liquids to soothe the throat and prevent dehydration. Warm drinks such as lemon and honey or a herbal tea can help; avoid milky drinks as they increase mucus production. Proprietary medications are not recommended for young children. Seek medical advice if your child is in discomfort, has a prolonged high fever or is unable to speak.

CROUP

A condition that affects young children, croup is an infection of the windpipe, the larynx (voicebox) and the main air passages into the lungs. It is generally caused by a virus. A child with croup has a distinctive short, barking cough and may

make a rasping sound, known as stridor, especially when she inhales. She may be hoarse and develop breathing difficulties.

What to do

Most cases of croup get better without medical help. During an attack, sit your child on your knee supporting her back. Stay calm, and reassure your child as an attack can be worsened if she panics. Create a steamy atmosphere as moisture can help breathing. For example, take her into the bathroom and sit her on your lap beside a bath filled with hot water. If she does not improve, call an ambulance.

HAY FEVER

This is a common condition that results when a person has an allergic reaction to pollen — the fine powder released by plants as part of their reproductive cycle. Symptoms include sneezing, runny nose and watery, itchy reddened eyes. It generally erupts during spring and into summer, but as different children are sensitive to different pollens, for example, it could be trees (early spring) grass (spring into late summer), or wheat (later summer). Hay fever often runs in families, especially if there is a history of asthma (below) or eczema (see page 257).

What to do

There is no cure for hay fever and many children who develop it when young will grow out of it in time. In the meantime, you can only treat the symptoms and try to avoid the triggers, though this can be difficult especially if grass is the cause. Antihistamine medication can alleviate most symptoms. Eye drops may help if your child's eyes are very red and uncomfortable; it can help to wear sunglasses too.

If your child suffers from severe hay fever, ask your GP to arrange for tests to ascertain exactly what the trigger is so you can try to avoid it.

ASTHMA

This is a long-term or chronic condition that affects the tubes that carry air in and out of the lungs. When a child comes into contact with something that irritates her airways (a trigger), the muscles around the walls of her airways tighten narrowing the airways and their linings become inflamed and start to swell. The linings make sticky mucus, which can further narrow the airways and can cause coughing.

Symptoms include a persistent cough, often with a wheezing sound in the chest. Your child will be short of breath and may say her chest feels tight.

Unlike other coughs, this type is often brought on by exercise. Other triggers include house mites, dust, a smoky atmosphere or pet hair. Asthma can also be brought on by a chest infection.

There is no cure for asthma, but with a combination of medication and lifestyle changes, it is possible to keep the condition under control. Children often outgrow their asthma by the time they reach their teens.

What to do

If your child has never had an asthma attack before and she develops breathing difficulties, take her to hospital, or call an ambulance. She will probably need oxygen, and may be given a short course of steroids. The doctor will then assess her and she is likely to be prescribed inhalers, one to use everyday that helps prevent attacks (normally brown or white) and another to ease the symptoms when they occur. Children are given inhalers with a special spacer. You place the inhaler in the base of the spacer and administer the medication into it. The child then puts her mouth over the mouthpiece and breathes in and out normally.

4 steps to take if your child has an asthma attack

1   Give your child the recommended dose of the reliever inhaler.

2   Sit him down in the most comfortable position for breathing and encourage him to take slow, steady breaths.

3   If the attack is not easing, repeat the dose of the inhaler.

4   If the attack is still not improving, call an ambulance

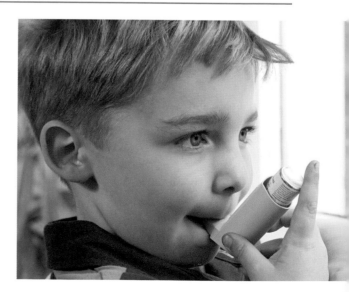

SKIN CONDITIONS

Because your child's skin is far more sensitive than an adult's, it is more susceptible to skin disorders. These can vary from irritation by sun, detergents, skin infections, or rashes caused illnesses or fever. Most of the skin problems are not serious and will clear up on their own. If in any doubt, always consult your GP.

ECZEMA

This is a long-term condition that causes the skin to become itchy, red, dry and cracked. Atopic eczema, which mainly affects children, is the most common form (about one child in 20 develops it), and those affected by it often have a family history of eczema, asthma (see page 256) or hay fever page (see page 255). However, it may also be a result of intolerance to certain foods.

Atopic eczema commonly appears in areas with folds of skin such as, behind the knees, the inner side of the elbows, on the side of the neck and around the eyes and ears. It can vary in severity but most children are only mildly affected and have periods where it is not noticeable, and flare-ups where additional treatment is needed.

Severe eczema can cause cracked, very sore skin that's red and oozing fluid and may even bleed if the child scratches the skin. Eczema can be very irritating for a child at night and cause her to scratch more. Very cold or very hot conditions can bring on a flare-up.

What to do

If you suspect that your child has eczema talk to your GP. Use emollient creams on her skin and put some in her bath too. While some eczema develops for no particular reason, sometimes there is a trigger. Your GP will work with you to find out the possible cause. If the problem persists, your child will be referred to a dermatologist for additional tests.

Try to dress your child in clothes that are less likely to irritate the skin, for example cotton. Keep your home fairly cool as heat can aggravate the condition.

If the eczema is severe, your GP may prescribe the weakest effective corticosteroid cream to rub onto her skin to reduce the redness and swelling in flare-ups. In very severe cases, your child may need special bandages and dressings to help keep her skin moist and prevent scratching. If the skin becomes infected, a course of antibiotics may be required. Other medication such as immuno-suppressants may also be prescribed.

Keep your child away from anyone who has cold sores.

CONTACT DERMATITIS

This is a type of eczema caused by an irritant such as the adhesive on plasters, rubber, metal from a bracelet, some plants, bubble bath, scented soap, washing detergents and fabric softeners. The symptoms may take a few days to appear. Your child's skin will be red and inflamed and there may be a scaly rash. Her skin will be itchy and may blister, or even break especially if she scratches a lot. Depending on the trigger, the rash may be localised or widespread.

What to do

Relieve the symptoms by dabbing calamine lotion on the affected area. If it is widespread, an antihistamine may be needed. If you know the cause, restrict your child's contact with it.

If you are not sure of the cause, think about any recent changes you have made, for example, to washing routines. If the rash started after you changed your detergent and/or softener, it may be worth changing back to the previous one. If the symptoms persist and you are unable to identify the cause, talk to your GP. He or she may arrange for some tests to try and identify the cause.

IMPETIGO

This is a highly contagious skin condition that causes large fluid-filled blisters and sores to develop on the skin — mainly around the mouth and nose. Bacteria enter and infect the skin where it is broken by a cut, an insect bite or a pre-existing skin condition such as eczema (see page 257) or scabies (see page 258). The most infectious type results in sores that burst and leave a distinctive yellow crust on the skin. It is rarely serious, and would heal on its own, but generally treated with antibiotics because it is so contagious.

What to do

Take your child to your GP. He or she will want to confirm the diagnosis and will probably prescribe an antibiotic cream to put on the sores. Your child will remain infectious until the sores have dried and healed or for 48 hours after starting treatment. In the meantime, keep her away from nursery or playgroup and encourage her not to touch the sores to stop the infection from spreading. Make sure she uses her own towels and face cloths and showers or bathes daily. Keeping her nails short may discourage the infection from spreading.

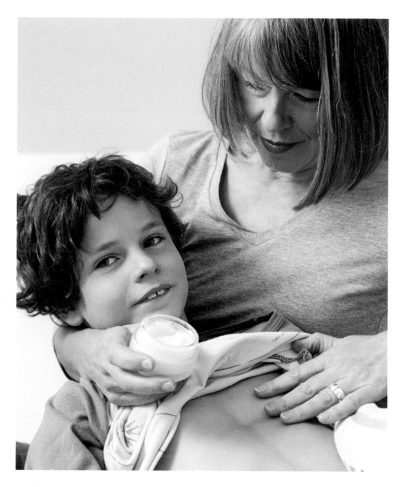

URTICARIA

Also known as hives, or nettle rash, urticaria is a raised itchy rash that may be limited to one body part, or it can spread over the entire body. It is caused by an allergic reaction to something a child has touched (for example, a nettle) or eaten. The trigger causes high levels of histamine and other chemical messengers to be released in the skin, so the blood vessels in the affected area open up (causing the redness or pinkness) and become leaky. The extra fluid in the tissues causes swelling and sometimes itchiness.

Urticaria normally subsides in a few hours, but occasionally lasts for a few weeks.

What to do

Dab calamine lotion on the affected part of the skin or give your child a coolish bath to soothe her skin. If the rash persists, your child may benefit from some antihistamine medication suitable for children; your pharmacist should be able to advise you. Contact your doctor immediately if the rash affects your child's face as it could cause her mouth to swell resulting in breathing difficulties.

If your child has frequent attacks, try to identify the cause to prevent the attacks occurring.

WARTS AND VERRUCAE

These are small, brown or flesh-coloured rough lumps that often develop on the skin, in particular the hands (warts) and the soles of the feet (verrucae). They are caused by the human papilloma virus and are not serious, but they are contagious. They can be spread directly by skin-to-skin contact, or indirectly from contact with a contaminated surface — for example the area around a swimming pool, or even the bathroom floor. Warts and verruccae can appear singly or in clusters and while not usually painful, verrucae can be uncomfortable to walk on.

What to do

Most warts and verruccae disappear without treatment, but this can take a couple of years.

You can treat them with a proprietary medication; ask your pharmacist for advice. If the warts are on your child's genital area, speak to your doctor straight away; never use proprietary medicines on this part of the body. If your child has a verruca, she should wear a special rubber swimming sock on her foot at the pool to prevent spreading the infection.

MOLLUSCUM CONTAGIOSUM

This is a highly contagious viral infection that causes small, raised, itchy spots. It usually affects children under the age of five, or those with a weakened immune system, as a result of cancer treatment, for example.

What to do

Talk to your GP who can confirm the diagnosis. Treatment is not normally recommended as molluscum contagiosum clears up on its own, although it can take 12–18 months. If your child has the virus, keep affected areas of her skin covered and avoid sharing towels, flannels and clothing or baths. Make sure your child does not scratch the spots because this may lead to other areas of skin becoming infected and prolong the infection.

SCABIES

Scabies is a contagious, intensely itchy skin condition. It occurs when tiny parasitic mites (Sarcoptes scabiei) burrow into the skin. There may be a rash where the mites have burrowed. It is spread by close contact with an affected person: children are especially at risk if there is an outbreak at their playgroup or nursery, as are their parents.

Scabies mites can survive outside the human body for between 24 and 36 hours, and an infestation can spread quickly because people are usually unaware they have the condition until two to three weeks after exposure.

What to do

Take you child to your GP as without effective treatment, the scabies mite life cycle can continue indefinitely — mites are resistant to soap and hot water and cannot be scrubbed out of the skin. Your doctor is most likely to prescribe permethrin cream, or if that does not work, malathion lotion. The lotion or cream is applied to areas where the scabies mites often burrow, such as the wrists, elbows, armpits, and under the fingernails, then left on for a few hours. Treatment is repeated every few days. Wash your child's bed linen, nightwear and towels after each treatment.

To prevent re-infection, all members of your household and any close contacts, should be treated, even if they do not have any symptoms.

RINGWORM

This is a highly contagious and common fungal infection that causes round, reddish-grey scaly, and sometimes itchy, patches on the skin (or bald patches if it appears on the scalp). It is not serious and in spite of its name, it has nothing to do with worms. There may be only one patch or several and they spread outwards as they progress.

What to do

Consult your GP. He or she will prescribe an anti-fungal cream if the skin is affected or shampoo, and possibly medication, if the infection is on the scalp.

It is important to prevent the ringworm spreading to other members of the family; don't share towels, or let other children share the affected child's bath. Your child does not need to stay away from playgroup or nursery, but let the caregivers know she has the condition. You may be asked to cover the affected area with a plaster.

BOILS

Pus-filled painful lumps can arise if bacteria infect hair follicles. Generally a boil will clear up on its own in about two weeks but there are things you can do to make the boil drain itself of pus and to make your child more comfortable.

If the boil lasts for more than two weeks or is very painful or large, take your child to your GP. He or she may prescribe oral antibiotics and/or may make a cut in the boil to release the pus.

What to do

Apply a warm compress several times a day to the affected area.

Infections or allergic reactions are responsible for most rashes and spots, so suspect this is the case with your child if a rash or spots appear and she is otherwise well. If, however, your child is under the weather, and/or the rash is itchy or sore, ask your doctor for advice. Your doctor may need to see it to confirm a diagnosis and even if it's not serious, he or she can suggest ways to soothe discomfort and calm the rash.

Many infectious diseases (see charts on pages 246–251) are characterised by different types of spots, some of which can be uncomfortable. Dabbing calamine lotion on the spots can cool the spots and relieve itching.

If you suspect an allergic reaction, try to work out the cause. For example, have you started using a different soap on your child's skin or a new detergent to wash her clothes? This could be contact dermatitis, see page 257. Has she brushed against a leaf or cuddled a new household pet (see urticaria page 258).

One disease in particular — meningitis, which is inflammation of the layers around the brain (see page 270) — can result in blood-poisoning, or septicaemia, which causes a rash that begins as red or brown pinprick marks, and develops into larger red or purple blotches in the late stages. This is a very serious condition.

Glass test

If your child has been unwell with flu-like symptoms and a fever and develops a rash, press the side of a glass against the rash. This rash is caused by bruising under the skin and, unlike other rashes and spots, will not disappear if pressed. If you can see the rash through the glass, call an ambulance, even if you have already spoken to your doctor.

When it does drain, carefully wipe the pus away using a cotton ball soaked in antiseptic solution. Cover the affected skin with a plaster. Don't poke or squeeze the boil to make it burst as you may spread the infection. If your child gets frequent boils try using an antibacterial soap.

GASTROINTESTINAL PROBLEMS

Children often get infections that cause diarrhoea and vomiting. These infections are very easily transmitted from person to person, and very young children are especially vulnerable because of their tendency to put everything in their mouths. One of the major risks is dehydration from the loss of fluid.

GASTROENTERIITIS

This highly contagious infection of the stomach and bowel (large intestine) can be caused by a virus, bacteria or parasite. If affected, your child may begin by vomiting, and then have diarrhoea (several loose, watery stools in a 24-hour period). She may also have a fever. If she is suffering from 'food poisoning', she will probably also have stomach cramps.

What to do

Most cases of gastroenteritis suffered by children are mild and pass within three to five days without the need for treatment, but it is best to seek medical advice for your preschooler if she suffers from persistent vomiting or diarrhoea that lasts longer than 24 hours, or eight hours if she has not been able to hold down any fluids, as there is a serious risk of dehydration. Rarely, children need to be hospitalised and given fluids intravenously. Always consult your GP if your child has been abroad recently (the cause may be a parasite); there are symptoms not usually associated with gastroenteritis, for example headache or stiff neck; of if there is blood or mucus in her stools.

Don't give your child over-the-counter anti-diarrhoea medications (they are not recommended for children under

5 ways to prevent spread of tummy bugs

1 **Encourage your child to wash her hands properly** after going to the toilet and before eating.

2 **Clean the toilet thoroughly** using disinfectant after each episode of diarrhoea and/or vomiting, making sure that you also clean the handle and seat, and then wash your own hands.

3 **Don't let other members of your household share** your child's towels, flannels, cutlery or eating utensils.

4 **Keep her at home** for at least 48 hours after she has recovered.

5 **Don't take your child to a swimming pool** for at least two weeks after the last episode of diarrhoea — rotavirus can be spread in water.

the age of 12), or medicines that prevent vomiting (anti-emetics) because of the risk of side effects, such as muscle spasms or allergic reactions.

Provide your child with a bowl to vomit into just in case she can't get to the bathroom on time. Wipe her mouth when she has been sick. Give her water, diluted squash, diluted fruit juice or semi-skimmed milk to drink and encourage her to sip it often. If she is feverish, give her infant paracetamol. Bedrest is not essential but make sure she has easy access to the toilet.

Initially your child may not have much of an appetite, but when she feels hungry again start her off with bland foods that won't upset her stomach, such as toast or rice, and gradually introduce other foods. Don't send her back to nursery or playgroup until at least 48 hours after the

last episode of diarrhoea and vomiting.

TODDLER DIARRHOEA
Some children (more commonly boys) up to the age of five suffer from persistent diarrhoea, even though they are not unwell. Sometimes called chronic nonspecific diarrhoea, affected children may have soft stools several times a day and pass recognisable pieces of food, for example vegetables. Some children complain of mild tummy pain as well.

Diet, especially one that contains too much fruit juice and sweet drinks is often the cause; one theory is that the balance of fluid, fibre, undigested sugars and other foods that reach the large bowel (colon) becomes upset. Children grow out of it as the bowel becomes more efficient. It is not caused by food intolerance.

What to do
The condition is not serious but your doctor will want to eliminate other causes or infections. He or she will measure your child to make sure she is growing normally. A change of diet often helps. Reduce the amount of sweetened drinks, and make sure that your child eats foods containing fat such as whole milk and cheese and easily digested fibre (broccoli, carrots, sweet potato); If necessary, mash foods that she finds hard to digest.

CONSTIPATION
If your child passes hard, dry stools infrequently, she may be constipated. This can happen if she becomes dehydrated following an illness such as fever or vomiting, or due to dietary reasons, for example her diet has changed recently or if she is not eating sufficient fibre-rich foods, such as fruit, vegetables or wholemeal bread. It can also result from withholding stools while being toilet trained.

What to do
Children do vary in their toilet habits and some children go for two to three days without passing a stool. If you are concerned, however, encouraging your child to drink more fluids and adding more fibre-rich foods to her diet may solve the problem but consult your doctor if constipation persists for more than a week, or your child is in pain when she tries to defecate.

Your doctor will ask about your child's diet and if a change has not made a difference, he or she may prescribe stool softening medication or a laxative.

Encouraging your child to use the toilet at the same time everyday can establish a more regular habit, but this can take a couple of months. If the problem persists, your child should be referred to a gastrointestinal specialist.

THREADWORMS

Also known as pinworms, these are tiny parasitic worms that look like little pieces of white thread. They infect the large intestine and lay their eggs around the anus.

Threadworms are very common and spread easily from person to person as a result of poor hygiene. You may see them in your child's stool or around her bottom. They often cause itching around the anus, especially at night, which may disturb your preschooler's sleep. When she scratches, the eggs get stuck on her fingernails and are transferred to her mouth or clothes.

What to do

Your doctor can prescribe medication in the form of tablets or liquid medicine or it can be bought over the counter from the chemist. If any member of the household has threadworms, everyone needs to be treated. Threadworms have a six-week lifecycle so it is essential to follow a very strict hygiene regime for at least six weeks to prevent re-infection. The day after the family has been given the medication, wash everyone's night clothes and bedding. Clean the house thoroughly, and insist that everyone wash their hands frequently, particularly before eating and always after using the toilet. Keep your child's fingernails short, and discourage your child from putting her hands in her mouth. Put underwear on your child at night, and change it every morning. Make sure everyone in the house uses a separate towel and face cloth.

APPENDICITIS

This is inflammation of a small finger-like pouch connected to the large intestine called the appendix. The condition starts as a pain in the centre of the abdomen, which then travels towards the lower right-hand side, gradually worsening as it moves. Appendicitis is a medical emergency and the appendix needs to be removed surgically; if left untreated, it can burst and cause potentially life-threatening infections. Appendicitis is more common in children over the age of 10.

What to do

If your child complains of a severe pain in the abdomen that is worsening, call your doctor immediately. Appendicitis can be difficult to diagnose and there may be another cause of the pain, such as a bladder infection. If in doubt, take your child to the hospital, or call an ambulance.

---

more about | Causes of gastroenteritis

Rotavirus is the leading cause of gastroenteritis in children. It is often spread when an infected child does not wash her hands properly after going to the toilet. The first infection by rotavirus tends to be the most severe as the body has no resistance to it. After being infected with the virus once, the body starts to build up a resistance (immunity) to it. This is also why rotavirus infection is extremely rare in adults. All young babies are currently immunised against it as part of their routine vaccination programme.

Norovirus is sometimes known as the winter vomiting bug and it affects people of all ages. It is highly infectious and will last a couple of days. It develops 12–48 hours after contact with an infected person and you are infectious during that period.

Food poisoning. Food may be contaminated with bacteria such as salmonella or E.coli, as a result of poor food hygiene or insufficient cooking. Or it can be contaminated with a virus.

MOUTH AND TOOTH CONDITIONS

The skin around the mouth is even more delicate than the skin that covers the rest of the body. The soft lining of the mouth and the tongue is easily damaged by a sharp tooth, or food or drink that is too hot or too cold. Children commonly put lots of things — from hands to toys in their mouths — so this area is very exposed to a variety of potentially damaging infections.

COLD SORES

These are small fluid-filled blisters that appear around the mouth, generally on the lips. They are secondary infections caused by the herpes simplex virus, which has entered the body as a result of an earlier illness. Cold sores often start as a tingling, or even burning sensation at the site of the infection, and a few days later, the blisters appear. These will burst forming a weeping sore with clear fluid oozing out. As the fluid dries, a crusty scab will form, under which healing takes place.

Cold sores are highly contagious.

What to do

Cold sores usually clear up without treatment within 7–10 days but antiviral creams can help alleviate the symptoms and may speed up healing. Ask your pharmacist for a cream suitable for young children; always wash your hands after applying the medication. Encourage your child not to touch or pick at the sore.

Your child may not want to drink if her lips are very sore and risks becoming dehydrated. In this case, try letting her drink through a straw.

Cold sores are at their most contagious when they burst, and remain so until they are completely healed. To prevent family and friends becoming infected, make sure no one shares a towel or face cloth and that you don't come in contact with the sore through kissing.

MOUTH ULCERS

These are small open sores in the lining of the mouth or on the tongue. They are not serious and will normally heal on their own within four to 10 days, but they can be very painful and if your child has one, she may be reluctant to eat. Ulcers mostly appear for no apparent reason, but can occur because a child has a very sharp tooth, or as a symptom of gingivostomatitis (see opposite); rarely, they may be caused by an underlying disorder.

What to do

If the ulcers are painful, give your child infant paracetamol or ibuprofen to relieve the pain. You can buy anaesthetic gels at the chemist; ask your pharmacist for one suitable for young children. Give your child bland and soft food to eat and make sure she continues brushing her teeth properly (use a softer brush if

---

*more***about** | The herpes simplex virus

After an initial infection (symptoms include swollen gums, sore throat, producing more saliva than usual, fever or even dehydration, headache or feeling sick), the herpes simplex virus remains dormant in the nervous tissue, but triggers such as strong sunlight, colds or stress may cause it to be reactivated.

necessary). Consult your GP if the ulcer has not healed after 10 days, your child has repeated ulcers, or she has a fever as well.

GINGIVOSTOMATITIS

This is a viral infection accompanying the first infection by the herpes simplex virus — the same one that is behind cold sores (above). Gingivostomatitis generally affects children under the age of three.

Your child will develop a fever and a sore mouth, which is followed by small, yellowish painful ulcers that rupture, and red swollen gums. Her neck glands will be swollen, and she may have bad breath. She'll find it difficult to chew or swallow, and may be reluctant to drink.

What to do

Call your doctor. He or she will prescribe pain relief and possibly anti-viral medication. If your child is very unwell, she may need to be admitted to hospital so that fluids and anti-viral medication can be given intravenously.

GINGIVITIS

Not to be confused with gingivostomatitis, this is an inflammation of the gums that is caused by not brushing teeth and gums properly. The bacteria in the plaque that collects around the base of the teeth and in the gum margins irritate the gums. The first sign you may see is that your

child's gums bleed when she brushes her teeth; she may tell you her gums are sore. If left unchecked, gingivitis can cause the teeth to loosen.

What to do

Take your child to the dentist for a check-up. If the attack is mild, then just a better dental hygiene routine may be sufficient.

If the condition is severe, an antibacterial mouthwash may be recommended.

Once the gums have recovered and are less tender, the dentist may want to scrape away the plaque to prevent another attack.

TOOTH DECAY AND DENTAL ABSCESS

The same bacteria that contribute towards gingivitis, can cause tooth decay. They break down the sugars in food and drink to provide them with energy and in

so doing create acids, which, if left on the teeth, will de-mineralise the hard outer tooth enamel (cause loss of calcium and phosphate). This eventually breaks down the enamel and the layers beneath, causing decay.

If bacteria enter the teeth through the decay, the tooth can become infected (an abscess). Pus will collect beneath the tooth and can enter the tooth's sensitive core, damaging the nerves and blood vessels beneath it.

What to do

Good dental hygiene (see page 65) can prevent tooth decay and routine dental check-ups can pick up signs of problems early.

If you see a blackened area on one of your child's teeth, or she complains of toothache, take her to the dentist.

If the decay is at an early stage, the dentist will scrape away

LIP LICKER'S ECZEMA

Some young children who still suck their thumbs or excessively lick their lips are prone to a rash around the mouth caused by saliva. Saliva can be irritating; it makes the lips dry and chapped while inflaming the surrounding skin, which becomes scaly.

Applying a moisturising lip balm frequently and treating the adjoining skin with petroleum jelly is the best way to deal with the problem. The problem resolves as soon as the lip licking stops.

any plaque, allowing the surface of the tooth to come into contact with saliva. The saliva helps re-mineralise the tooth, allowing it to heal over time. If decay is severe, the dentist may need to remove the damaged area of tooth and insert a filling.

If an abscess has developed, take your child to the dentist straight away. The dentist will need to drill into the tooth to relieve the pressure and then remove the damaged area. If the damage is severe, the tooth may have to be removed altogether.

MALOCCLUSION

Ideally, all upper teeth sit directly over the lower teeth and the points of the molars fit the grooves of the opposite molar. A malocclusion is a misalignment of upper and lower teeth and the condition tends to run in families.

Treatment may be needed eventually if the teeth are so crooked or out of position that a child finds eating and talking difficult. Malocclusion can also interfere with speech development.

Malocclusion can be caused by a difference between the size of the upper and lower jaws or between jaw and tooth size (especially in adult teeth), which can result in overcrowding of teeth or in abnormal bite patterns. However, it can also result from early childhood habits such as thumb sucking, use of a dummy beyond the age of three years and continuing to use a bottle for a prolonged period.

What to do

Very few people have perfect teeth alignment and most problems are so minor that they do not require treatment.

If there is a family history of malocclusion that needed treatment, your dentist will check your child as she grows, as early detection and treatment may optimise the time and method of treatment needed.

Many types of malocclusion are not preventable but you can help by discouraging thumb sucking or the use of dummies. Treatment will not be carried out until your child is much older (normally 11–13 years), and may include extraction of some teeth, and/or wearing of braces over the teeth.

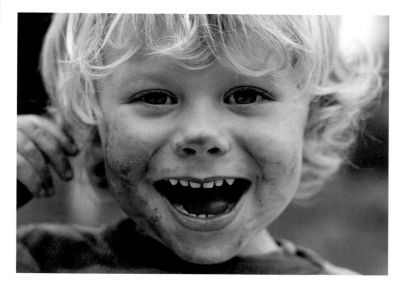

EAR AND EYE PROBLEMS

Ear and eye infections are very common in young children and need prompt treatment. If left untreated, persistent ear infections can result in short-term hearing impairment. Some eye problems can cause impaired vision. Other problems with hearing and vision are often present from birth and these, too, may impact on a child's development.

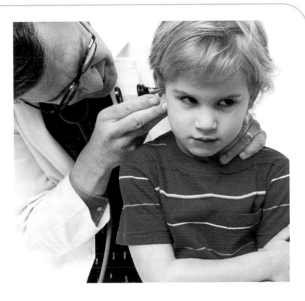

EAR INFECTIONS

Infections can occur in the outer (otitis externa) or inner ear (otitis media) and can be painful. The latter is often a complication of a virus such as cold or throat infection, but can also be caused by a bacterial infection. A young child's Eustachian tube, which connects the nose to the middle ear, is short and horizontal, so infections can pass easily from one area to another. Many children suffer from recurrent ear infections.

Suspect that your child has an infection if he has a fever and feels generally unwell. If young, he may pull at his ear but if older, he may tell you it hurts. His hearing may be temporarily impaired.

What to do

Take your child to your doctor. He or she will examine the ear with an auriscope and is likely to recommend the appropriate dose of infant paracetamol or ibuprofen to reduce pain and fever.

If your doctor suspects a bacterial infection, a course of antibiotics may be prescribed.

Occasionally an eardrum will burst; if this happens, the pain may ease because pressure on the eardrum is relieved, and mucus will weep from the ear.

A perforated eardrum will heal within a few weeks, but you should not take your child swimming until it does.

EXCESSIVE WAX

Earwax protects and lubricates the ear canal and is made up mainly of dead cells, hair and dust. A child's earwax is generally wet and soft but if he has too much or the wax is hard, it can block the ear canal and cause temporary hearing impairment, so may need to be removed.

What to do

Discuss it with your GP. He or she may suggest waiting to see if the wax clears on its own or, if your child's hearing is affected, eardrops to soften the earwax and encourage it to clear more quickly may be prescribed.

GLUE EAR

If your child becomes unable to hear, his middle ear may be filled with fluid or it's the result of a persistent cough or cold.

What to do

Take your child to your GP who will refer your child for a hearing test either at the hospital or child health clinic. The tests may be repeated over a few months as most cases of glue ear clear up within three months. If there is no improvement, you will be referred to an ear, nose and throat (ENT) specialist for further assessment; intervention is normally only

NERVOUS SYSTEM PROBLEMS

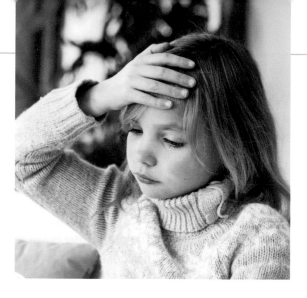

The nervous system is made up of the brain, spinal cord and nerves, which between them control many body functions. Any injury or infection that affects this system can have long-lasting consequences.

HEADACHE

Most children complain of occasional headaches. However, some children suffer from recurrent headaches that interfere with their everyday activities.

A tension headache is one resulting from emotional stress, for example, a problem at nursery or an event that the child is worried about, or it can even be caused by him clenching or grinding his teeth.

Headache can also be a symptom of migraine, which is often felt as a throbbing pain on one side of the head, and may be accompanied by vomiting, sensitivity to light (your child may say lights are sparkling) or noise.

Migraine can last for anything from a couple of hours to a couple of days. Attacks can be triggered by emotional stress, but some foods, in particular chocolate, oranges and cheese also trigger attacks, as can tiredness or too much sun.

What to do

Try to establish the cause of the pain; sometimes children say they have a headache when they mean an earache or toothache or an ache they can't explain.

If you suspect a tension headache, give your child the recommended dose of infant paracetamol or ibuprofen. If headaches are frequent, discuss this with your doctor so that he or she can eliminate other more serious causes, although these are very rare.

If you think the problem is migraine, give your child the recommended dose of infant paracetamol or ibuprofen and encourage him to rest in a darkened room. When you are able, take him to the doctor. He or she will want to identify trigger factors and may offer an anti-emetic to minimise vomiting during an attack as well as prescribe other medications in case of repeated attacks.

MENINGITIS

This is a serious infection, as a result of either a virus or bacteria, which causes inflammation of the meninges, the layers, or membranes around the brain and spinal cord. Bacterial meningitis is particularly serious as the same bacteria also cause septicaemia (blood poisoning), which can be fatal. The most common disease-causing bacteria are Neisseria meningitidis and Streptococcus pneumoniae but there are also several others. Meningitis can develop very quickly, but with prompt medical attention in hospital most children make a full recovery. However, some will suffer after-effects, which can range from mild to more serious, and occasionally disabling, because the infection damages an area of the brain.

What to do

Call your doctor immediately if you notice any of the symptoms (see box opposite page). If you have already seen the doctor and any of the symptoms worsen, do not hesitate to call again, and if you notice a rash developing call an ambulance; tell the control that you suspect meningitis. Your child will be admitted to hospital and given intravenous antibiotics.

The diagnosis will be confirmed by blood tests and a lumbar puncture (fluid taken from around the spinal cord). Anyone who has been in contact with him should also be given a short course of antibiotics as a precaution.

EPILEPSY

This is a life-long condition in which a person has a tendency to suffer from seizures (a disturbance in the electrical activity in the brain); it can develop at any age. (See box on page 272 on types for help in diagnosis).

Sometimes epilepsy develops after a child has sustained a head injury or has had an illness that affects the brain such as meningitis; some children have a family history of epilepsy. In many cases, however, the cause is unknown. Neither are all seizures the result of epilepsy. The condition will not be confirmed on the basis of only one seizure; specialist tests such as an electroencephalogram (EEG), and possibly brain scans such as a CT and/or MRI are needed. If your child has had seizures as a result

of a raised temperature, he does not have epilepsy although he has a slightly higher chance of developing it than children who have never had one.

What to do

Call an ambulance if this is his first seizure, or if he's had them before and the seizure lasts more than five minutes, if he is having repeated seizures, or if he is unconscious for more than 10 minutes. Call your doctor for advice in any other circumstance. If possible, ask someone to video the seizure so that your doctor can see the seizure pattern.

Your doctor will want to know what your child was doing

In focal seizures, only part of the brain is affected but in tonic–clonic seizures, the whole body is involved; both follow a pattern. A focal seizure can be followed by a tonic-clonic seizure.

Focal, or partial, seizures

In these seizures, the epileptic activity starts in part of a child's brain. They normally only last a couple of minutes. A child may appear fully conscious and alert, or he may be unaware of what is happening. He may have unusual sensations or feelings, his skin may be hot and flushed or even very pale, he may start chewing, swallowing or smacking his lips, scratching his head for no reason, or may wander off into another room.

Tonic–clonic or generalised seizures

In the first (tonic) phase, the child loses consciousness and, if he is standing, will fall to the floor. His body stiffens as all the muscles contract; he may let out a loud sound at the same time because the muscle contraction forces air out of the lungs. His breathing pattern changes, so there is less oxygen than normal in his lungs, and in his blood, causing his skin to look bluish (cyanosis). This will be most noticeable at his mouth, ears and fingernails. He may bite his tongue and the inside of his cheeks.

In the second (clonic) phase, convulsions begin. His limbs begin jerky movements as groups of muscles tighten and relax in turn. He may clench his jaw so breathing may be noisy. If he bites his tongue, the saliva may be blood-stained. He may also lose control of his bladder and/or bowel.

After a few minutes the convulsive movements will stop and he will regain consciousness, but may be completely unaware of what happened. He may say that he is very tired and fall into a deep sleep.

immediately before a seizure as it may help identify what triggered it — fatigue, lack of sleep and stress are common triggers, and for a few children, flashing or flickering lights.

If epilepsy is confirmed, your child will be monitored carefully. He may be given anti-epileptic drugs to help control his tendency to have seizures; with the right medicine, many children have few or no seizures. If a trigger is identified, avoiding it can help, although this can be difficult. An epilepsy specialist will review your child regularly, and his medication will be adjusted as he grows. Surgery or a special diet sometimes may be recommended.

FIRST AID FOR EPILEPSY

It is not possible to stop a seizure, and never try to control your child's movements during one. Never put anything in his mouth as he could choke but make sure he cannot hurt himself.

If it is a focal seizure, sit him down somewhere quiet. Clear a space around him and move any objects such as hot drinks out of harms way. Stay with him until he is better.

If it is a tonic–clonic seizure, clear a space around him, removing any objects that could hurt him or place rolled-up towels or cushions around him, especially by his head, to prevent injury. Make a note of when the convulsions start.

When the convulsive movements stop, he may be unconscious for a short time. Open his airway and check breathing (see page 224). Once he is breathing, place him in the recovery position. Monitor him until he has completely recovered.

GENITALS AND URINARY SYSTEM PROBLEMS

Most conditions that affect the genitals or the urinary system are minor and clear up quickly with treatment. Some conditions, however, are caused by underlying structural defects and may not be picked up by on regular health checks.

URINARY TRACT INFECTION (UTI)

An Infection can occur in any part of the body used to make and get rid of urine — the kidneys (pyelonephritis), ureters, bladder (cystitis) or urethra (urethritis); the urethra is most commonly infected. Bacteria can easily pass from the rectum to the urethra and result in urethritis.

UTIs are not usually serious, but must be properly diagnosed and treated to prevent scarring of the kidneys, which can cause problems in later life. Girls tend to suffer more UTIs than boys.

Suspect one if your child is passing urine more frequently than usual (especially if he is bed-wetting having previously been dry at night), and complains of pain or a burning sensation when he is passing urine. He may be irritable and/or appear lethargic, vomit, have a temperature of 38°C (100.4°F) or above and tell you he has a pain in his lower back or abdomen.

What to do

Always contact your doctor as soon as possible (within 24 hours) if you think your child has a UTI. A urine sample from your child will be tested and if an infection is confirmed, your child will be given a course of antibiotics. If the infection is serious, he may need to be admitted to hospital, but usually can be treated at home. Another urine sample will be needed a few days after treatment to demonstrate the infection has cleared. If your child is prone to recurrent infections, he may be given a low dose of antibiotics for a few months, and may even require surgery. While your child is unwell, make sure he drinks plenty of fluids as they dilute the urine and ease discomfort while urinating; they also help flush out the bacteria. Teach your child to always wipe his bottom from front to back to prevent bacteria spreading.

TIGHT FORESKIN

At birth the inner surface of the foreskin is attached to the head of the penis (glans). From about the age of two, the foreskin begins to separate naturally from the glans until it can be pulled back — you should never attempt force it. In some boys, this does not happen until they are about four years old. If the tissue that holds a baby's foreskin in place remains for longer than normal a tight foreskin can result. Tight foreskin can also occur if there is an abnormally narrow opening in the penis (phimosis).

What to do

If your son is over four years old and is having trouble urinating or his foreskin cannot be retracted, take him to your GP. If left untreated he is at greater risk of UTIs. Circumcision to remove the foreskin, or surgery to separate the tissues may be recommended; both operations would be performed under anaesthetic.

BALANITIS

This is an inflammation of the foreskin and the head of the penis (glans) and it can be caused by a fungal or bacterial infection. It most commonly results from not cleaning the penis properly, but a tight foreskin (see above) can also increase the likelihood of balanitis. It can also be a reaction to chemicals used in soaps and detergents. Suspect balanitis if your child has a red rash at the tip of his penis (it may be scaly or ulcerated) or there is tenderness, pain, swelling, itching and discomfort, a discharge or pus from underneath the foreskin (this may smell unpleasant), and he is unable to pull back his foreskin.

What to do

Take your child to your GP so the cause can be identified. You will be prescribed either an anti-viral or antibiotic ointment and be advised to keep the head of the penis and foreskin as clean as possible using only warm water and not anything that might

irritate the area, such as soap or detergent. Occasionally, especially if there are recurrent infections, circumcision will be advised

VULOVAGINITIS

This is a common condition that causes minor inflammation or irritation of the vagina and vulva. The linings of both can be quite thin in young girls, making the area susceptible to irritation especially from some soaps and detergents, or even wearing underwear that is too tight. Poor hygiene can also contribute.

You may notice your child scratching her vaginal area. There may also be a vaginal discharge (greenish yellow if it's a bacterial infection; white if it's a fungal infection), redness of the skin between the labia majora and burning or stinging on passing urine. Threadworms (see page 263) may also be to blame.

What to do

Good hygiene, avoiding possible irritants such as bubble bath, and changing to looser cotton underwear will clear up most mild cases. However, take your child to your GP if she complains of pain when passing urine, is very uncomfortable or symptoms persist for more than two weeks, as other causes need to be eliminated. If there is an infection, an anti-fungal or antibiotic ointment will be prescribed.

GLOMERULONEPHRITIS

This is a potentially serious kidney disorder that affects the tiny filters inside the kidneys. Your child may have a rash, complain of pain in his lower back and possibly in his joints, and exhibit tiredness or breathing problems. But often there are no noticeable symptoms and this infection of the glomeruli may only be picked up as a result of urine or blood tests done for another reason.

What to do

If your child complains of any of the above symptoms, see your doctor. If glomerulonephritis is suspected, your child will be referred to a kidney specialist and put on a low-sodium low-protein diet to ease the strain on his kidneys; his fluid intake may be restricted. If a bacterial infection is suspected, he will be given antibiotics. Glomerulonephritis normally clears up within a week.

BONE, MUSCLE AND JOINT DISORDERS

Any serious or long-term problems must be treated in order to prevent problems with muscle development and mobility. If your child has started limping, find out if she has injured her leg or foot or trodden on a sharp object. Inspect the soles of her feet and look between her toes for a wound. If she complains of joint pain, pain in her bones, or develops a limp for no apparent reason, always take her to see your doctor.

IRRITABLE HIP

Also known as transient synovitis, this is a condition in which the lining around the hip joint becomes inflamed and fluid accumulates within the joint. It can be very painful and your child will find it difficult to walk.

It may follow a hip injury, but in some instances it develops after a minor viral infection of the chest, throat or digestive system. It is more common in children over the age of four, and it affects boys more than girls.

What to do

If your child complains of severe pain in her hip, groin, thigh or knee, and/or is limping for no apparent reason, take her to your doctor. He or she will examine her leg and hip and ask her to try and walk on it and order an X-ray, blood test to rule out infection, and possibly an ultrasound scan to confirm the diagnosis and rule out Perthes disease (see page 276). The recommended treatment is anti-inflammatory medication such as infant ibuprofen, and bed rest (or on the sofa) until the pain is resolved — normally 7–10 days. If there is an infection, fluid may need to be drained from the joint, and antibiotics will be prescribed. It can help to massage your child's hip and hold a covered hot-water bottle against it. Your child should not to be too active too soon as the problem may flare up again.

BONE INFECTION

Children are forever getting superficial cuts and grazes, which usually heal on their own. In deeper wounds, however, dirt can be carried further into the body and bacteria can more easily travel to other parts of the body. If bacteria, most commonly Staphylococcus aureus, reach bone they can cause a serious infection called osteomyelitis. A bone can also become infected when the blood supply to that area is disrupted, but this is rare in children. Osteomyelitis most commonly affects the long bones of the arms and legs, but can affect other bones too. If your child has the condition, she will complain of severe pain in the infected bone and may be generally unwell. She may have a fever and feel tired or nauseated. The skin above the infected bone may be sore, red and swollen.

What to do

If your child complains of bone pain and has a fever, take her to your GP straight away. She will need blood tests to confirm the diagnosis and be given antibiotics to treat the infection. If the infection is caught early, she should make a complete recovery but rarely, infected bone may need to be surgically removed.

RICKETS

This is a condition that affects bone development in children. It is caused by a lack of vitamin D and calcium, the vitamin and mineral needed for healthy bone growth. Without them, developing bones become soft and malformed, which can also lead to deformities such as bowed legs and curvature of the spine. A child can become deficient if her diet is lacking in vitamin D or calcium or if she cannot absorb one or both nutrients.

What to do

If your child has bone pain, delayed growth (as measured against the appropriate developmental chart) or skeletal problems, take her to your GP. A routine check may not pick up the changes as older children are not routinely undressed to be examined. Rickets can be successfully treated in most children by ensuring they eat calcium- and vitamin D- rich foods and/or take the appropriate supplements. If your child has problems absorbing vitamins and minerals, or cannot take supplements, she may be given a yearly vitamin D injection. Sun light also contains vitamin D, which is absorbed by the skin, so try to increase the amount of time your child spends outside.

If your child develops a bone deformity, your GP may suggest treatment to correct it. For example, she may need to wear a brace to support the affected area as her bones grow, or she may need surgery.

PERTHES DISEASE

This is a childhood condition that affects the head, or top, of the femur (thighbone) where it fits into the pelvis. Occasionally the blood supply to the growth plate in the top of the femur becomes temporarily inadequate, causing softening of the surrounding bones. When the supply returns, the tissue reforms and remodels itself over a few years. If diagnosed early, most Perthes disease sufferers heal without intervention, but some children need a temporary cast to prevent deformity. Perthes disease affects boys more than girls and tends to develop around the age of four.

What to do

If your child complains of hip pain or develops a noticeable limp, take her to your GP as soon as possible. An X-ray will be needed to confirm the cause of the problem. For less severe cases, pain relief and bed rest for 7–14 days, or until the pain subsides, will be recommended. If there is a risk of deformity, your child may need to wear a temporary cast as a preventative measure. Regular X-rays or scans will monitor your child's recovery and bone growth. Treatment is aimed at promoting the healing process and ensuring that the head of the femur remains aligned in the pelvis. In very severe cases, deformity is not preventable and the child may develop arthritis later on in life.

ARTHRITIS

Your child may suffer pain, redness and swelling and stiffness in one or more of her joints due to one of three types of juvenile idiopathic arthritis (JIA). Oligo-articular JIA is the most common and affects up to four joints in the body, generally the knees, ankles and wrists. Polyarticular JIA, or polyarthritis, affects five or more joints — often the small joints of the hands and feet. Systemic onset JIA affects the whole body and symptoms such as a fever, rash, lack of energy and swollen glands, may develop some time before the joint becomes painful.

What to do

If your child complains of severe joint pains or stiffness, or starts to limp, or you notice a rash with a fever, take your child to the GP. Your doctor will arrange for blood tests to identify the cause. Anti-inflammatory drugs such as infant ibuprofen will be prescribed; if they do not help there are stronger medications. There is no cure for arthritis, but regular physiotherapy and exercise, especially swimming, can help maintain mobility and strength.

BEHAVIOURAL PROBLEMS

It's important to separate 'normal' disruptive behaviour (see page 139) from that which might have a genetic or medical cause. It's also vital that the problem is correctly identified so it can be treated effectively; some higher-functioning autistic children will often be diagnosed with other conditions such as Attention Deficit Hyperactivity Disorder (ADHD), Attention Deficit Disorder (ADD), dyspraxia, dyslexia (see box, page 281) or epilepsy.

Autism

Also known as ASD (Autism Spectrum Disorder), this is a lifelong developmental condition that impairs a child's ability to interact socially, understand social situations and communicate successfully with others. Children with autism find it difficult to pick up on social cues that other children understand intuitively and need to be taught basic social skills and helped to make sense of the world around them.

Autistic children have difficulty interpreting facial expressions and tone of voice, which prevents them from understanding how other people feel. An autistic child may also not appreciate the reciprocal nature of conversation, so he will appear to behave eccentrically and insensitively to others. A child with autism will usually have some form of language delay and when he does talk, he will take speech literally and struggle to understand jokes or figures of speech. He may also speak in a stilted manner or at length about a topic of special interest to him, and will be oblivious to his listener's level of interest.

Autism is a spectrum condition. This means that although there are common traits in all children with autism, each child will be affected by the condition in different ways and to different degrees. Children with classic or lower-functioning autism, defined as lower by reference to the child's IQ, may also have learning disabilities but there also exist autistic children with normal-to-above average IQs who are able to function competently.

It is a popular misconception that autistic children are savants with special or prodigious talents and abilities. Although savants are more common amongst autistic people, in fact, only ten per cent of the autistic population exhibit these traits as opposed to one per cent of the normal population.

The causes of autism are currently unclear save that there is no link between the MMR vaccine (see page 217) and autism. The fact that the MMR is given to children at around 18 months, when the first signs of autism can appear, is coincidental rather than causative. A combination of genetic and environmental factors is probably responsible for the condition. There is currently no single test available that can determine whether or not a child has autism.

About one in a hundred of the population are on the autistic spectrum and autism is more common in boys than girls. About four times as many boys are diagnosed with autism as girls but in higher-functioning forms of autism, such as Asperger Syndrome (see page 278), this figure is thought to be as high as 16 boys diagnosed to every girl. It is not known whether boys are genetically predisposed towards having autism or whether autism is under-diagnosed in girls. The traditional view of high-functioning autistic boys as trainspotters and science geeks does not take into account the fact that a girl's special interests may extend to subjects such as fairies, horses or fashion instead. Girls may be less commonly diagnosed with higher-functioning autism or Asperger Syndrome because they are better at masking their difficulties than boys. It appears that girls with autism are more severely affected than boys. The ratio of autistic girls to boys with lower-functioning autism is two to one.

Diagnosing autism

A diagnosis is not usually made before the age of 18 months because it is very difficult to assess a child's level of interpersonal skills before this age. A child with higher-functioning autism will usually not be diagnosed until he is about three years old, when the difficulties in relating to others become more obvious. Talk to your doctor if you are concerned about your child and you observe any of the traits set out below. Your child will be assessed by a specialist developmental paediatrician acting as part of a multi-disciplinary team, which may be made up of speech and language therapists, occupational therapists, family workers and psychologists. As part of the assessment, the team will take a full developmental history, usually interview you in detail as well as

*more***about** | Asperger Syndrome

This is a form of high-functioning autism where the child is of average or above average intelligence and is on the autistic spectrum. It is not usually diagnosed before the age of three. It is named after Austrian paediatrician Hans Asperger who, in the 1940s, studied a group of children he called his 'little professors'. The term 'Asperger Syndrome' was coined by English psychiatrist Lorna Wing in 1981 and became formally recognised as a diagnosable condition in 1989. A child with Asperger Syndrome does not suffer from a language delay and this is what differentiates Asperger Syndrome from other forms of high-functioning autism. This is why it is often referred to as a hidden disability as it is not immediately obvious when a child has Asperger Syndrome.

talk to your child, and may want to visit his nursery or playgroup and home.

You may be concerned that a diagnosis of autism will affect your child adversely by labelling him as different. In fact, the diagnosis of autism can be beneficial to you and your child as he can make significant progress with the right help. Adjustments can be made to your home and nursery or school environment to enable your child to cope better.

Recognising the signs

Some of these characteristics are common in young children with or without autism and it is important to remember that none or all of these signs on their own or together necessarily mean that your child has autism. But if you are concerned that your child is

not reaching his developmental milestones, ask your doctor if a developmental paediatrician can assess your child.

- Speech is delayed or non-existent or your child talks in an eccentric way that may sound robotic or monotonous.
- Difficulty understanding simple directions, instructions or questions.
- Doesn't make eye contact or appears to look straight through people.
- Sensitivity to smells, bright lights and loud noises such as vacuum cleaners, motorbikes and hairdryers.
- Soothes self by flapping hands, rocking, spinning wheels on toy cars or switching lights on and off.
- Doesn't like being touched, cuddled or picked up.

- May have a blank facial expression and doesn't pick up on other people's (including parents') facial expressions or tone of voice.
- Little interest in playing with toys; may only be interested in organising toys or groups of objects in a repetitive way, for instance by lining up cars or grouping toy soldiers in strict order of rank.
- Obsessions with objects or topics such as train timetables, makes of cars or a favourite dvd.
- May have problems with sleep — either getting to sleep initially or staying asleep once settled.
- Suffers severe temper tantrums that are especially difficult to control.
- Exaggerated interest in visual stimuli especially television screens, computers and dvds.
- Prefers rigid routines and finds change difficult.

What to do

There's no known cure for the condition but special educational programmes and speech and language therapy could help your child improve and gain a certain level of independence

ADHD

Attention Deficit Hyperactivity Disorder leads to problems with attention and/or hyperactivity and impulsivity that are inappropriate

MEDICATION FOR ADHD

If your child is diagnosed with ADHD, medication may make a big difference. It can help a child focus her thoughts better and ignore distractions. This will enable her to pay more attention and to control her behaviour, with the aim of improving her school performance and ability to succeed in social activities. The medications most commonly prescribed are stimulants; the most common is Ritalin®. These medications help to focus attention, control impulses, organise and plan, and stick to routines. They are prescribed in a variety of doses and schedules. Some children respond to one type of stimulant but not another. In addition, there are some non-stimulant medications that are used to treat ADHD. It may take some time to find the best medication, dose and schedule for your child. The paediatrician or child psychiatrist will follow your child closely and adjust the medication as needed.

for your child's developmental level and are impairing her performance. There are three common types:

- **Inattentive only:** Children with this type (formerly known as ADD) are not overly active. They do not disrupt the classroom or other activities, so their symptoms may not be noticed. This is the most common form found in girls.
- **Hyperactive/impulsive:** Children with this type show both hyperactive and impulsive behaviour, but are able to pay attention.
- **Combined inattentive/ hyperactive/impulsive:** Children with this type show all three symptoms; this is the most common type.

A child with ADHD is on the go all the time, has difficulty in concentrating and is impulsive (does things without thinking). Since most preschool children normally show these symptoms, the diagnosis is often not made before the age of six. In the UK. 5–10 per cent of the population have symptoms of ADHD and boys are the primary sufferers. ADHD may be problemmatical for parents, and if untreated, can significantly affect learning and progress in school. Therefore it is important to get help if you think your child is affected.

ADHD is one of the most common chronic conditions of childhood. The cause is not known but genetic factors may be involved. There is no specific test to diagnose it, but a diagnosis can be made following an appropriate clinical assessment. If you suspect that your child has ADHD, you should consult your doctor, who should check if there are other conditions present that may account for the symptoms, and if not, should involve a paediatrician and/or a child psychologist.

Since it is very common for children to exhibit behavioural problems, parents, teachers (if appropriate) and other caregivers

SYMPTOM	BEHAVIOUR
Inattention	Has a hard time paying attention, daydreams and forgets things. Does not seem to listen. Is easily distracted from work or play. Does not seem to care about details, makes careless mistakes. Does not want to do things that require ongoing mental effort. Does not follow through on instructions or finish tasks. Is disorganised. Often loses important things.
Hyperactivity	Is in constant motion, as if 'driven by a motor; cannot stay seated but squirms and fidgets. Runs, jumps and climbs when this is not permitted. Cannot play quietly. Talks constantly.
Impulsivity	Acts and speaks without thinking. Has trouble taking turns and cannot wait for things, such as calling out answers before a question is complete or interrupting others. May run into the street without looking for traffic first.

need to provide information on the core symptoms, their duration and the degree to which they interfere with a child's ability to function. Special checklists are often used to identify the key symptoms, which the diagnostician will use, and he or she may observe your child's behaviour in different settings as well as taking a careful history.

Diagnosing ADHD

The behaviours on page 280 must:

- Occur in more than one setting, such as home, school and social situations, making it difficult for your child to function in these settings;
- Be more severe than in other children the same developmental age;
- Start before your child reaches age seven. (However, symptoms may not be recognised as those of ADHD until your child is older);
- Continue for more than 6 months.

Once the diagnosis is made, management will be discussed. The possible modes of treatment include medication, behaviour therapy, dietary changes and support in school. In addition to the above, education, parent training and counselling may all be needed. You may also be able to get help from a hyperactive or ADHD support group.

*more **about*** | Dyspraxia and dyslexia

Dyspraxia is a developmental disorder affecting about 5% of children, most commonly boys. It is a motor learning problem demonstrated by a child's inability to plan and produce smoothly coordinated movements such as those needed for sitting, crawling and walking initially and then later on to hop, skip, peddle a bike or tie shoelaces or fasten buttons. Although occupational and physical therapy can help, and most children improve with age, it often goes unrecognised and can lead to educational, social and emotional problems.

Dyslexia is a condition where a child has trouble reading and spelling because while she is able to recognise individual letters, she is unable to put them in the right order. A child may also have difficulty recognising specific sounds, processing language at speed and with short-term memory. The problem affects between 4–10% of children but is not generally diagnosed until a child starts learning to read at school. Once the problem is recognised, special programmes and strategies should help her develop the necessary skills to learn effectively. Most affected children are still able to reach their full academic potential.

TICS AND TOURETTE SYNDROME

Tics are rapid, repetitive involuntary body movements. They usually affect the facial and neck muscles and may appear as grimaces, twitches of the eye or shoulder shrugging. Tics tend to run in families and affect more boys than girls. Tourette syndrome is a tic disorder that is frequently associated with ADHD.

What to do

Tics often appear during stressful periods, so it's important that your child's life has minimal pressure — not too many commitments, for example. Discuss the problem with your child if he is old enough to be aware of it in order to suggest ways of dealing with any of his playmates who may comment derogatorily on the behaviour or make fun of him.

INDEX

ACKNOWLEDGEMENTS

Carroll & Brown would like to thank

Jemima Dunne for supplying text for the health and medical section

Rachel Nixon for supplying text on autism

St. John's Ambulance Brigade for the loan of first-aid pictures on pages 236, 237, 238, 239, 240 and 245.

Getty Images for supplying cover photograph

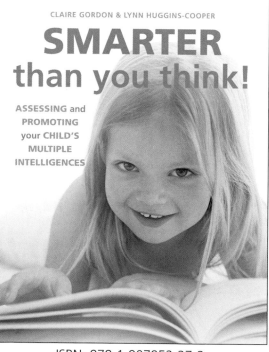